ABOUT THIS BOOK

'Globalization is irreversible and irresistible.'

TONY BLAIR

This book gives the lie to that claim. Greg Buckman argues that economic globalization has never been an inevitable part of human history. This is persuasively articulated in the first half of the book, where a readable and readily comprehensible overview is provided of how globalization came about. Globalization is eminently reversible and hugely resistible – as Buckman shows in the second half of the book, where he introduces and explains the alternatives of the anti-globalization movement.

Buckman argues there are two broad policy approaches within the anti-globalization movement. One, perhaps the most widely supported and influential strand today, he calls the Fair Trade/ Back-to-Bretton-Woods school. This is a moderate school that argues for immediate reform of the world's trading system, capital markets and global institutions, notably the World Bank, IMF and WTO. The other school, an equally broad church, advocates Localization, taking a more radical root-and-branch position that argues for the abolition of these institutions and an outright winding back of economic globalization. Buckman explains the details of each school's outlook and proposals, the criticisms that can be made of them, where they disagree among themselves, and – perhaps most importantly – where they share common ground and can come together in their campaigning.

This book attempts to give an informed hope to those dedicated to resisting and reversing economic globalization, a hope based on real and viable positive alternatives.

CRITICAL PRAISE FOR THIS BOOK

'So refreshing and useful to read a book that goes beyond the usual bleatings about the problems of globalization in order to analyse in detail the alternatives that are at last emerging.'

COLIN HINES, author of
Localization: A Global Manifesto

'Greg Buckman has done the global justice movement a valuable service in clearly outlining the major debates around taming versus scrapping globalization, and then attempting to find common ground. I urge everyone who wants a fairer, safer and more sustainable world to read this book.'

ROD DONALD MP, Co-leader,
Green Party of Aotearoa New Zealand

'Greg Buckman's work opens up the all-important debate between the ideas of localization and fair trade, on the one hand, and economic globalization, on the other.'

SENATOR BOB BROWN,
leader of the Australian Greens

'The clearest and most succinct explanation of the origins and processes of economic globalization yet to appear in English, plus the best coverage of the debates over what to do about it. A useful tool for anti-globalization activists everywhere.'

CHRISTINE DANN

GLOBALIZATION: TAME IT OR SCRAP IT?

Mapping the Alternatives of the Anti-globalization Movement

GREG BUCKMAN

University Press
Dhaka

White Lotus
Bangkok

Fernwood Publishing
Nova Scotia

Books for Change
Bangalore

SIRD
Kuala Lumpur

David Philip
Cape Town

ZED BOOKS
London & New York

Globalization: Tame It or Scrap It? was first published in 2004 by

In Bangladesh: The University Press Ltd,
Red Crescent Building, 114 Motijheel C/A, PO Box 2611, Dhaka 1000

In Burma, Cambodia, Laos, Thailand and Vietnam:
White Lotus Co. Ltd, GPO Box 1141, Bangkok 10501, Thailand

In Canada: Fernwood Publishing Ltd,
8422 St Margaret's Bay Road (Hwy 3) Site 2A, Box 5,
Black Point, Nova Scotia, B0J 1B0

In India: Books for Change,
139 Richmond Road, Bangalore 560 025

In Malaysia: Strategic Information Research Development (SIRD),
No. 11/4E, Petaling Jaya, 46200 Selangor

In Southern Africa: David Philip (an imprint of New Africa Books),
99 Garfield Road, Claremont 7700, South Africa

In the rest of the world: Zed Books Ltd, 7 Cynthia Street, London N1 9JF,
UK, and Room 400, 175 Fifth Avenue, New York, NY 10010, USA
www.zedbooks.co.uk

Copyright © Greg Buckman 2004

Designed and typeset in Monotype Bembo by Illuminati, Grosmont
Cover designed by Andrew Corbett
Printed and bound in the EU by Cox & Wyman, Reading

Distributed in the USA exclusively by Palgrave Macmillan, a division of
St Martin's Press, LLC, 175 Fifth Avenue, New York, NY 10010

A catalogue record for this book is available from the British Library
Library of Congress Cataloging-in-Publication Data available
Canadian CIP data is available from the National Library of Canada

ISBN 1 55266 137 7 Pb (Canada)
ISBN 81 87380 98 5 Pb (India)
ISBN 983 2535 31 X Pb (Malaysia)
ISBN 0 86486 657 7 Pb (Southern Africa)

ISBN 1 84277 380 1 Hb (Zed Books)
ISBN 1 84277 381 X Pb (Zed Books)

CONTENTS

PART I   THE EVOLUTION AND CONSEQUENCES OF
          ECONOMIC GLOBALIZATION

CHAPTER I Introduction   3

CHAPTER 2 The Evolution of the Global Supermarket
           (A History of World Trade)   6
           World trade in the nineteenth century 7
           World trade in the twentieth century 8
           World trade after the Second World War 10
           The shocks of the 1970s 10
           Causes of the spread of world trade 14

CHAPTER 3 The Evolution of the Global Bank
           (A History of World Capital Flows)   18
           Pre-Industrial Revolution global finance 18
           The influence of the Industrial Revolution 19
           The emergence of the gold standard 20
           The First World War and the inter-war years 21
           The Bretton Woods twins 23
           *The world economic order from the 1950s to the
             1970s* 25
           The shocks of the 1970s 25
           Today's casino economy 28

CHAPTER 4   The Engines of Globalization   35

Transnational corporations 36
The World Trade Organization 43
The International Monetary Fund and the
World Bank 51
The Washington Consensus 57
The technological engines of globalization 60
The environmental price of world trade 62

CHAPTER 5   Rich versus Poor in the Global Economy   68

The polarization of global wealth 68
Concentration of economic globalization around
rich countries 73
Relative size of poor economies 76
The Third World debt crisis 76
Poor countries and global trade 80
Trade winners and losers 83
Poor-country raw material exports 85
Poor-country trade winners 87
Export-processing zones 87
Rich-country trade losers 89
Aid to the rescue? 90
Ecological debt 92

CHAPTER 6   Rich-country Double Standards   96

Rich-country double standards on trade 96
Rich-country double standards on patents 99
Rich-country double standards on agricultural
and textile trade 100

PART II   THE POLICY ALTERNATIVES OF THE
            ANTI-GLOBALIZATION MOVEMENT

CHAPTER 7   The Anti-globalization Movement   107

The global loss of democracy 109
The anti-globalization movement 110
Origins of the anti-globalization movement 112
The anti-globalization protests 115

Policy formulation by the anti-globalization movement 116

NGOs and non-mainstream parties 118

CHAPTER 8   The Fair Trade/Back to Bretton Woods School   122

Trade 124

The future of the IMF, the World Bank and the WTO 129

Capital market and TNC regulation 137

CHAPTER 9   The Localization School   150

Advocates of Localization 151

Trade 154

The future of the IMF, the World Bank and the WTO 155

Capital market and TNC regulation 159

CHAPTER 10   Globaphobes versus Globaphiles   166

The Oxfam Rigged Rules report debate 166

Short-term versus long-term strategies 168

Corporate engagement 169

Rich-country versus poor-country anti-globalization organizations 171

Changing fashions within the anti-globalization movement 172

Policies that straddle both schools 174

Policies that stand outside the Localization/Fair Trade divide 175

CHAPTER 11   Deficiencies of Both Schools   180

Deficiencies in Fair Trade school policies 180

Deficiencies in Localization school policies 186

Deficiencies common to both schools 189

CHAPTER 12   The Policy Future of the Anti-globalization Movement   194

Common ground between the two schools 195

Broader areas of agreement between the two schools 197

Potential areas of greater consistency between the two schools 199
The general policy future of the anti-globalization movement 201

CHAPTER 13   Conclusion   207

             Useful Globalization Websites   213

             Suggested Reading   217

             Index   220

LIST OF TABLES, FIGURES AND BOXES

Box 2.1	Timeline of global trade	12
Figure 3.1	Increase in world currency turnover	27
Box 3.1	Timeline of global capital flows	30
Box 4.1	Causes of modern economic globalization	38
Table 4.1	International trade negotiations held since World War II	45
Table 4.2	World's largest companies	61
Figure 4.1	World fossil fuel emissions	63
Figure 5.1	Per capita incomes of world's richest and poorest countries	69
Figure 5.2	Poor-country share of world manufacturing	74
Table 5.1	World's largest economies	75
Figure 5.3	Third World and Eastern bloc foreign debt	79
Table 5.2	Aid given by top fifteen world donors	91
Figure 7.1	Growth of non-governmental organizations	119
Box 8.1	The Fair Trade/Back-to-Bretton Woods agenda	142
Box 9.1	The Localization school agenda	161

ABOUT THE AUTHOR

GREG BUCKMAN is a former national finance manager for the Wilderness Society of Australia. Currently treasurer of the Australian Greens, he has also been co-editor of their magazine, *Green*. He has undertaken much economic research, particularly on issues concerning globalization, forestry and energy. His long involvement with the environmental movement goes back to the successful international fight to save the Franklin river in Tasmania in the early 1980s.

To Derek Brown, whose idealism lives on

PART I

THE EVOLUTION AND CONSEQUENCES OF ECONOMIC GLOBALIZATION

CHAPTER I

INTRODUCTION

Every era has its defining influences. In the post-Second World War decades of the 1950s, 1960s and 1970s it was technology. The world then was either awestruck or horrified by Sputnik, the moon landing, the Aswan Dam, the 'green' (fertilizer) revolution, the Thalidomide scare, the birth-control pill and mainframe computers.

In the 1980s, the 1990s and the present decade, the defining influence is money – particularly global money. We've become familiar with the Nasdaq and the Dow Jones indexes. Everyone knows what Enron is. Most of us have a pretty good idea what the latest national exchange rate is or what the daily spot prices for oil and gold are. We've seen the Asian 'meltdown' of 1997, the Argentinian collapse of 2002 and the post-September 11 stock-market gyrations played out on our television screens. There's no escaping the all-pervading influence of economic globalization. We are all caught up in it now.

This book holds a mirror to the face of economic globalization. It charts the rise and negative consequences of economic globalization and profiles the policy responses of the anti-globalization movement, which, like the Nasdaq and Dow Jones indexes, has become ubiquitous, particularly since the 'Battle for Seattle' protests of 1999.

The anti-globalization movement is a very broad church which takes in activists concerned with nonviolence, feminism, poverty, the rights of indigenous people, the rights of the unemployed, preservation of the environment and responsible media, to name just a few issues. This book concentrates exclusively on economic globalization. Economic globalization is necessarily connected to all the myriad issues covered by the anti-globalization movement but it deserves specific attention. It is the dominant influence behind many of the world's present-day ills and needs to be examined in its own right. This does not mean the other issues covered by the anti-globalization movement are not important; they are important, but for the purposes of understanding and reasoned response it is necessary to pull the globalization machine apart and specifically examine its economic parts.

Many would have you believe that economic globalization is the product of an inevitable rightward swing in politics over the past few decades. Others say it is the predictable consequence of the march of technology. Many in the anti-globalization movement say it is the product of the irrepressible greed of transnational corporations. In reality it is the result of all these things, and more. It is the convergence of many haphazard and planned influences. As a result this book tries to avoid pigeon-holing economic globalization, and its origins, into neat boxes, and instead tries to take a holistic overview of its various defining influences and consequences.

Like economic globalization in general, the anti-globalization movement has evolved haphazardly with resulting significant internal policy differences on economic globalization. But increasingly there is common ground, common purpose and common hope that economic globalization can be redesigned in a sustainable way. The first half of this book (Chapters 2 to 6) examines what economic globalization is, how it has emerged and what its consequences have been. The second half of the book (Chapters 7 to 13) presents an overview of the anti-globalization movement, paying particular attention to its policy alternatives to economic globalization. It focuses on the radical and more mainstream policy schools within the movement and assesses the strengths and weaknesses of each school's policies, as well as the areas of agreement and disagreement between them.

In 1998 British prime minister Tony Blair said 'globalization is irreversible and irresistible'. This book gives the lie to that claim. Economic globalization has never been an inevitable part of human evolution and is therefore eminently reversible and hugely resistible. This book attempts to give hope to those dedicated to resisting and reversing it – not a naive hope but one based on real and viable alternatives.

CHAPTER 2

THE EVOLUTION OF THE GLOBAL SUPERMARKET (A HISTORY OF WORLD TRADE)

Today's global trade network is very much a product of history, a history that at times has been convoluted and unpredictable. To understand economic globalization you have to understand its origins and where it has come from.

You could get involved in a long and complex debate about when, exactly, economic globalization began. You could argue it began as early as two thousand years ago when the Silk Road was established between the Mediterranean and China. Or you could argue it began when Christopher Columbus sailed to the Americas in 1492. Historian Robbie Robertson claims there have been three major 'waves' of globalization. He says the first wave began with Columbus's voyage in 1492, and that of Vasco da Gama in 1497, and ended before the Industrial Revolution (which began in the eighteenth century). He says the second wave went from the Industrial Revolution through to the start of the Second World War. His third wave went from the Second World War through to the present day.[1] Many regional trade networks existed around the world before the start of the first wave, but Robertson says the European conquest of the Americas, during the first wave, gave it wealth that allowed it to engage with those regional trade networks for the first time[2] (although trade in the first wave of globalization was mainly only concerned with luxury items). This chapter and the next chapter mainly look at Robertson's second and third waves of globalization.

The British invention of the steam engine kicked off both the Industrial Revolution and the second wave of globalization. The steam engine allowed two things to happen for the first time that were vital to the growth of economic globalization. It allowed countries to produce large surpluses of produce and it allowed those surpluses to be transported over vast distances.

It is oversimplifying things, however, to ascribe all of the birth of the second wave of economic globalization to the Industrial Revolution. Independent of the Industrial Revolution had been the creation and refinement of an international payments system that started in the fourteenth century. This progressed to the development of 'forward exchange systems' in the seventeenth and eighteenth centuries that allowed exporters and importers to reduce currency fluctuation risk through being able to contract on the basis of agreed spot prices.[3] And separate to all this had been the spread of European colonization ushered in by da Gama's and Columbus's voyages. By 1800 extensive fertile and mineral-rich areas of the Americas and the Pacific, in particular, had been settled by Europeans whose colonized area by then already exceeded that of Western Europe. These newly colonized areas fed the raw material hunger of Britain's emerging Industrial Revolution. The infamous British colonizer Cecil Rhodes even once remarked, 'we must find new lands from which we can easily obtain raw materials and at the same time exploit the cheap slave labour that is available from the natives of the colonies.'

World trade in the nineteenth century

The upshot of these influences was an explosion of industrialization and world trade that Britain managed to keep largely to itself until the mid- to late nineteenth century. At about that time the Industrial Revolution crossed the English Channel and began to take root in continental Europe. Steam-based transport in the form of railways (which enjoyed an explosion in popularity from the 1820s) and steam ships (which took off much later, in the nineteenth century) provided the arteries for the spread of the Industrial Revolution. They were augmented by the development of telegraph communication, a huge migration of nearly 50 million people out of Europe and the opening of the Suez Canal in 1869. The upshot was that by 1900 Europe had established itself as the world's centre of industrialization, with raw materials being fed into it from 'regions of recent settlement' like the United States, Canada, Argentina, Uruguay, South Africa, Australia and New Zealand. All of this had enormous implications for world trade. World trade doubled between 1830 and 1850, then trebled between 1850 and 1880.[4] In 1800 world trade only equalled about 3 per cent of the world's combined gross domestic product but by 1913 it equalled 33 per cent[5] – a proportion similar to that which exists today. During the nineteenth century the foundations of today's global supermarket were well and truly established, leading some supporters of economic globalization to characterize the century as the 'golden age' of capitalism.

Today it is easy to think that the tentacles of economic globalization must have spread quickly once the Industrial Revolution crossed the English Channel, but in fact they remained fairly constrained for a long time. Even by the First World War it was really only Europe, Japan and the United States that had experienced any significant degree of industrialization.

World trade in the twentieth century

Although a clear periphery/core template of global trade, centred around Europe, had been established by 1914, the First World War, and the years between it and the Second World War, altered Europe's domination of the world economy. The First World War ushered in a major shift in the architecture of global trade. The war hugely disrupted Europe's production but left the economies of most of the rest of the world, particularly that of the

United States, unscathed. The result was that between 1913 and 1937 Europe's share of world trade fell from two-thirds to half.[6] But the First World War did little to stop the spread of world trade. The economy of the United States kept growing quite rapidly, enabling world trade to continue expanding, with the result that the United States became the new giant of the global trade network. This status was confirmed by its large post-war reconstruction loans to Europe and its large level of post-First World War foreign investment.

Europe emerged from the First World War in a vulnerable state with reconstruction and inflationary pressures upon it. It was just starting to get those under control when the tumultuous stock-market crash of October 1929 heralded the start of the Great Depression. This had a major dampening effect on world trade, with the result that after expanding by 40 per cent between 1881 and 1913 it grew by only 14 per cent between 1913 and 1937.[7] As well as shifting the spotlight of world trade away from Europe for the first time, the inter-war years also introduced some crucial qualitative changes in world trade, some of which were to have profound ramifications in years to come. Food and agriculture lost their dominance of the world's trade in raw materials, while minerals significantly increased their share.[8] Oil, the 'blood' of world trade, began to take off as a major globally traded raw material for the first time.[9] The mix of trade in globally traded manufactured items also began to change with a shift away from trade in mainly 'capital' goods (machinery etc.) to a greater share of consumer goods. And, most crucially for exporters of raw materials (poor countries mainly), the first wave of downward pressure on world raw material export prices began to be felt. Many farming and mining processes were becoming increasingly mechanized, which increased world supply, while new influences like synthetic substitutes for wool and cotton fabric, which decreased world demand for those materials, also began to take root. The result of all these influences was the start of a long-term global slide in raw material prices that is still happening today.

World trade after the Second World War

Unlike the First World War, the Second World War did significantly disrupt the expansion of world trade. Europe in particular finished the war with acute shortages that resulted in high inflation and low economic growth, which depressed world trade. As with the First World War, however, the economy of the United States finished the Second World War relatively unscathed, with the result that its dominance of the world trade market reached its peak in the early 1950s when a full third of all the world's exports came out of the country.[10] Shortages after the Second World War persisted for five or six years when, among other things, the start of the Korean War raised world production and broke the post-Second World War downturn.

If the nineteenth century had been capitalism's first 'golden age', then once the world economy had recovered from the Second World War it entered what supporters of globalization sometimes describe as its second golden age. With the exception of a few very brief periods in a few particular economies (which each lasted less than a year), from the early 1950s right through to 1973 the world experienced two decades of continuous high economic growth that gave a major push to the expansion of world trade. By the 1960s world trade was growing by 8 per cent per year, which had it nearly doubling every decade.[11] This major push took the relative size of the world trade network back to the proportions it had assumed prior to the First World War.[12] After the slowdowns of two world wars, and the Great Depression, the global supermarket was back in business.

The shocks of the 1970s

The rapid expansion of the 1950s and 1960s came to a dramatic halt, however, in 1973 when the first big oil price increase induced by the Organization of Petroleum Exporting Countries (OPEC) and the Yom Kippur war in Israel caused a sudden slowdown in world growth and the hitherto breakneck post-war expansion of world trade. A second sharp oil price increase in 1979–80 (caused by the fall of the Shah of Iran) induced another major slowdown in 1981–82.

The trade in oil is massive; by weight it exceeds the combined total of the world's next three most traded raw materials, iron ore, coal and grain.[13] During the years after the Second World War rich countries hugely increased their appetite for oil. Between 1949 and 1972 Europe's oil consumption grew fifteenfold, for instance.[14] Middle Eastern oil producers realized the increased power this gave them, and after Colonel Qaddafi seized power in Libya in 1969 they were increasingly prepared to use it. From 1970 OPEC began demanding increased prices for oil, which by 1973 saw the price of oil reach a level more than five times what it had been in 1970.[15]

The 1970s not only reduced the pace of world trade expansion; the decade also reduced the economic domination of the United States. For all of the first half of the twentieth century the US had enjoyed uninterrupted trade surpluses with the rest of the world and had been self-sufficient in oil. The US had, in fact, been the world's largest producer of oil until the 1950s and had also been a major world oil exporter (which helped boost its trade surpluses).[16] But in the 1950s all that changed. In 1950 the vast US thirst for oil began to outpace its production and the US started importing oil for the first time.[17] And in 1958 the US recorded its first trade deficit since the late nineteenth century.[18] By the 1970s the occasional US trade deficits had become a permanent feature and the US became a long-term, large, net importer of goods and services in general and of oil in particular. Between 1967 and 1971 the US trade deficit increased from US$2.9 billion to US$19.8 billion.[19] Ongoing US trade vulnerability, which has continued to this day, is not helped by the fact that today it imports half the oil it consumes and by 2020 is projected to be importing as much as two-thirds.[20] Nor is it helped by the fact that the US accounts for a quarter of all the world's current oil consumption.

Box 2.1   Timeline of global trade

1492, 1497	Voyages by Christopher Columbus and Vasco da Gama begin era of European colonization, allowing Europe to connect with pre-existing regional trade networks around the world.
1700s	Start of Industrial Revolution makes the United Kingdom centre of world industrialization.
1800s	Extensive areas of the Americas and the Pacific become colonized by Europeans, making those areas raw material suppliers to European industrialization.
1830–80	World trade increases rapidly; is twelve times larger by end of period.
1913	Value of world trade reaches a level equal to one-third of world GDP.
Early 1900s	Western Europe, Japan and United States become industrialized.
1913–37	US becomes dominant global economy. Food, agriculture and capital goods lose world trade market share to minerals, oil and consumer goods.
1929	US stockmarket crash begins Great Depression, which slows expansion of global trade.
1944	Bretton Woods conference establishes International Monetary Fund and World Bank.
1947	World trade conference in Havana establishes International Trade Organization and less ambitious General Agreement on Tariffs and Trade (GATT).
1950	United States President Truman confirms the US will not endorse the establishment of the International Trade Organization.
Early 1950s	US accounts for one-third of all global trade.
1950s–1970s	Most economies in the world experience almost uninterrupted high economic growth, leading to rapid expansion of world trade. World trade doubles every ten years.

1963, 1964	Joint United Nations Declaration of Developing Countries made; United Nations Conference on Trade and Development (UNCTAD) created.
1962–67	Kennedy round of global trade talks leads to major reductions in some rich-country tariffs.
Early 1970s	US trade deficits become persistent.
1973	First oil price shock leads to slower world growth and slower expansion of world trade.
1979, 1980	Second oil price shock also leads to slower world growth and slower expansion of world trade.
1986–93	Uruguay Round of global trade talks leads to further reductions in rich-country tariffs.
1980s–1990s	Poor countries implement rapid reduction of tariffs.
1995	World Trade Organization established.
1999	50,000 people protest against attempted start of new world trade talks in Seattle.
2001	Doha Round of world trade talks begins.
2002	World trade reaches level twenty times that of 1950, equal to 40 per cent of world GDP. Trade in services accounts for a quarter of total world trade.
2003	Doha Round of WTO trade talks collapses at Cancún.

Another key trade development of the 1970s was the rising trade power of Japan, which by the end of the 1970s had established itself as a third major giant in the global trade network. After accounting for just 3 per cent of world exports in 1950, Japan was producing 15 per cent by 1987.[21] This rise in trade power allowed Japan to take its place alongside Western Europe and the US as one of the 'triad' of dominant players in the global trade network. Japan's new East Asian influence over global trade was augmented in the 1980s by the rising trade power of its four neighbouring East Asian 'tiger' economies: Hong Kong, Singapore, South Korea and Taiwan.

During the 1970s the pace of world trade expansion slowed to about half its speed of the 1960s and early 1970s. After the global recession of 1981–82 the world trade network continued to grow but at a slower pace. This did not stop it, however, expanding at a rate faster than general economic activity in most major world economies with the result that over the past two decades world trade has grown at roughly twice the pace of world production[22] and is now equivalent to about 43 per cent of world production.[23] This is an unprecedented level of influence for the global supermarket, a level higher than it had been before the start of the First World War. By 2000 world trade was twenty times larger than it had been in 1950, while the world's overall production of goods and services was only six times larger.[24]

The period since the Second World War has also seen major shifts in the make-up of world trade. Since the war, world trade in raw materials has waned and by 1987 it made up less than 30 per cent of the global trade in goods.[25] Meanwhile, global trade in manufactured goods has increased (72 per cent of global goods trade in 1987).[26] Not only have manufactured goods risen in importance; so too has the trade in commercial services like banking, business, design and tourism services. The volume of services trade around the world has grown incredibly quickly in recent times, with a trebling in volume over the past fifteen years to now account for about a quarter of total world trade.[27]

Causes of the spread of world trade

There has been a large raft of influences behind the expansion of the global trade network. Some of the influences are dealt with in Chapter 4. One of the major influences has been large reductions in world tariffs that occurred throughout the post-war years (the 1980s and 1990s in particular).

Major cuts in world tariffs gave the post-Second World War expansion in world trade a big boost. The cuts largely occurred through the General Agreement on Tariffs and Trade (GATT), established in 1947, and its successor, the World Trade Organization (WTO), established in 1995. The GATT in particular held several major post-war 'rounds' of global trade negotiations aimed at reducing world tariff levels. The Kennedy Round of world trade negotiations, conducted between 1964 and 1967 (mainly between rich countries), had a particularly large influence in reducing tariffs and was responsible for average cuts in industrial tariffs of between 36 and 39 per cent.[28] The Uruguay Round of trade talks, completed in 1993, that led to the establishment of the WTO, was also responsible for large cuts in world tariffs. It resulted in a halving of average rich-country tariffs from 10 per cent in the early 1980s to 5 per cent in 1999.[29] And although slower to cut tariffs than rich countries in the three decades after the Second World War, in the 1980s and 1990s poor countries also hugely reduced their tariffs.

Falling tariffs and rising transport and communication capacity have not been solely responsible for the post-Second World War spread of global trade, however. The expansion of global trade has led to the emergence of a global factory where components can be sourced from several countries around the world and then assembled in yet another country and this intra-company trade has also hugely increased world trade. In Delhi the Fashun Wears company, for instance, manufactures childrens' corduroy dresses for the chainstore Gap using synthetic lining and buttons made in China, zips made in South Korea and linen collars made by another supplier in India.[30] In 1988 subsidiaries of Japanese companies based in the United States purchased over 80 per cent of their inputs from their parent company in Japan, then exported more than 60 per cent of their output back to the same company.[31] The age of Henry Ford's production line using local employees producing products for local demand made from local materials is fast disappearing.

Another major globalizing influence has been transnational corporations (TNCs). Much of today's global manufacturing is dominated by TNCs. Nearly 70 per cent of world trade is currently controlled by the largest five hundred TNCs in the world and about a third of world trade is conducted between different arms of the same company.[32] This means two dollars in every three dollars of world trade is controlled by TNCs, and one dollar in every three is represented by trade within the same company.

So, today's global trade supermarket is the product of misguided free-market economic globalization ideology and a lot of opportunism, both of which have failed to take into account either the big world picture or our long-term future. The global supermarket is based on short-termism and has evolved into a system that has little vestige of sustainability.

Notes

1. Robbie Robertson, *The Three Waves of Globalization: A History of a Developing Consciousness*, Zed Books, London, 2003.
2. Ibid., p. 88.
3. A.G. Kenwood and A.L. Lougheed, *Growth of the International Economy 1820–1990: An Introductory Text*, Routledge, London, 1992, p. 103.
4. Ibid., p. 67.
5. Ibid., p. 79.
6. Ibid., p. 211.
7. Ibid., p. 209.
8. Ibid., p. 216.
9. Ibid., p. 217.
10. Ibid., p. 241.
11. Ibid., p. 286.
12. Kevin Watkins et al., *Rigged Rules and Double Standards: Trade, Globalisation and the Fight Against Poverty*, Oxfam International, Washington DC, 2002, p. 33.
13. 'The Stuff of Wars', *The Economist*, 12 January 1991, p. 66.
14. 'Oil Equals Power', *The Economist*, 12 January 1991, p. 83.
15. Daniel Yergin, *The Prize: The Epic Quest for Oil, Money and Power*, Free Press, New York, p. 625.
16. Joan E. Spero and Jeffrey A. Hart, *The Politics of International Economic Relations*, 5th edn, Routledge, London, 1997, p. 277.
17. Ibid.
18. Kenwood and Lougheed, *Growth of the International Economy*, p. 262.

19. Robertson, *The Three Waves of Globalization*, p. 194.
20. Michael Klare, 'United States Energy and Strategy', *Le Monde Diplomatique*, November 2002, p. 1.
21. Kenwood and Lougheed, *Growth of the International Economy*, p. 289.
22. Watkins et al., *Rigged Rules*, p. 34.
23. Based on figures in World Bank, *World Development Report 2002*, Oxford University Press, New York, 2002, pp. 237, 239.
24. Malcom Waters, *Globalization*, 2nd edn, Routledge, London, 2001, p. 69.
25. Kenwood and Lougheed, *Growth of the International Economy*, p. 290.
26. Ibid., p. 290.
27. Watkins et al., *Rigged Rules*, p. 225.
28. Kenwood and Lougheed, *Growth of the International Economy*, p. 281.
29. Watkins et al., *Rigged Rules*, p. 102.
30. Ibid., p. 41.
31. Kenwood and Lougheed, *Growth of the International Economy*, p. 290.
32. John Madeley, *Hungry for Trade: How the Poor Pay for Free Trade*, Zed Books, London, 2000, p. 91.

CHAPTER 3

The Evolution of the Global Bank (A History of World Capital Flows)

Like the global trade network, today's global capital market is very much a product of history. And also like the global trade network, to understand the problems of the global capital market you have to understand its evolution.

Pre-Industrial Revolution global finance

Global capital movements, of the sort we are used to today, only became possible with the creation of two things: currencies and banks. The first currency in the world was developed between 640 and 630 BC by the little-known Lydian city-state situated on the Anatolian Peninsula where modern-day Turkey is located.[1] Lydia was a rich mini-kingdom made considerably richer by its invention of coins, which, for the first time, enabled people easily to transport a standard measure of wealth around the kingdom generally worth no more than a few days' labour or a small part of a farmer's harvest. Banking took much longer than currency to be developed and didn't emerge until about nearly two thousand years later when the Templar crusade order of knights created it in the twelfth century.[2] The Templars fought in the Holy Land to wrest control of the area from Arabs, but most of their wealth was raised in Europe, so banking allowed them to transfer wealth between continents from the donors' European pockets to the

Middle Eastern battlefront. By the fourteenth century banking on an international level was made easier by the development of a simple, global multilateral clearing system.[3]

At the start of the nineteenth century Amsterdam was the most important global capital centre in the world, closely followed by London, but despite the developments of the previous six hundred years the total value of global capital movements was insignificant and played only a minor part in economic activity around the world at the time.[4] The mechanisms for a global capital market − a global bank − were in place by the start of the nineteenth century, but there was yet to emerge any major force to power them. Global capital flows took much longer to take hold, in any significant way, than global trade and have been a much more recent phenomenon of economic globalization.

The influence of the Industrial Revolution

As a result of Britain's eighteenth-century Industrial Revolution, and the new wealth it generated, the British began to invest more of their new-found wealth, instead of necessarily spending it all. Machinery, factories and infrastructure like new railways, roads and ports became the exciting things to invest in. Britons became richer and their population began to increase significantly, and as a result London overtook Amsterdam as the dominant financial centre of the world.

By the start of the nineteenth century the Industrial Revolution and European world colonization were well and truly pushing open the doors of a new world order of international capital flows. It was tentative at first, however, and very much dominated by the United Kingdom. British foreign investment was a steady trickle in the first half of the nineteenth century but by 1870 it was three times what it had been in 1850 and by 1900 it was eleven times its level of 1850.[5] As the Industrial Revolution spread throughout Western Europe other countries such as France, Belgium, Germany, the Netherlands and Switzerland became major foreign investors as well as the United Kingdom. By the start of the First World War, Britain still accounted, however, for just under half of all the world's foreign investment.[6] The growing wave of foreign investment in the nineteenth century was pushed along by large-scale European migration and by the development of more sophisticated and specialized global financial institutions, including commercial banks and investment houses.

As the nineteenth century progressed there was more and more European foreign investment, with the British Empire, Latin America and the United States being favoured destinations. Iconic European foreign investments included the railways of the United States and the Suez Canal. As remains the case today, however, most European foreign investment was based around its global trade network, with little of it concerned with the development of local economies. Although some European colonies, particularly those in North America and the Antipodes of Australia and New Zealand, experienced significant gains in wealth as a result of European foreign investment, the inhabitants of most colonies, particularly those of Africa, Asia and Latin America, gained little benefit from the foreign investment, with most of it concentrated around the export businesses of those colonies.[7]

The emergence of the gold standard

Many factors were responsible for the nineteenth-century explosion in global foreign investment. The spread of European trade networks was obviously key, but rivalling it in importance was the establishment of a complex multinational payments system based around the 'gold standard'. The gold standard, as its name suggests, was built around the ultimate convertibility of a nation's currency into gold. The gold standard did not mean that a country always paid for its imports, or its overseas investments, by shipping out gold, but it did mean that long-term international imbalances could ultimately be settled with gold. For much of the nineteenth century the currencies of many major economies were based on silver standards, or a combined gold and silver standard, but the discovery of large quantities of silver in America led to most countries switching to a gold standard by the 1870s. From the 1870s to the First World War the gold standard underpinned a global capital system that was fairly smooth and predictable, without the wild fluctuations in currency values and none-too-occasional foreign debt defaults that plague the global capital market today. There is disagreement about why, exactly, the gold standard worked so well during that period but suffice it to say that from the 1870s until 1914 there was a well-structured and secure system of global finance and investment that gave economic globalization a relatively good name, unlike the often manic and unpredictable global capital market we live with today.

The First World War and the inter-war years

Major convulsions within the world's capital markets occurred during the First World War. The First World War saw the end of Britain's dominance of the world capital market, with the United States taking over its paramount role. It also saw the end of the gold standard, which wasn't to be revived until the late 1920s.

As the First World War dragged on all the participant countries became starved of capital, but Britain and France were handed a lifeline in the form of loans from the US following its entry into the war in 1917. Germany and the the Austro-Hungarian Empire, which had become major European economic power-houses before the war, enjoyed no such wartime lifeline, however, and their economies were in a state of near collapse by the end of the war. After the end of hostilities the US became banker to the world, with US global lending more than doubling between 1919 and 1930.[8] Just as the pre-war global economy had depend-ed on British capital, the post-First World War global economy depended on US capital. This worked relatively well until the US began to withdraw its capital from the rest of the world in the late 1920s. High US interest rates and ever seductive stock market rallies began calling US capital home in a big way in the late 1920s. The withdrawal of US capital was further cemented by the US stock-market collapse of October 1929.

Until the late 1920s there had been a delicate balance of global financial flows, with capital flows from the US to Europe balancing a trade deficit that Europe ran with the US. But all that came crashing down with the withdrawal of US capital. This was the world's first big bitter taste of the price of overdependency on a global capital market. The withdrawal of US capital was the catalyst for the Great Depression of the 1930s, which was deepened by a string of complicating factors including a reluctance of governments and central banks to make money more freely available during the depression, a global collapse in raw material prices and overvalued currencies (particularly in Europe). A return to the gold standard in the late 1920s failed to return the global capital system to the stability it had known in the late nineteenth century or to stave off the depression.

By the early 1930s most countries that had returned to the gold standard had abandoned it again, and as the depression deepened global sentiment turned against economic globalization and world economic interdependence (in an echo of what may be beginning to happen today). Many countries introduced controls and limits on the amount of global capital and trade that could cross their borders. Countries abandoned the global economy and began to put the health and recovery of their own economies first. Although many current-day commentators claim these controls deepened the depression, particularly the trade controls, the truth is that the controls often allowed economies to follow expansionary policies, such as lower interest rates and expanded government spending, that allowed employment and economic activity to grow even though the world economy was in a downturn. The controls helped economies that used such controls out of the depression; they did not deepen it.

The outbreak of the Second World War increased the restrictions on international trade and capital flows, but in 1941 the US and UK governments began discussions on what they thought would be a desirable post-war world economic order. These discussions began a new era for the world's capital markets.

The Bretton Woods twins

The Second World War had a much more devastating effect on the world economy than the First World War had had, although in general terms most countries were able to recover from it faster than they had been able to recover from the First World War. The catalyst for discussions between the Americans and the British about the structure of the post-war global economy was the signing of their Mutual Aid Agreement in 1941, which, although mainly concerned with war-time lend–lease arrangements, committed both countries to post-war economic cooperation.[9] These discussions ended up having an enormous impact on the shape of today's global economy. Although no doubt well intended, they were confined to just the UK and US and their outcomes therefore necessarily had an exclusively Anglo-Saxon flavour, even though they were eventually to affect every country in the world.

Both countries agreed that the post-Second World War world economic landscape should be more stable than the pre-war landscape, and that that would necessarily require large amounts of global capital given that many of the pre-war economic woes were caused by the drying up of global capital, particularly US capital. But beyond that general goal the views of the UK and US differed markedly. The UK (headed by high-profile economist John Maynard Keynes) wanted post-war capital channelled through what it called an 'International Clearing Union' where participant countries would have an almost automatic right to loan funds. The Union would also have an arrangement where countries that consistently ran trade surpluses with the rest of the world would have as much pressure put on them to reduce their surpluses as countries that ran deficits would have on them to

reduce their deficits. Punitive rates of interest, and other penal-
ties, would be applied to both surplus and deficit countries. The
US, however, which knew it would be contributing most of the
world's post-war global capital, and which knew it would be running up trade surpluses with the rest of the world after the war,
wanted an 'International Stabilization Fund' where loans would
be much more conditional than they would be under the British
model. And they wanted no pressure applied to surplus countries.
The US chief negotiator, Harry Dexter White, said 'we have been
perfectly adamant on that point – we have taken the position of
absolutely no, on that'.[10] Needless to say the Americans won out
with the Stabilization Fund eventually becoming the International
Monetary Fund (IMF). Its dominance by the United States was
cemented by the Americans' insistence that it be based in the US.
The British had hoped it would be based in London but when
staking his claim for a US home Harry Dexter White said: 'we
are putting in twice as much money as anybody else, three times
as much … it is preposterous that the head office should be any
place else. We can vote it any place we want.'[11]

The US was also fairly unilateral in establishing the twin of
the IMF, the World Bank, through which significant amounts
of post-war capital would also be channelled. The US largely
modelled the World Bank on its own Reconstruction Finance
Corporation.[12] The Anglo-American arrangements for the IMF
and the World Bank were confirmed at a conference held in
Bretton Woods, New Hampshire, in July 1944, with 730 delegates
from 44 countries (there were only about 55 countries in the
world at the time). Many history books present this conference as an exercise in economic democracy with all attendee
countries having a say in the shape of the world's post-war public
economic institutions. But in reality most decisions had already
been taken by the Americans and the British, and the proceed-
ings were conducted in English, which many delegates could not
understand. The few decisions that were left to the conference
were largely sorted out at a pre-conference meeting in Atlantic

City and in backrooms of the Bretton Woods conference. This form of undemocratic decision-making unfortunately became a template for nearly all world financial conferences and negotiations held since.

The world economic order from the 1950s to the 1970s

Immediately after the Second World War many of the pre-war global financial structures remained in place. Most major economies kept currency controls in place until the late 1950s because they did not have enough foreign exchange to make their currencies freely convertible. In the late 1950s these rich-country currency controls were relaxed and in the 1960s a return to the gold standard was made, accompanied by a regime of fairly inflexible exchange rates. The IMF had a very limited role in the first ten years after the war because most US assistance was channelled through its Marshall Plan (which pumped about US$11 billion of aid into Western Europe immediately after the war[13]). The IMF's first loan was not extended until 1956 when it lent money not to a poor country but to the United Kingdom, which experienced foreign exchange problems after the Suez Canal crisis in the same year.

From the early 1950s the consistently high economic growth experienced by rich countries led to a high level of US foreign investment, which by 1960 was nearly three times what it had been in 1938.[14] But in among all this economic sunshine were the seeds of future destabilizing influences. The start of persistent US trade deficits in the 1960s planted the seeds of massive world economic uncertainty, which is still with us today.

The shocks of the 1970s

The 1970s began a global financial roller-coaster that the world economy has never managed to get off. The decade saw a major convulsion in the world's capital markets, which began a new era of instability in global capital flows that has remained since.

The instability of the 1970s was largely caused by the convergence of two major economic forces: the world's increasing dependence on Middle Eastern oil and the United States' loss of global trade dominance. By the 1970s the hitherto occasional trade deficits of the US had become permanent, made worse by the oil price increases of the 1970s, an overvalued US dollar, reconstructed European economies being increasingly able to compete with the US again, and inflationary pressures generated by US spending on the Vietnam War. Dollars were pouring out of the US economy, ultimately placing a lot of pressure on the country's gold reserves, at a time when the oil price increases were depressing world export markets. The US response to all these pressures, under President Nixon – without any international consultation whatsoever – was unilaterally to delink the US dollar from the gold standard, in August 1971, thus beginning the modern age of floating exchange rates. This act, more than any other, gave a big push to the modern era of world capital integration.

The US decision to go off the gold standard was an ill-considered act by a frightened, declining economic superpower, and we are still living with the consequences of it today. It ended the stability of world capital flows that had existed since the Second World War. By the late 1970s most major world economies had also floated their currencies, and from then on all of the capital controls of most rich countries around the world began to be dismantled. After the US floated its currency in 1971, Japan and major European countries floated their currencies in 1973. In 1974 the US began dismantling many of its non-currency capital controls, followed by the UK in 1979 (following the election of Margaret Thatcher). They were quickly followed by Japan and other major European economies. The controls on bond markets were then relaxed in the 1980s; controls on foreign investment in rich-country stock markets were relaxed in the 1990s. Until the

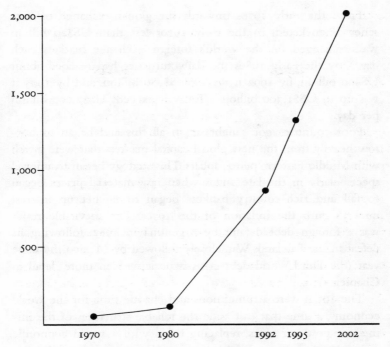

Source: *The Economist*, 23 September 1995, p. 73, for 1970, 1980, 1995 figures.

Figure 3.1 Increase in world currency turnover
(daily turnover in US$ billion)

1970s radical changes in exchange rates had been discouraged, and
were fairly rare, with most countries keeping a fixed rate to the
US dollar. As a result the world had known relatively stable exchange rates since the late 1940s. But the floating of rich-country
currencies, followed by the relaxation of non-currency capital
controls, meant the doors of a new world casino economy were
well and truly thrown open, and stable exchange rates became
less possible to maintain.

From the early 1970s onwards the global exchange of currency skyrocketed. In the early 1970s less than US$20 billion was exchanged on the world's foreign exchange markets each day.[15] By the early 1980s the daily turnover had reached about US$60 billion, by 1992 it was at US$880 billion, and by 1995 it was up to US$1,300 billion.[16] Today it exceeds US$2,000 billion per day.

Poor countries got caught up in all this and began to borrow heavily from the new global capital markets that were awash with Middle Eastern 'petro' dollars. This strategy began to unravel spectacularly in the late 1970s when raw material prices began to fall and rich-country bankers began to ratchet up interest rates to curb the inflation of the 1970s. The inevitable result was a foreign debt default by Argentina in 1982, following its defeat in the Falklands War, closely followed by Mexico the same year (the Third World debt crisis is dealt with in more detail in Chapter 5).

The 1970s were a tumultuous and chaotic time for the world economy, a time that cast aside the reliable structures of the immediate post-war years, replacing them with a world economic order whose only predictable feature was its unpredictability.

Today's casino economy

Today among rich countries, and increasingly among poor countries, there are few barriers to unhindered global transfers of enormous amounts of money. Huge amounts of money can be transferred these days – to take advantage of a short-term rise in interest rates or a quick rally on a stock market somewhere – with the mere pressing of a computer key. Increasingly the world's capital flows are made up of hot money chasing short-term profits. This hot money uses the world economy as little more than a glorified roulette wheel. Just before the US floated the dollar in 1971 as much as 90 per cent of world financial flows were associated with trade, or long-term investment, while less than 10 per cent was speculative; today those proportions are reversed with 90 per cent of flows being hot, speculative money.[17]

This extraordinary availability of cash has had a major effect on both rich and poor countries. For many 'bankable' rich countries the global casino economy has meant it is easier to avoid making difficult decisions and adjustments, particularly if they are persistently running high trade and current account deficits (the current account includes all the overseas non-capital transactions of a country, like trade, interest and profit transfers). Countries like Greece, Iceland, Portugal, Spain, Turkey, the United States, Australia, New Zealand, the Czech Republic, Hungary and Poland now have the luxury of continually borrowing from the rest of the world instead of addressing deep internal structural issues such as low domestic savings rates and high domestic import dependencies. The case of the United States is particularly telling. Although quick to lecture poor countries about the sins of overreliance on debt and the virtues of free trade, the US household savings rate has halved over the past decade to be among the lowest of all rich countries,[18] while at the same time its annual trade deficit has climbed from US$29.5 billion in 1991 to US$550 billion in 2004.[19] The net result has been that in 1988 the US went from being a net creditor to the world to being a net debtor, and today it is by far the world's largest debtor. By 2002 the net foreign liabilities of the US (the value of US overseas assets less the value of foreign assets in the US) equalled US$2,500 billion, to which about US$1.5 billion was added every day. Foreigners now hold US$7,000 billion in US assets.[20] In the 1980s Japan became the dominant capital supplier of the world, and it is capital from Japan, and several other Asian countries, that these days mainly keeps the US economy afloat.

For poorer economies today's casino economy has also had many downsides. Lending and investing in poorer countries went out of vogue after the Third World debt crisis began in 1982. But during the 1990s many restructured poor economies, particularly in East Asia and South America, began to record high rates of

Box 3.1   Timeline of global capital flows

640–630 BC	First currency developed by Lydian city-state, on Anatolian (Turkish) Peninsula.
1100s	Banking first developed by Templar crusade order.
1800s	Amsterdam becomes centre of global capital markets.
1850–1900	British foreign investment grows rapidly and London becomes new centre of global capital markets.
1870s–1914	Gold standard underpins relatively stable workings of global capital markets.
1914–1918	First World War sees the United States replace the United Kingdom as the dominant player in global capital markets with New York becoming the new global capital centre.
1919–1920s	US foreign investment doubles as the country becomes lender/foreign investor to the world.
Late 1920s	The US withdraws a huge amount of capital from global markets. A return to the gold standard fails to bring stability back to global capital markets. Capital controls around the world are reintroduced.
1941	The US and UK begin discussions on post-war world economic order.
1944	Conference at Bretton Woods creates the International Monetary Fund and the World Bank.
1950s	Post-Second World War currency controls are relaxed around the world.
1960s	Major world economies return to the gold standard. The US becomes largest world lender/investor again.
1971	US President Nixon takes the US dollar off the gold standard, beginning the modern era of floating exchange rates.
1974, 1979	The US and UK begin dismantling capital controls, followed by other major economies.

1980s	Major world economies relax controls on foreign investment in bond markets.
1980s	Japan becomes dominant world capital supplier.
1982	Debt defaults by Mexico and Argentina begin Third World debt crisis. Rich countries begin withdrawing capital from poor countries.
1988	The US becomes a net foreign debtor for the first time since the Second World War.
1990s	Major world economies relax controls on foreign investment in stock markets. Rich countries begin investing in poor countries again.
1994	Mexico experiences another foreign debt/ currency crisis.
1995	Turnover on world's foreign exchange markets reaches sixty times its level of the early 1970s.
1997	'Asian meltdown' foreign debt/currency crisis throws the economies of Malaysia, Thailand, Singapore, Taiwan, Indonesia, South Korea and the Philippines into turmoil. Russia also experiences major foreign debt/currency crisis.
1999	Brazil experiences major foreign debt/currency crisis.
2002	Argentina undergoes major foreign debt/currency crisis.

economic and export growth. This encouraged a new round of speculation and investment in poor countries by rich-country companies, banks and financiers.

During the colonial period, up to about 1960, European countries invested heavily in their colonies, mainly in their extractive and export industries. This investment accounted for as much as half of all the foreign investment around the world.[21] But the Third World debt crisis reduced rich-country investment in poor countries and by 1990 this had fallen to a fifth of total world foreign investment. As the 1990s progressed, however, foreign investment in poor countries climbed back to be nearly 30 per cent of the total by the end of the decade.[22] Today foreign investment makes up most of the global capital flows into poor countries. But all this new investor interest has two major problems. The first is that, like the trade performance of poor countries, it is highly concentrated. Some 60 per cent of all foreign investment in poor countries currently goes to just six countries: Brazil, Mexico, Argentina, Thailand, Indonesia and China, and 94 per cent goes to just twenty countries, including four major former Communist economies of Eastern Europe.[23] Meanwhile in 1999 only 0.5 per cent of all the world's foreign direct investment found its way into the world's poorest forty-nine economies.[24]

The second major problem is that many poor countries are not set up to be able to handle these huge inflows of capital. The large capital flows often push up the exchange rates of poor countries to unsustainably high levels, which punishes their export performance, leaving them in a vulnerable position when overseas capital pulls out. This was a major influence behind the 'Asian meltdown' of 1997. Poor countries would sometimes peg their exchange rates to the value of the US dollar but that often left them with overvalued currencies, particularly when the exchange rate of the US dollar was on the rise (as it was in the second half of the 1990s). This was a major factor in Argentina's debt default in 2002.

The net result of all the volatility generated by the free flow of capital around the world has been a series of currency, debt and investment crises that stand in stark contrast to the global stability that existed between the end of the Second World War and the early 1970s. There was the Third World debt crisis of the early 1980s, the US savings and loans debacle of the late 1980s, the European exchange rate crisis in 1992, the Mexican currency crisis in 1994, the East Asian meltdown of 1997, the Russian meltdown of 1998, the collapse of the Brazilian currency in 1999, and the Argentinian debt catastrophe of 2002. Nothing is certain any more and much depends on luck and the herd instinct.

From the 1980s onwards many poor countries became increasingly attracted to the borderless world capital market, often pushed along by IMF and World Bank conditions on their loans. But it was countries that kept, or reimposed, capital controls, like India, China and Malaysia, that were often best equipped to weather foreign exchange crises. As with borderless trade, by the late 1990s sentiment in many poor countries was beginning to turn against borderless capital markets. But rich countries keep pushing for an expansion of unhindered capital movements. There is now growing resentment about capital market crises in poor countries, fuelled by the pain of their past foreign exchange crises. It is that resentment, along with the increasingly loud voice of the anti-globalization movement, that hopefully will begin to close the doors of today's global casino economy and one day return some sanity and structure to the world's capital markets.

Notes

1. Jack Weatherford, *The History of Money*, Three Rivers Press, New York, 1997, p. 30.
2. Ibid., p. 64.
3. A.G. Kenwood and A.L. Lougheed, *Growth of the International Economy 1820–1990: An Introductory Text*, Routledge, London, 1992, p. 103.
4. Ibid., p. 26.
5. Ibid.
6. Ibid., p. 27.
7. Ibid., p. 41.
8. Ibid., p. 183.
9. Ibid., p. 235.
10. George Monbiot, *The Age of Consent: A Manifesto for a New World Order*, Flamingo, London, p. 165.
11. Robert Skidelsky, *John Maynard Keynes: Fighting for Britain 1937–1946*, Macmillan, London, 2000, p. 352.
12. Ibid., p. 307.
13. Kenwood and Lougheed, *Growth of the International Economy*, p. 242.
14. Ibid., p. 250.

15. 'Big', *The Economist*, 23 September 1995, p. 73.

16. Ibid., p. 73.

17. Robert Went, *Globalization: Neoliberal Challenge, Radical Responses*, Pluto Press, London, 2000, p. 13.

18. 'Economic and Financial Indicators', *The Economist*, 26 January 2002, p. 101.

19. 'The Other America the Facts', *New Internationalist*, November 2002, p. 19; and 'Economic and Financial Indicators', *The Economist*, 7 February 2004, p. 93.

20. Alan Wood, 'Foreign Investors Hold Key to Rate of US Dollar Descent', *The Australian*, 21 January 2003, p. 13.

21. Ankie Hoogvelt, *Globalization and the Post Colonial World: The New Political Economy of Development*, Palgrave, London, 2001, p. 78.

22. Went, *Globalization*, p. 45.

23. Hoogvelt, *Globalization and the Post Colonial World*, p. 84.

24. 'Emerging-market Indicators', *The Economist*, 19 May 2001, p. 108.

CHAPTER 4

THE ENGINES OF GLOBALIZATION

The spread of economic globalization around the world has been fed by many factors. One of the most important has undoubtedly been the ever compliant pro-globalization decisions made by the world's governments. Yet just as important have been the institutions created by economic globalization, which, once allowed to take root, have had a vested interest in the ongoing expansion of the world economy. Also of crucial importance has been the technology that allowed globalization to happen in the first place, particularly transport and communications technology. This chapter profiles these 'engines' of globalization and the all-important influence they have brought to its spread. The political decisions of economic globalization get all the headlines, but it is the institutions and technology of economic globalization that power it along.

There are two groups of institutions that are relentless in their promotion and expansion of economic globalization. One is the world's transnational corporations (TNCs). This group wields enormous influence. It controls most of the investment, trade and employment decisions of economic globalization and, as a result, often has an influence that exceeds that of many governments. The second group is made up by the public international financial institutions created to oversee the management of economic globalization. These organizations are: the International Monetary Fund (IMF), the World Bank and the World Trade Organization (WTO). Although, in theory, ultimately answerable to the world's governments, in practice each of these public international financial institutions has become a major global bureaucracy wielding enormous, largely unaccountable, influence.

Transnational corporations

One group that always stood to do well out of economic globalization is TNCs – companies that operate across borders, based in several countries at once. The reduced trade and investment barriers of economic globalization created vast new markets and almost limitless expansion possibilities for these companies. And they have exploited the opportunities to the hilt. In the 1970s there were about 7,000 TNCs in the world.[1] By 1997 the United Nations Conference on Trade and Development (UNCTAD) estimates there were 53,000 of them, with 448,000 foreign affiliates.[2] The value of the overseas investments owned by these TNCs came to US$3,500 billion in 1997, while their estimated total sales were US$9,500 billion.[3] It is almost impossible to underestimate the power this gives TNCs. Today the largest 500 TNCs control about 80 per cent of all foreign investment in the world and about 30 per cent of global output.[4] Estimates of the total employment of TNCs are notoriously difficult, but UNCTAD calculates their global workforce at between 17 and 26 million.[5]

Like so much of globalization, TNCs are very much a creation of the rich parts of the world. Although much of their workforce is spread throughout the world, TNCs are nearly always owned by shareholders in rich countries, are managed from rich countries, and have very Western/hierarchical structures. And although their production is spread around the world, most TNCs are headquartered in rich countries. Of the 100 largest TNCs, 38 have their headquarters in Western Europe, 29 in the United States and 16 in Japan.[6] In fact, of the largest 500 TNCs in the world only 29 are headquartered in poor countries.[7]

The anti-globalization movement often claims TNCs account for about half of the largest 100 economies in the world, but this statistic confuses sales with gross domestic products. The two are different concepts. Gross domestic products are an expression of the value added by an economic unit whereas sales figures are not; as a result of this confusion, this statistic is not a particularly sound one to quote. Some TNCs are very large but at least 44 of the world's 193 economies are larger, in value-added terms, than the largest TNC; of the world's largest 100 economic entities, measured in value-added terms, TNCs make up less than a third.[8]

The area where TNCs wield some of the greatest influence is trade. Today the largest 500 TNCs control nearly 70 per cent of global trade.[9] They also control up to 80 per cent of trade in information technology.[10] About a third of world trade is conducted between different arms of the same TNC.[11] TNCs have a particularly large influence over trade in the world's raw materials. Seven TNCs control 85 per cent of the world's trade in grain, eight control up to 60 per cent of world coffee trade, seven account for 90 per cent of all the trade in tea, three account for 83 per cent of world trade in cocoa, and three control 80 per cent of the global trade in bananas.[12]

The power of TNCs, and of rich countries in general, is further augmented by their domination of the world's patent research and development. Rich countries account for 97 per cent of the world's patents, and roughly the same proportion of international research and development spending, with 40 per cent of the global total spent in the United States alone.[13] Within the US just fifty companies account for half of all the nation's research and development.[14]

Box 4.1   Causes of modern economic globalization

Post-Second World War dominance by the United States

The United States was economically very dominant after the Second World War and used the dominance to shape the International Monetary Fund (IMF) and World Bank, as well as global trade agreements, in the form they desired. US clout also ensured the IMF and World Bank were headquartered in Washington.

Technology

Modern-day transport and communications technology have hugely reduced the cost of moving goods and capital around the world and have made global business information more available than it has ever been before.

Compliant governments

The United States began the modern era of economic globalization when it floated the US dollar in 1971 in a panic move induced by increased post-war trade competition from European economies and loss of competitiveness caused by its spending on the Vietnam War. Since then most governments around the world have progressively reduced their trade and capital controls. The free-market ideologies of Friedrich von Hayek, Milton Friedman, Margaret Thatcher and Ronald Reagan have become the order of the day.

The influence of the IMF, World Bank and WTO

The start of the Third World debt crisis in 1982 gave the IMF and World Bank enormous power, which allowed them to impose pro-globalization, free-market conditions on their loans to poor countries. Past or present IMF and World Bank debtors account for about 40 per cent of all the world's economies. Meanwhile the World Trade Organization has increasingly pushed the boundaries of trade globalization through harsh trade rulings and new areas – such as patents, investment and services trade – included in the Uruguay and Doha Rounds.

TNCs, speculators and global investors

TNCs have perpetrated the influence of economic globalization through their domination of world trade, investment,
and research and development. The largest 500 TNCs control
70 per cent of world trade, 80 per cent of global foreign investment and 30 per cent of world output. Currency speculation
is now rife, with daily foreign currency turnover more than
one hundred times its volume of the early 1970s.

The political influence of TNCs

Predictably, the ever-increasing economic clout of TNCs has
given them growing influence that they have not been shy
to wield. TNCs are now *the* dominant influence of economic
globalization politics. Several developments have shown what an
unassailable influence they have become in the global economy.

In 1995 the rich-country Organization for Economic Cooperation and Development (OECD) began work on its proposed
Multilateral Agreement on Investment (MAI). The MAI would
have been the world's first investment treaty. It would have given
foreign investors unprecedented rights. Under the agreement they
would have been able to invest where they liked, with governments having little power to stop them. The proposed deal sent
shock waves around the world and was eventually squashed in
1998 after a public backlash and resistance from countries like
France. Although it appeared to be the brainchild of the twenty-
nine governments belonging to the OECD, a dominant player in
its formulation was the US business group the US Council for
International Business, which includes 150 top-level executives
from companies like IBM and AT&T.[15] There is renewed pressure,

these days, to have an agreement much like the MAI included in the current Doha Round of World Trade Organization trade talks, which again is being pushed by TNCs. It was the relentless pursuit of such an investment agreement, particularly by Europe and Japan, that was most responsible for the collapse of WTO trade talks at Cancún, Mexico, in September 2003.

Similar TNC influence lies behind one of the side deals of the Uruguay Round of trade negotiations, the Trade Related Aspects of Intellectual Property Rights (TRIPS) agreement, which locks in global TNC patent control over a broad range of strategic goods and services sold around the world. Agitation for the TRIPS agreement followed lobbying of the Reagan administration by a number of large US software, pharmaceuticals and chemical companies, which wanted the administration to quantify the amount of revenue they claimed they were losing around the world through patent piracy.[16] Companies like Pfizer, Merck and Du Pont succeeded in getting the US government to force the TRIPS agreement into the Uruguay Round of international trade talks. A former chief executive of Pfizer, Edmund Pratt, even admitted: 'our combined strength enabled us to establish a global private sector/government network which laid the ground for what became TRIPS.'[17] In its assessment of the Uruguay Round, Credit First Suisse Boston described the pharmaceuticals industry as the 'greatest beneficiary' of the TRIPS agreement.[18]

Large TNC finance companies, including American Express, Credit First Suisse Boston and the American International Group, were similarly involved in getting another devastating side deal of the Uruguay Round in place, the General Agreement on Trade in Services (GATS). They even formed themselves into the 'Coalition for Service Industries'.[19] This group was also sometimes known as the 'AMEX coalition'.[20]

Many TNCs are responsible global players, but the history of TNCs wielding dubious political influence goes back a long way. From 1970 to 1972 the International Telephone and Telegraph Company, for instance, sought to prevent the election of Salvador

Allende in Chile, and then, once he was elected, helped to secure his overthrow.[21] During the Spanish Civil War the US oil giant Texaco gave huge assistance to the forces of General Franco through the supply of nearly 2 million tons of oil on unsecured credit.[22] During the Vietnam War the computer company Honeywell lent its support to the US war effort.

Unsurprisingly there is no particularly thorough regulation of TNCs at an international level. There are some codes and principles developed by UNCTAD, as well as declarations of principles and codes developed by the International Labor Organization (ILO) and the World Health Organization.[23] There are also Guidelines for Multinational Enterprises drawn up by the OECD. But there is nothing that could pass as international law governing the behaviour of TNCs. Throughout the 1980s the United Nations Centre on Transnational Corporations attempted to develop a UN code of conduct for TNCs, but it was eventually scrapped in the early 1990s.[24] TNCs don't necessarily feel beholden to follow the OECD's Guidelines for Multinational Enterprises. In 2003 the anti-globalization movement campaigned against an oil pipeline being built by a BP-led consortium that went through Azerbaijan, Georgia and Turkey. During the approval process for the pipeline the consortium sought, and gained, a large number of exemptions from national social, labour, tax and environmental laws in blatant breach of the OECD guidelines.[25]

The on-the-ground influence of TNCs

Like economic globalization in general, the foreign investment that TNCs bring into a country can be a positive or a negative influence. If it brings in new technology, new employment and a significant level of new foreign exchange, it can be a positive influence. If it crowds out existing businesses in a country, transfers little technology or know-how and ends up having an insignificant net influence on a country's foreign earnings, it can have a negative influence. There are examples of both around the world. In countries like South Korea and Taiwan, which have invariably insisted on TNC links with the local economy that must be of net benefit to local businesses, TNCs have expanded the country's trade base and have brought in a lot of new employment, but in many Latin American and African countries the reverse is true. In Latin America up to half of all foreign investment in the late 1990s was used just to merge or take over local firms.[26] And a lot of the foreign investment that has come into Latin America has left again as repatriated profit that reduced the benefit of the initial injection of foreign capital by as much as half.[27] In Africa most foreign investment by TNCs is based around raw material extraction and up to three-quarters of it leaves as transferred profit.[28]

Changing attitudes towards TNCs

The decades since the Second World War have seen several changes in government attitude towards TNCs. Even though poor countries generally kept fairly closed economies after the war, they often had a benign attitude towards TNCs in the 1950s and 1960s. That changed in the 1970s when attitudes hardened. Between 1977 and 1980 the Indian government forced 400 TNCs to reduce their foreign ownership by selling shares to Indians.[29] In 1972 the governments of Saudi Arabia, Qatar and Abu Dhabi began forced negotiations with oil companies that eventually gave them majority ownership of their oil operations.[30] Even several rich-country governments sought to increase their control over TNCs in the 1970s. In 1972 the Canadian government established a Foreign Investment Review Agency that screened all foreign investment, rejecting any that did not meet import-substitution, export, local ownership and research expenditure targets.[31] But all that changed in the 1980s. Governments of both rich and poor countries now increasingly roll over for TNCs and allow them in on virtually any terms. It's quantity, not quality, that matters these days and TNCs rule the roost as a result.

The World Trade Organization

Just as powerful as TNCs in influence over the global economy are three international financial 'sister' institutions: the International Monetary Fund (IMF), the World Bank and the World Trade Organization (WTO). All have their origins in international economic talks held at the end of the Second World War or in the years following its conclusion. The WTO is a global trade bureaucracy which took over from the General Agreement on Tariffs and Trade.

The IMF and the World Bank were created at the international finance conference held in Bretton Woods, in the United States, in 1944 (which was detailed in the previous chapter). A new world trade regime required a separate conference, however. The global conference which aimed to establish the trade sister to the World Bank and the IMF was held in Havana in 1947. The conference gave birth to the International Trade Organization and a fairly bold accompanying charter. The Havana Charter was the product of much compromise and negotiation between rich and poor countries. But the charter was very different from the global trade document envisaged by the United States. In addition to encompassing a commitment to post-war free trade, as the US had hoped, it also included proposals for agreements to stabilize the price of raw material exports and the export incomes of poor countries in general, as well as various anti-monopoly measures that the US had strong objection to. The result was that the US Congress refused to ratify the charter and it was finally ditched by President Truman in 1950 (which was ironic because Truman had originally lent a lot of support to the Havana conference, thinking it was important to have broad agreement on trade from all the world's economies to avoid the trade troubles of the Great Depression). The Havana conference also produced a much less ambitious General Agreement on Tariffs and Trade (GATT); this, however, was much more minimalist and less interventionist than the Havana Charter. It was the GATT charter that went on to form the template for all international trade negotiations held since.

Trade negotiations

Since the Second World War there have been eight rounds of world trade negotiations, with a ninth started in Doha, Qatar, in November 2001. Of the eight rounds the last three have been particularly influential in shaping world trade. These were: the Kennedy Round, negotiated between 1964 and 1967; the Tokyo Round, negotiated between 1973 and 1979; and the last completed round, the Uruguay Round, negotiated between 1986 and 1993. The Uruguay Round broke with earlier rounds by covering many more countries (twice the number that had taken part in the Kennedy Round) and by including several new trade-related issues for the first time. The Uruguay Round ended up having a massive influence on the pace of economic globalization. After the Uruguay Round the WTO was established (in 1995). Like the GATT the WTO stands for 'rules based' international trade where all countries are supposedly equal. Unlike GATT, however, the rules and agreements of the WTO have much more binding force and have pushed the boundaries of economic globalization much further than they ever went under the GATT. The WTO has become an infamous Geneva-based institution that for many in the anti-globalization movement epitomizes all that is wrong with economic globalization.

The Doha Round

Following the completion of the Uruguay Round, global reaction to the spread of world trade, and economic globalization in general, entered a new, divisive phase. It was the attempt by the WTO to launch a fresh ninth round of international trade negotiations in Seattle in December 1999 that sparked the first high-profile international mass protests against economic globalization

Table 4.1 International trade negotiations (rounds) held since World War II

Year	Name of round	No. of participants
1947	Geneva	23
1949	Annecy	13
1950	Torquay	38
1956	Geneva	26
1960–61	Dillon	26
1962–67	Kennedy	62
1973–79	Tokyo	99
1986–93	Uruguay	125
2001–03	Doha	146

Note: By 2002 the the United Nations had 191 members.

(although there had been a large protest against a G8 meeting held in Birmingham, UK, in 1997). The 'Battle for Seattle' saw thousands of protestors hit the streets of the city protesting against the impact of economic globalization on the world's poor and the world's environment. It shocked the global community and was soon followed by major protests in Prague, Melbourne, Washington, Quebec City and Gothenburg. The result was the collapse of the Seattle Round with a new attempt to start the round delayed for two years. The new round was finally kicked off in Doha, Qatar, in November 2001, where protests are illegal, thereby denying a voice to those opposed to economic globalization. Like the Uruguay Round, the Doha Round is attempting to introduce new issues and push the boundaries of economic globalization even further. The new issues proposed for the Doha Round include: more WTO control over national investment policy, WTO control over national competition policy, greater exposure of government purchasing policies to world competition and trade facilitation. Poor countries never agreed to including these new issues in the Doha Round and it was disagreement over these new issues that in the end led to the collapse of WTO trade talks at Cancún in September 2003. The Doha Round is scheduled to be completed in January 2005 – although there is now virtually no chance of this deadline being met, following the Cancún collapse.

Poor countries entered the current Doha Round of trade negotiations with unprecedented suspicion of rich countries. Most (rightly) feel that too many rich-country promises from the Uruguay Round remain unfulfilled and want to see them kept before they will countenance further trade liberalization. At the Cancún talks a group of twenty-one poor countries, the G21, successfully stood up to rich countries for the first time at WTO talks. This was a great victory for poor countries and represented a major coming-of-age for them. The group was led by the large poor-country economies of Brazil, India and China and also included Argentina, Bolivia, Chile, Colombia, Costa Rica, Cuba, Ecuador, Egypt, El Salvador, Guatemala, Mexico, Pakistan, Paraguay, Peru, the Philippines, South Africa, Thailand and Venezuela. The main sticking points for them were ongoing rich-country reluctance to reduce agricultural subsidies and the introduction of the new ('Singapore') issues. Through being well organized and not breaking ranks they were able to scuttle WTO trade talks – the second time in four years that WTO talks had collapsed. Before the Cancún talks, poor-country access to affordable medicines under the TRIPS agreement had also been a major sticking point. This was diluted as an issue before Cancún with an agreement that gave poor countries access to affordable generic medicines – although there is so much red tape associated with the agreement that it represented only a modest advance on the issue.

Another major problem for poor countries taking part in international trade negotiations is that they often lack the resources to be able to participate in them properly. About thirty of the world's poorest countries, or roughly a quarter of all the poor countries that belong to the WTO,[32] can't even afford to maintain delegations at the WTO's base in Geneva and sub-Saharan African countries often send only one, or no, representative to key negotiations while rich countries send a small army.[33]

The bizarre rulings of the WTO

One of the biggest differences between the GATT and the WTO is that members of the GATT had a fair bit of discretion about observing its rules. Members of the WTO have very little discretion. The WTO has a disputes settlement process whose free-trade rulings are binding on its members. It's these non-negotiable rulings of the WTO that have been the focus of a lot of anger by anti-globalization protestors.

Probably the most infamous ruling of the WTO was one handed down in 1998 which found against a US law restricting the importation of shrimps from countries whose fishing industries caught them with nets that harmed turtles. The US had originally enacted the law under its Endangered Species Act. It was designed to put pressure on foreign fishing industries to use turtle excluder devices. But the WTO ruled that the environmental measure was an inappropriate barrier to free trade. Free trade came before the world's fragile environment, it seemed. This bias had been established by an earlier, similar, trade ruling. That ruling overturned a law enshrined in the US Marine Mammal Protection Act that banned the importation of tuna caught by foreign fisheries that harmed dolphins. This free-trade anti-environment bias of WTO rulings was also echoed in a 1996 WTO ruling against a US law that prohibited the importation of high-pollution petroleum from Venezuela and Brazil. Australia was forced to accept the importation of potentially diseased salmon from Canada under an equally bizarre WTO ruling. In other incredible rulings, European countries have been forced to stop preferential importation of bananas from poor African countries and have also been forced to allow the importation of hormone-treated beef from the US and Canada (which they defied). A ban in Massachusetts, in the US, on purchases from companies that invest in Burma was also overturned by a WTO ruling. WTO rules have similarly been used to strike out container return legislation. In 2003 the US government announced that it would try and use a WTO ruling to overturn the European Union's (then) moratorium on the importation of genetically modified food.

The new trade boundaries pushed by the WTO

The Uruguay Round of international trade negotiations embraced many new areas that hadn't been touched by earlier rounds. Consequently the WTO oversees, and enforces, new global trade rules in areas previously relatively unaffected by economic globalization. Among the new areas affected by the Uruguay Round were: agriculture, textiles, patent rights, services and trade-related investment.

The new rules on patents, enshrined in the Trade Related Aspects of Intellectual Property Rights (TRIPS) agreement, were particularly radical. For the first time minimum patent-protection rights lasting twenty years were hammered out, along with protection for trademarks, copyrights, commercially based designs and other intellectual-property rights. At first glance such rules might seem reasonable but they were designed to make sure the goods and services of TNCs weren't undercut by cheaper rivals in poor countries. In many cases these TNCs have also been keen to patent plant and genetic material long considered public property in poor countries.

The TRIPS agreement meant that, starting in 2000 for most poor countries, or 2016 for very poor countries, laws had to be introduced that outlawed products that use copies of patented technology. This had a particularly nasty effect on the sale of pharmaceuticals in poor countries. Before the TRIPS agreement generic drug companies had been able to market medicines in poor countries at a fraction of the price they sold for in rich countries. Indian generic drug companies, for instance, were able to sell anti-viral triple therapies for less than US$1,500 in poor countries, whereas patented equivalents sold for between US$10,000 and US$15,000 in rich countries.[34] The TRIPS agreement, however, meant people in poor countries could no longer afford essential drugs that had been within their reach under previous, looser international patent laws. This threatened to have a particularly devastating effect on the huge number of HIV/Aids sufferers in poor countries. Despite the TRIPS agreement, however, the South African government enacted laws in 1997 that made generic HIV/Aids drugs available to its people. The laws were soon challenged in court, under the TRIPS agreement, by a coalition of thirty-nine drug companies, most of them large TNCs. Luckily a huge international campaign was mounted against the court action by the South African Treatment Action Campaign, Médecins sans Frontières and Oxfam (among others) that was loud enough to shame the drug companies into withdrawing their action.[35]

The TRIPS agreement could have a similar effect upon plants and genetic materials traditionally used in poor countries. Patents have already been awarded in Europe, and in the US, for products and formulas long known to farmers in poor countries and long considered public property there. US companies have already patented the Mexican Yellow Enola Bean, Basmati rice and selected maize genes, while a European company has patented a process for extracting medical substances from the Indian Neem tree, a process known to Indian farmers for centuries.[36] Other patents in the US, Japan and Europe have been given for kava from the Pacific and turmeric and bitter lemon from Asia. International free trade, in the form of the TRIPS agreement, means that both the health and food security of poor countries could in future be owned by wealthy TNCs.

Another new area that the Uruguay Round pushed economic globalization into was services. The rules about the trade in services that came out of the Uruguay Round also threaten to make poor-country consumers the preserve of rich-country TNCs. The new services trade rules were enshrined in an agreement called the General Agreement on Trade in Services (GATS). The GATS agreement was aimed at a progressive liberalization of the global trade in services, starting in February 2000. It may end up resulting in the privatization of a large number of hitherto government-run services like health, education and water supply in poor countries. Big European TNC water supply companies could end up owning water provision services throughout Africa and South America. Like the TRIPS agreement, the GATS agreement has become a major focus of the anti-globalization movement in recent years.

The GATS agreement is buttressed by yet another Uruguay Round side deal, the agreement on Trade Related Investment Measures (TRIMS). TRIMS is the trade investment 'sister' of TRIPS and GATS. It prohibits investment laws that may discriminate in favour of local businesses in areas of local investment and ownership linked to trade. The TRIMS agreement was mainly aimed at removing trade impediments to the free flow of components between different arms of the same TNC located in different countries.

Regional trade deals

Although the WTO is meant to stand for rules-based trade being applied, in equal measure, across the entire globe, it was obvious long before the WTO was established that regional trade deals would undermine its claim to being a truly international trade regime. Regional trade agreements exploded during the 1990s after taking root soon after the Second World War. No fewer than 109 regional trade agreements were signed between 1948 and 1994, with a third of them signed between 1990 and 1994 alone.[37]

One of the early significant regional trade agreements was that which underpinned the establishment of the European Economic Community in 1957. Other major regional trade agreements since include the North American Free Trade Agreement (which began as a free-trade agreement between the US and Canada) in 1993, the ASEAN (Southeast Asian) free-trade area formed in 1992, and the South American Mercosur free-trade area agreement (between Argentina, Brazil, Paraguay and Uruguay), signed in 1995. One very controversial free-trade agreement currently being formulated is the Free Trade Agreement of the Americas, designed to take in nearly all the countries of North and South America, which is due to be signed in 2005. As well as locking all signatory countries into the globalization web of the United States, the US is also keen that the agreement lock signatory countries into its foreign policies as well. In May 2003 US trade representative Robert Zoellick said the US seeks 'cooperation, or better, on foreign policy and security issues' from its potential free-trade agreement partners.[38]

The International Monetary Fund and the World Bank

Like the WTO, the International Monetary Fund (IMF) and the World Bank are frequent targets of the anti-globalization movement. Indeed their annual general meetings are often specific targets for anti-globalization protestors. And like the WTO, the IMF and the World Bank are also major forces behind the ongoing expansion of the world economy.

During the 1950s and 1960s both institutions had reasonably benign and predictable functions during the climate of relatively stable exchange rates and limited world capital mobility that existed at the time. The IMF concerned itself with the short-term stabilization of countries experiencing balance-of-payments difficulties, while the World Bank concerned itself with long-term development through specific project loans.[39] During

the immediate post-war years the IMF had limited influence
and was overshadowed by US post-war reconstruction aid for
Europe channelled through its Marshall Plan. The IMF didn't
make its first loan until 1956 (to the United Kingdom) and did
not have much power until the early 1960s.[40] The World Bank
had more power than the IMF straight after the Second World
War but, like the IMF, was initially mainly concerned back then
with European countries, making its first loans to France, the
Netherlands, Denmark and Luxembourg.[41]

The rise of the IMF and the World Bank

The massive increase in world capital flows, kicked off in the
1970s with the floating of rich-country currencies, and the start
of major private bank lending to poor countries, significantly
changed the role of the IMF and the World Bank. In the 1950s
and 1960s world capital flows had been insignificant, exchange
rates relatively stable, and poor countries had generally enjoyed
steady increases in per capita wealth. But the 1970s changed all
that. World capital flows began to skyrocket, many poor countries
began to borrow heavily and at the same time the ongoing development of some poor countries began to falter for the first time
since the Second World War. In 1982 it all came to a head with
the start of the Third World debt crisis. These influences hugely
changed the role of the IMF and the World Bank.

The 1970s and 1980s saw a significant increase in lending by
the IMF and the World Bank; the World Bank's lending alone
quadrupled between 1968 and 1981.[42] But by far the most radical change was that both institutions began long-term lending
to poor countries with major policy-based strings attached to
their loans. With these loans the IMF became more than just a
short-term currency crisis lender. It claimed that the solvency
of its short-term loans was necessarily connected to the long-
term viability of the relevant poor-country debtor economy
and started extending conditional long-term loans with titles

like Extended Fund Facility, Structural Adjustment Facilities and Systemic Transformation Facility. It started having a major say in the overall management of the economies of its debtors. The World Bank similarly began to operate beyond its original narrow ambit of project-based lending, claiming, like the IMF, that the viability of its loans was necessarily connected to the long-term economic health of its poor-country debtors. It too began extending conditional long-term loans, in their case with titles like Structural Adjustment Loans and Sector Adjustment Loans. The IMF and World Bank began tripping over themselves to extend these new loans, often failing to coordinate with each other, all the while assuming more and more economic powers.

In some ways the logic behind these new loans made sense; the short term is indeed often connected to the long term. But it was the flavour and philosophy of the conditions that raised the ire of many poor-country governments and, eventually, the anti-globalization movement. The conditions of both IMF and World Bank loans were significantly influenced by the original reaction of the two institutions to the Third World debt crisis in South America. Part of the cause of that crisis had been chronic over-spending by South American governments. When coupled with low interest rates this led to high inflation. Since raising taxes was sacrilegious to the US-based free-market philosophy of the IMF and the World Bank, they insisted that government spending be cut as a way of financing the problem South American loans. This often involved cutting food subsidies to the poor and reducing essential services like health provision. And the IMF and the World Bank didn't stop there. They also insisted on tariff cuts, higher interest rates, less restriction on foreign investment, deregulation of the labour force and widespread privatization: in short a wholesale imposition of American free-market economic liberalization. Unsurprisingly both institutions quickly developed reputations for the unthinking application of predictable, doctrinaire economic liberalization that would not tolerate dissent. Poor countries felt unable to upset the IMF and the World Bank because if they refused to lend to them, everyone else, especially private banks, would refuse as well. Peru, for instance, was ostracized by international finance institutions after it limited its debt repayments to 10 per cent of its foreign earnings.

Over time both institutions began applying the same free-market prescription to every poor-country crisis, regardless of its cause. Indeed, one-time chief economist of the World Bank Joseph Stiglitz even claims the IMF once drew up a loan agreement that, as a result of sloppy word processing, still had the name of the previous poor country it had been applied to sprinkled throughout.[43] The autocratic reputation of the two institutions was reinforced by the resignations from the World Bank of dissident economists Herman Daley in 1994 and Joseph Stiglitz in 1999, followed by the resignation of the probing editor of the World Bank's *World Development Report* in 2000. Ravi Kanbur, one-time head of the World Bank's World Development Task Force, was also forced to resign.

Because the loans of the two institutions often touch on areas of government activity that are crucial to the human and economic health of poor countries, their one-size-fits-all prescriptions have frequently had devastating consequences. These consequences have included:

- the outbreak of bubonic and pneumonic plague in India in 1994 as a direct result of IMF/World Bank loan-mandated budget cuts in 1991;[44]
- the collapse of the agricultural industry of Somalia as a result of IMF/World Bank intervention in the early 1980s, which led to a huge loss in agricultural self-sufficiency in Somalia with a resultant significant increase in dependency on imported grain;[45]
- the escalation of the prices of essential fuel and consumer goods at the height of the Rwandan civil war in 1992, significantly worsening the impact of the war;[46]

- the bankruptcy of small and medium-sized farmers in Bangladesh in the early 1980s as a result of IMF-mandated elimination of agricultural subsidies;[47]
- consumer prices in Lima, Peru, in 1991, becoming higher than New York's while, at the same time, the after-inflation earnings of most Peruvians fell by 60 per cent;[48]
- the fuelling of the war in Bosnia as a result of IMF/World Bank-driven budget cuts in the amount of federal government assistance the central government in Yugoslavia provided to its provinces;[49]
- the escalation of a recent severe drought in Malawi through the sell-off of its national grain buffer stock stipulated by the IMF in 2001.

The fall of the IMF and the World Bank

Despite these devastating consequences, in its 1991 *World Development Report* the World Bank claimed that global economic opinion was increasingly behind its policies and even that there was an 'emerging consensus' about it all. But just as the IMF and the World Bank appeared at the height of their power and respect, their reputations were severely dented by the East Asian meltdown in 1997. That crisis was largely caused by the exit of huge volumes of 'hot' money that had particularly focused on short-term real-estate gains in the region, specifically the economies of Indonesia, Malaysia, South Korea, Thailand and Taiwan. The exit of the money left these economies depressed, with huge increases in unemployment and bankruptcy as a result. The IMF/World Bank standard formula brought on even lower growth just when higher economic growth was needed. It prescribed huge cutbacks in government spending, higher interest rates and continuing overvalued currencies. The net result was that the East Asian economies went further under and in the process the credibility of the IMF and World Bank took a battering.

As a result of the dented reputations of the two institutions, as well as the failure of a string of ongoing Third World debt strategies, some changes have taken place within the IMF and the World Bank. In 1999 the Heavily Indebted Poor Country Initiative was announced, which undertook to cut the foreign debts of forty-one of the world's poorest countries by nearly half (although it went on to have a much more modest net effect).[50] At the same time poverty reduction was made a higher priority, with the IMF and the World Bank introducing Poverty Reduction Support Credit and Poverty Reduction and Growth Facility loans. Both institutions even admitted to some minor failings during the Asian meltdown (although they were inclined to blame it all on poor 'sequencing' of economic liberalization instead of on fundamental problems with the policy itself). In the early 1990s the World Bank also introduced increased environmental awareness into its programmes and in 1994 even introduced a complaints mechanism.

The big body blow to the IMF and the World Bank, however, has been growing agreement between the left and the right of politics, particularly in the United States, that the policies of neither institution are working. The clearest expression of this sentiment, from the right of US politics at least, came in 2000 when the US government-appointed Meltzer Commission review of the IMF and the World Bank delivered its findings. They were unforgiving. They said World Bank projects had a high failure rate (up to 70 per cent in very poor countries), few countries enjoyed much benefit from the two institutions (eleven countries have received 70 per cent of World Bank loans), the IMF and the World Bank were largely irrelevant to poverty reduction in poor countries and they often did the bidding of vested interests in rich countries.[51] The conservative US think-tank the Heritage Foundation has also been very critical of the World Bank.

The net result of their dubious policies and ever-diminishing support is that both the IMF and the World Bank are now very unpopular. A recent poll conducted by the World Bank itself among 2,600 global opinion leaders in forty-eight countries found that most thought it was too arrogant, too bureaucratic, too ineffective and too closely aligned with the United States.[52] A majority of the opinion leaders in Latin America, the Middle East and North Africa also thought World Bank reforms did more harm than good.

Core problems persist in both the World Bank and the IMF and, as a result, they have never looked more vulnerable. Both institutions continue to display an inordinate inability to consult and work with local societies, a trait that often undermines their poverty-reduction strategies. They both continue to override local authorities and show blatant disregard for the social and environmental impact of their programmes. Their debt-reduction strategies also fail to address the basic causes of Third World poverty. The World Bank continues to favour large, capital-intensive projects over smaller, community-based projects that may have more lasting effect. And, most crucially of all, neither institution shows any sign of lessening its faith in free-market economics. It is sometimes said the IMF and the World Bank have overthrown more governments than all the world's armies.

The Washington Consensus

Underpinning the influence of the WTO, IMF, World Bank and TNCs is what is known as the 'Washington Consensus' or the 'Wall Street–Treasury Complex'. These are labels for the common free-market ideology of the IMF, the World Bank, the US stock-market, large US TNCs and the US Treasury. The Washington Consensus is more than just a group of influential people, based in the same city, who share the same economic philosophies, however. Over the past two decades it has become a tightly knit, self-reinforcing club. Invariably the US Treasury calls the shots, then the other institutions fall into line. The *New York Times* even went so far, on one occasion, as to call the IMF 'a proxy for the

United States'.[53] They all sing from the same song sheet and the sum of their separate voices makes for an unassailable free-market economic force.

Several factors reinforce the influence of the Washington Consensus. The first is historical. The Washington Consensus perpetuates an Anglo-Saxon free-market view of how the economic world should be shaped, which carries on the free-market tradition established by Britain in the nineteenth century and which was continued by the US in the twentieth century. It was the US and Britain that crafted the IMF and the World Bank; it was the US that first floated its currency in 1971; and it was the US and Britain that first relaxed their capital controls in the 1970s. The second influence is size. Although not as dominant as it was after the Second World War, the economy of the United States still represents 21 per cent of the world's combined gross domestic product (GDP) (measured by purchasing power parity, or 30 per cent of world GDP if measured by exchange rate)[54] and takes in 19 per cent of all the world's imports.[55] Two-thirds of all the world's reserves of foreign exchange are held in US dollars.[56] The third influence is personnel. There is a high degree of cross-fertilization between different parts of the Washington Consensus. Stan Fischer, a one-time deputy managing director of the IMF, left his job there to become vice-chairman at Citigroup (which owns Citibank);[57] Robert Rubin, US Treasury Secretary under President Clinton, was a senior bank executive at Goldman Sachs; Lewis Preston, former president of the World Bank, was chief executive at J.P. Morgan;[58] and Peter Sutherland, former director-general of the WTO, is now chairman of Goldman Sachs International. And the fourth influence is, of course, proximity. All are located in Washington (and New York in the case of the Wall Street stock market). The IMF and World Bank were even located in the same building at one time.

Historically, you could broaden the Washington Consensus by calling it the 'Anglo–Washington–Chicago School Consensus'. Much of the current economic liberalization ideology pursued by the Washington Consensus was originally drawn from the philosophies of a high-profile free-market economist, Milton Friedman, who from 1948 was Professor of Economics at the University of Chicago. He, in turn, was inspired by a free-market contemporary of John Maynard Keynes, Austrian economist Friedrich von Hayek (who strenuously opposed the interventionist ideas of Keynes). The philosophies of both Friedman and von Hayek were championed and implemented by Margaret Thatcher, following her election as British prime minister in 1979, then by Ronald Reagan, following his election as US president in 1980.

All these influences are reinforced by the decision-making structures of the IMF, the World Bank and the WTO. In the IMF and World Bank, voting power is largely determined by the number of shares a country can afford to buy, which gives the US, and rich countries in general, enormous clout and influence over all decisions. The US has a permanent seat on the World Bank board, can veto any decision, and has 17.6 per cent of all the votes (it had as many as 42 per cent of all the votes immediately after the Second World War).[59] The US has 18 per cent of the votes on the IMF board and, along with other rich countries and a requirement that some decisions require 'super' majorities, effectively runs that organization as well.[60] When the IMF and the World Bank were established, chief US negotiator Harry Dexter White said, 'the US should have enough votes to block any decision'.[61] The WTO is ostensibly operated along more consensual lines with each country having, in theory, an equal vote; but in reality most decisions are made in 'green rooms', away from the main meeting, where the 'quad' of the European Union, Japan, the US and Canada dominates, with poor countries only given a say if they represent a regional or political grouping.

All these myriad factors coalesce into making the Washington Consensus the new Roman Empire of today's global economy.

The technological engines of globalization

Although economic globalization is very much the product of political decisions taken to reduce barriers to economic globalization, like tariffs and capital controls, as well as of the influence of the all-powerful institutions it has created, it was technological change that allowed economic globalization to happen in the first place. Politicians gave economic globalization permission to take place but technology has given it the means. Technological change, especially since the Second World War, has massively shrunk the world, making it more able than ever before to converge into one giant world supermarket and bank.

In 1956 it was possible for only eighty-nine simultaneous telephone conversations to occur via the cable that then linked Europe to North America; today it is possible to have up to a million simultaneous conversations taking place through the satellite and fibre-optic communications links that now exist between the two continents.[62] Computers have similarly shrunk the world. In 1993 there were only about 1 million Internet hosts around the world; within just six years the number had increased twentyfold to about 42 million.[63] An equivalent revolution has taken place in transport technology. According to the Boeing aircraft corporation world air traffic cargo trebled between 1985 and 1997 and is predicted to treble again by 2015.[64] Annual world car production increased fivefold between 1950 and 2000.[65] Similarly, world shipping, which carries about 90 per cent of global freight, was revolutionized by containerization, beginning in the 1950s, and has expanded rapidly ever since. World shipping grew about tenfold between 1950 and the late 1990s and is expected to increase by about 85 per cent between 1997 and 2010.[66]

The explosion in global freight is the result of a complex interplay between ever lighter trucks, ships and so forth, more efficient and powerful engines, and cheaper oil. Increasingly cars, trucks, aeroplanes and ships are being built from lighter material and are being fitted with ever more dynamic engines. Between

Table 4.2 World's largest companies (1999)

	Name	Headquarters	Sales (US$ billion)
1	General Motors	US	176.6
2	Wal-Mart Stores	US	166.8
3	Exxon Mobil	US	163.9
4	Ford Motor	US	162.6
5	Daimler Chrysler	US	160.0
6	Mitsui	Japan	118.6
7	Mitsubishi	Japan	117.8
8	Toyota Motor	Japan	115.7
9	General Electric	US	111.6
10	Itochu	Japan	109.1
11	Royal Dutch/Shell Group	UK/Netherlands	105.4
12	Sumitomo	Japan	95.7
13	Nippon Telegraph and Telephone	Japan	93.6
14	Marubeni	Japan	91.8
15	AXA	France	87.6
16	IBM	US	87.5
17	BP Amoco	UK	83.6
18	Citigroup	US	82.0
19	Volkswagon	Germany	80.1
20	Nippon Life Insurance	Japan	78.5
21	Siemens	Germany	75.3
22	Allianz	Germany	74.2
23	Hitachi	Japan	71.9
24	Matasushita Electric Industrial	Japan	65.6
25	Nissho Iwai	Japan	65.4
26	US Postal Service	US	62.7
27	ING Group	Netherlands	62.5
28	AT&T	US	62.4
29	Philip Morris	US	61.8
30	Sony	Japan	60.1
31	Deutsche Bank	Germany	58.6
32	Boeing	US	58.0
33	Dai-ichi Mutual Life Insurance	Japan	55.1
34	Honda Motor	Japan	54.8
35	Assicurazioni Generali	Italy	53.7
36	Nissan Motor	Japan	53.7
37	E.ON	Germany	52.2
38	Toshiba	Japan	51.6
39	Bank of America Corp.	US	51.4
40	Fiat	Italy	51.3

Source: The Economist, *Pocket World in Figures 2002 Edition*, Profile Books, London, p. 60.

the mid-1970s and mid-1990s nearly half a tonne was shaved from the weight of a new car, for instance, contributing to large increases in the distance that could be travelled on a litre of fuel. At the same time the average price of fuel has fallen. From the mid-1980s onwards the price of oil began to plummet, and, even though it has increased somewhat since, after factoring in the influence of inflation, oil prices today are close to the cheapest they have been since the Second World War.

All these technological changes mean that both money and goods can be moved anywhere around the world less expensively than ever before. And there has been no shortage of business-people eager to exploit the new opportunities this has created. There is also no shortage of businesspeople eager to guide more technological change along the path of globalization instead of developing sustainable alternatives.

The environmental price of world trade

The explosion in world freight, in particular, has had a punishing impact on the global environment. Nearly all global freight is powered by fossil fuels. A study in 1997 by the Organization for Economic Cooperation and Development and the International Energy Agency found that the transport sector accounted for between 20 and 25 per cent of the world's total carbon emissions.[67] Within the transport sector, freight accounts for 55 per cent of total emissions.[68] Road transport accounts for about 80 per cent of all the transport emissions, but aviation is the fastest growing contributor.[69] It's easy to see why freight accounts for so much carbon emission. Flying a kiwi fruit from New Zealand to Europe results in carbon emissions equal to five times the weight of the fruit.[70] Most orange juice consumed in Europe is produced in Brazil; to move all the juice between those two areas requires a consumption of fuel equal to 10 per cent of the weight of the juice.[71] A plate of food eaten in a typical rich trade-orientated

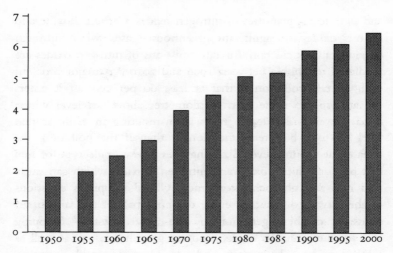

Source: Worldwatch Institute, *Vital Signs 2002–2003*, London, Earthscan, 2002, p. 63.

Figure 4.1 World fossil fuel emissions
(billion tonnes of carbon)

country these days has travelled about 2,000 miles from source to consumer.[72]

The steep rises in global fossil fuel use since the Second World War have meant that annual global carbon emissions are now nearly four times what they were in 1950.[73] This has led to a 16 per cent increase in world carbon dioxide concentrations over the same period.[74] These increased greenhouse gas emissions may eventually see world temperatures rise by up to 4°C by about 2070. This is only one or two degrees less than total global warming since the end of the last ice age. In no small measure, the world's environment is paying the price of the spread of economic globalization.

The specific pollution effects of aircraft and shipping are also alarming. Aeroplanes produce large quantities of carbon dioxide and significant quantities of nitrogen oxides. Carbon dioxide and nitrous oxide are significant greenhouse gases, while nitrogen dioxide causes acid rain. Aircraft emissions of nitrogen oxides are predicted to double between 1996 and 2010.[75] A major problem with aircraft pollution is that at least 60 per cent of it enters the atmosphere more than 9 kilometres above sea level where it has fewer molecules to react with, resulting in a life at that level up to a hundred times longer than if the pollution was released at ground level. Shipping uses a low-grade type of fuel that produces nitric oxide and nitrogen dioxide, which can cause acid rain and photochemical smog. Global shipping's emissions of these two pollutants is equal to about half of the land-based emissions of them generated by the United States.[76] Shipping also produces nitrous oxide, a potent greenhouse gas, as well as sulphur oxides, which cause acid rain. Most regrettably, however, pollution from world freight is exempt from the Kyoto greenhouse gas protocol.

Economic globalization has been around long enough now for it to have developed powerful vested interests, in the form of the IMF, the World Bank, the WTO and TNC institutions that power it along, in addition to the powerful new technologies that enable it to keep operating and expanding. These ensure that there is enormous self-perpetuating force behind the global economy these days, which means the anti-globalization movement is now up against a very powerful foe.

Notes

1. Oswaldo de Rivero, *The Myth of Development: The Non-Viable Economies of the 21st Century*, Zed Books, London, 2001, p. 46.
2. Robert Went, *Globalization: Neoliberal Challenge, Radical Responses*, Pluto Press, London, 2000, p. 18.
3. Ibid., p. 18.
4. John Madeley, *Hungry for Trade: How the Poor Pay for Free Trade*, Zed Books, London, 2000, p. 91.
5. Kevin Watkins et al., *Rigged Rules and Double Standards: Trade, Globalisation*

and the Fight against Global Poverty, Oxfam International, Washington DC, 2002, p. 190.

6. Went, *Globalization: Neoliberal Challenge*, pp. 44, 45.

7. George Monbiot, *The Age of Consent: A Manifesto for a New World Order*, Flamingo, London, 2003, p. 195.

8. Saul Estlake (Chief Economist, ANZ Bank, Australia), *Globalization: Keeping the Gains*, presentation to a series of workshops arranged by the Department of Foreign Affairs and Trade (Trade Advocacy and Outreach Section) in Australia in 2003, p. 20.

9. Colin Hines, *Localization: A Global Manifesto*, Earthscan, London, 2000, p. 14.

10. Robbie Robertson, *The Three Waves of Globalization: A History of a Developing Consciousness*, Zed Books, London, 2003, p. 198.

11. Madeley, *Hungry for Trade*, p. 91.

12. John Madeley, *Food for All: The Need for a New Agriculture*, Zed Books, London, 2002, p. 122.

13. Watkins et al., *Rigged Rules*, p. 210.

14. Ibid.

15. Ankie Hoogvelt, *Globalization and the Postcolonial World: The New Political Economy of Development*, Palgrave, London, 2001, p. 149.

16. Vandana Shiva, *Protect or Plunder? Understanding Intellectual Property Rights*, Zed Books, London, 2001, p. 19.

17. Hines, *Localization*, p. 213.

18. Watkins et al., *Rigged Rules*, p. 212.

19. Ann Capling, *Australia and the Global Trade System: From Havana to Seattle*, Cambridge University Press, Cambridge, 2001, p. 149.

20. Ibid.

21. Joan E. Spero and Jeffrey A. Hart, *The Politics of International Economic Relations*, 5th edn, Routledge, London, 1997, p. 259.

22. Russell Martin, *Picasso's War: The Extraordinary Story of an Artist, an Atrocity and a Painting that Changed the World*, Scribner, London, 2002, p. 151.

23. Martin Khor, *Rethinking Globalizaion: Critical Ideas and Policy Choices*, Zed Books, London, 2001, p. 104.

24. Ibid., p. 102.

25. 'Groups File Claim against BP and Pipeline Partners in 5 Countries: "Green" Company Violating International Norms in Controversial Caspian Oil Pipeline', published by Deb Foskey via WTO Watch email list (debf@webone.com.au), 1 May 2003 (#156), p. 1. (For archive copy, see www.nwjc.org.au/avcwl/lists/archives.html.)

26. Watkins et al., *Rigged Rules*, p. 182.

27. Ibid., p. 179.

28. Ibid., p. 178.
29. Spero and Hart, *International Economic Relations*, p. 264.
30. Ibid., p. 281.
31. Ibid., p. 129.
32. Mike Moore, *A World without Walls: Freedom, Development, Free Trade and Global Governance*, Cambridge University Press, Cambridge, 2003, p. 130.
33. Watkins et al., *Rigged Rules*, p. 252.
34. Ibid., p. 213.
35. Ibid., p. 216.
36. Ibid., p. 220.
37. Went, *Globalization*, pp. 21, 22.
38. 'Zoellick Says Fta Candidates Must Support US Foreign Policy', published by Deb Foskey via WTO Watch email list (debf@webone.com.au), 12 June 2003 (#169). (For archive copy, see www.nwjc.org.au/avcwl/lists/archives.html.)
39. Carol Sherman, *A Look inside the World Bank*, Envirobook, Sydney, 1990, p. 4.
40. A.G. Kenwood and A.L. Lougheed, *Growth of the International Economy 1820–1990: An Introductory Text*, Routledge, London, 1992, p. 262.
41. Sherman, *A Look inside the World Bank*, p. 6.
42. Walden Bello, *Deglobalization: Ideas for a New World Economy*, Zed Books, London, 2002, p. 38.
43. Joseph E. Stiglitz, *Globalization and Its Discontents*, Allen Lane, London, 2002, p. 47.
44. Michel Chossudovsky, *The Globalisation of Poverty: Impacts of IMF and World Bank Reforms*, Zed Books, London, 1999, p. 72.
45. Ibid., pp. 101, 102.
46. Ibid., p. 117.
47. Ibid., p. 140.
48. Ibid., p. 191.
49. Ibid., p. 246.
50. Worldwatch Institute, *Vital Signs 2001–2002: The Trends That Are Shaping Our Future*, Earthscan, London, 2001, p. 58.
51. Bello, *Deglobalization*, pp. 70, 93.
52. Anna Willard, 'World Bank Poll Finds Bank Arrogant, Tied to US', published by Deb Foskey via WTO Watch email list (debf@webone.com.au), 19 June 2003 (#171), p. 1. (For archive copy, see www.nwjc.org.au/avcwl/lists/archives.html.)
53. Ibid., p. 62.

54. The Economist, *Pocket World in Figures: 2002 Edition*, Profile Books, London, 2001, p. 24.
55. Based on figures in World Bank, *World Development Report 2002*, Oxford University Press, New York, 2002, p. 239.
56. 'Financial Indicators', *The Economist*, 7 October 2000, p. 133.
57. Stiglitz, *Globalization and Its Discontents*, pp. 207, 208.
58. Chossudovsky, *The Globalization of Poverty*, p. 25.
59. Bello, *Deglobalization*, pp. 59–60.
60. Ibid., p. 61.
61. Monbiot, *The Age of Consent*, p. 166.
62. Went, *Globalization*, p. 16.
63. World Bank, *World Development Report 1999/2000*, New York, Oxford University Press, 2000, p. 4.
64. Wayne Ellwood, *The No-Nonsense Guide to Globalization*, New Internationalist Publications, Oxford, 2001, p. 18.
65. Worldwatch Institute, *Vital Signs 2001–2002*, p. 69.
66. Edward Goldsmith and Jerry Mander, eds, *The Case against the Global Economy: And for a Turn towards Localization*, Earthscan, London, p. 226.
67. Andrew Simms, *Collision Course: Free Trade's Free Ride on the Global Climate*, New Economics Foundation, London, 2000, p. 9.
68. Ibid., p. 11.
69. Ibid.
70. Worldwatch Institute, *Vital Signs 2001–2002*, p. 69.
71. Simms, *Collision Course*, p. 8.
72. Bello, *Deglobalization*, p. 113.
73. Worldwatch Institute, *Vital Signs 2001–2002*, p. 53.
74. Ibid., p. 53.
75. Gardner et al., 'A Global Inventory of Aircraft Nox Emissions: A Revised Inventory (1996) by the European Civil Aviation Conference/Abatement of Nuisances Caused by Air Transport and EC Working Group'. Discussion of this paper can be found at: www.grida.no/climate/ipcc/aviation/137.htm.
76. James J. Corbett and Paul Fischbeck, 'Emissions from Ships', *Science* 278, October 1997.

CHAPTER 5

RICH VERSUS POOR
IN THE GLOBAL ECONOMY

It is often claimed by supporters of economic globalization that it 'lifts all boats' – that is, ultimately everyone grows richer from it. The anti-globalization movement counters that it 'lifts all yachts' – that is, only the rich benefit. Although there are some significant exceptions to this, in general economic globalization does seem to have mainly benefited the rich. Since the start of the Industrial Revolution rich countries have done much better out of economic globalization than poor ones. In recent decades some poor countries have even become significantly poorer as a result of economic globalization. Both the structure and the politics of today's globalized world are unambiguously tilted in favour of rich countries; if it is left as it is, today's global supermarket and global bank will make the rich richer and the poor will get left behind with devastating consequences.

The polarization of global wealth

The wealth record of poor countries, taken as a group, since the start of the Industrial Revolution (and the start of Robbie Robertson's second wave of globalization) does not make for heartening reading. Whatever else the Industrial Revolution and economic globalization may have brought to the world, they definitely have not made it a more financially egalitarian place.

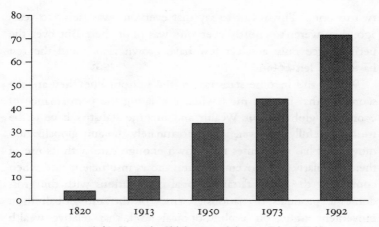

Source: Ankie Hoogvelt, *Globalization and the Post Colonial World*, Palgrave, London, 2001, p. 90.

Figure 5.1 Per capita incomes of world's richest and poorest countries (richest as a multiple of poorest)

Since the start of the Industrial Revolution the gap between the world's richest and poorest countries has grown wider and wider and is now a yawning chasm. The United Nations Development Program (UNDP) estimates that in 1820 the difference between the per capita incomes of the world's richest and poorest countries was 3:1, by 1913 they estimate it had grown to 11:1, by 1950 35:1, by 1973 44:1, and by 1992 they say it had blown out to a horrendous 72:1.[1] This analysis is echoed by David Landis, Professor Emeritus of History and Economics at Harvard University. He says, 'the difference in income per head between the richest industrial nation, say Switzerland, and the poorest non-industrial country, Mozambique, is about 400 to one. Two hundred and fifty years ago, this gap between richest and poorest was perhaps five to one, and the difference between Europe and, say, East or South Asia (India or China) was around 1.5 or two to one'.[2] This is not to say that everyone was rich 250 years ago; they weren't – nearly everyone was poor then. But over the period since only a select few have grown richer and the rest have been left behind.

Wealth and income statistics are the bottom line: they are the scorecard that matters most when evaluating the performance of economic globalization. Wealth and income statistics have to be treated carefully, however, and, unfortunately, the anti–globalization movement has sometimes not shown enough care with its use of them (similarly, the movement often shows insufficient care when comparing the sales of transnational corporations with the gross domestic products of nations). Critics of the anti–globalization movement argue, on a philosophical level, that relative wealth differences don't matter – it's changes in the absolute wealth, or bottom-line poverty, of poor people that matter. They also (rightly) argue that a lot of wealth and income statistics, covering the past few decades in particular, are based on exchange rate conversions which don't take into account the fact that a loaf of bread in, say, China costs only a fraction of the cost of an equivalent loaf in the United States (i.e. they don't take into account relative purchasing power, or purchasing power parity). Some supporters of globalization even claim that if you take relative purchasing power into account there has actually been a decrease in world income distribution polarization over the past three decades, not an increase.

The changes in world income distribution since the Industrial Revolution are of such a magnitude, however, that factoring in relative purchasing power does not change the big-picture message that rich countries have done much better out of economic globalization, in the long term, than poor ones. Nor is there any denying that, in the long term, wealth, finance and trade have all become much more concentrated around the triad of Western Europe, East Asia and North America than they were before the Industrial Revolution. Supporters of economic globalization often focus on short-term changes in global poverty but generally concede that the long-term trend in global wealth distribution has not been good. The pro-globalization Centre for International Economics in Australia, for instance, admits that 'for nearly two centuries, productivity improvements did not spread quickly, and international inequality widened'.[3] Like the anti-globalization movement, supporters of globalization also show a lack of sufficient care, at times, with global income statistics. They often compare movements in national per capita income statistics without factoring in that per capita income statistics are averages that can mask polarizations in income that may have occurred within countries. On the relative-versus-absolute-poverty argument, it is broadly agreed that today about 1.2 billion people live on US$1 or less per day and that about 2.8 billion people live on $2 or less per day.[4] The number living on $1 or less per day has not changed much over the past two decades, so this has meant there has been a slight reduction in the proportion of the world's population living on $1 or less per day (given ongoing increases in total world population). Supporters of globalization often point to this as further evidence that economic globalization reduces, rather than increases, poverty. But even if you are only concerned with absolute poverty, 2.8 billion people living on 2 dollars or less per day is about half of the world's population and is an unacceptable level of absolute poverty in anyone's book. Critics of globalization are often portrayed as irrational but there is nothing rational about half the world's population still living on roughly the same incomes their forebears lived on before the Industrial Revolution. Supporters of globalization are often obsessed with measures of bottom-line poverty and don't pay enough attention to relative poverty (which is often scarcely better than bottom-line poverty).

Apart from inadequate access to wealth, the world also suffers from inadequate access to other essentials of life. Over 1 billion people do not have adequate access to water and about 2 billion do not have adequate access to essential medicines.[5] Also, about 840 million people in the world are malnourished.[6]

Absolute poverty of the sort that persists today is an inter-national disgrace. No one could argue that economic global-ization has delivered enough benefit to those 2.8 billion living on $2 a day or less, most of whom rely on subsistence farming. Perhaps most frightening of all, global wealth distribution has now reached a point where it is self-perpetuating, especially with re-gard to the distribution of potentially wealth-creating technology. In most rich countries at least half the population has access to the Internet but in India, for instance, fewer than 1 per cent do.[7] The city of New York has more Internet connections than all of Africa.[8] There is a telephone connection for about every two people in rich countries but in the world's poorest countries there is only one for every 200 people.[9]

It is also difficult not to argue that within many poor countries the benefits of economic globalization have been very unevenly spread. China, for instance, in recent decades has experienced one of the biggest export booms of any country in history, yet only a quarter of its population has seen much benefit from it while about 800 million of its 1.2 billion population remain peasants. In Mexico 50 per cent of the population are poor despite the fact that the country's exports have trebled since it signed the North American Free Trade Agreement in 1994.[10] In Africa the proportion of the continent's population living on $1 per day or less has increased from 56 per cent in the mid-1960s to 65 per cent in the late 1990s.[11] In Argentina more than half its 36 million population live in poverty.[12] In Nigeria two-thirds of the population live on less than US$1 per day despite the fact that the country has exported US$300 billion worth of oil over the past two decades.[13] Even in rich countries wealth is often very unevenly distributed. In the United States the wealthiest 1 per cent of households own 30 per cent of the nation's net wealth.[14] No one could be proud of these statistics and they give the lie to claims that economic globalization necessarily lifts all boats. In 1996 the Organization for Economic Cooperation and Development adopted the goal of reducing the number of people in the world living in extreme poverty by half by 2015 (a goal reiterated at the 2000 United Nations Millennium Summit held in New York) but no one seriously thinks this goal will be met. Some historically poor countries such as the 'tiger' economies of East Asia (South Korea, Singapore, Malaysia and Taiwan), as well as some oil-exporting economies, have undoubtedly done well out of economic globalization, but they are very much the exception. Half the world's population have never made a telephone call[15] and for that half of the world, at the very least, the benefits of economic globalization remain abstract. It is often claimed there are about 1 billion 'bankable' people living in the world. That 1 billion have done well out of economic globalization but the other 5 billion people in the world have not.

Concentration of economic globalization around rich countries

Much of the cause of the massive drift in wealth away from today's poor countries over the past two centuries has been the equally massive concentration of the world's manufacturing in the hands of rich countries that has occurred over the same period. In 1750 today's poor countries accounted for nearly three-quarters of the world's manufacturing activity but by the start of the First World War their share had fallen to less than 10 per cent[16] (although it has recovered slightly since). The past two and a half centuries of economic globalization have led to a huge concentration of world production that has entrenched the financial power of rich countries. Today most of the world's industrial production takes place in the triad of Western Europe, East Asia and North America and there is no evidence that this is likely to change any time soon.

Like global manufacturing, global flows of trade and capital are also highly concentrated around the triad. And, like the concentration of global manufacturing, this concentration has also contributed hugely to the ongoing poverty of much of the

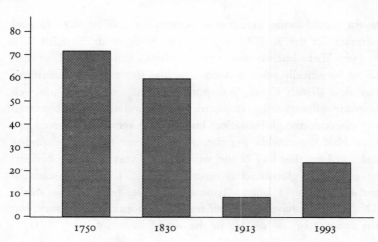

Source: *The Economist*, 1 October 1994, p. 10, Survey.

Figure 5.2 Poor-country share of world manufacturing (%)

world's population. In 2000 those countries that the World Bank classifies as 'high income', which between them account for just 16 per cent of the world's population, exported 73 per cent of the world's exports and imported 75 per cent of the world's imports.[17] Similarly, in 1997 high-income countries provided 90 per cent of the world's foreign direct investment, but 68 per cent was invested back into other high-income countries.[18] Poor countries sit very much on the sidelines of today's world economy and the select few that do get a look in account for the lion's share of trade and capital that doesn't go to rich countries. Just six countries – Brazil, Mexico, Thailand, Argentina, Indonesia and China – get 60 per cent of the 32 per cent of total global foreign direct investment that goes into poor countries.[19] Fourteen countries – Argentina, Brazil, China, India, Indonesia, South Korea, Malaysia, Mexico, the Philippines, Saudi Arabia, Singapore, South Africa, Thailand and Venezuela – account for a huge 72 per cent of the 27 per cent of total world exports that leave the shores of

Table 5.1 World's largest economies, 1999 (GDP, US$ billion)

Twenty largest economies using exchange rate

1	United States	9,152.1
2	Japan	4,346.9
3	Germany	2,111.9
4	United Kingdom	1,441.8
5	France	1,432.3
6	Italy	1,171.0
7	China	989.5
8	Brazil	751.5
9	Canada	634.9
10	Spain	595.9
11	Mexico	483.7
12	India	447.3
13	South Korea	406.9
14	Australia	404.0
15	Russia	401.4
16	Netherlands	393.7
17	Taiwan	288.7
18	Argentina	283.2
19	Switzerland	258.6
20	Belgium	248.4

Twenty largest economies using purchasing power parity

1	United States	8,878.0
2	China	4,452.0
3	Japan	3,186.0
4	India	2,226.0
5	Germany	1,930.0
6	France	1,349.0
7	United Kingdom	1,322.0
8	Italy	1,268.0
9	Brazil	1,163.0
10	Russia	1,022.0
11	Mexico	780.0
12	Canada	776.0
13	South Korea	728.0
14	Spain	704.0
15	Indonesia	550.0
16	Taiwan	467.0
17	Australia	452.0
18	Argentina	437.0
19	Turkey	415.0
20	Netherlands	386.0

Source: The Economist, *Pocket World in Figures*, London, Profile Books, 2002, p. 24.

poor countries.[20] Economic globalization has made for a select few centres of global commerce from which most poor countries are unambiguously shut out.

Relative size of poor economies

Until the early 1990s not only were poor countries left behind in the division of global wealth, they were also left behind in the calculation of the size of the world's economies. Until then economists had always converted the gross domestic products (GDPs) of the world's economies into a common currency (usually US dollars) using current exchange rates. But, as previously mentioned, exchange rates don't necessarily reflect the varying costs of a standard product in different countries. In 1993 the International Monetary Fund caused a stir by calculating the world's GDPs using relative purchasing power, instead of exchange rates, for the first time. Overnight the relative world economic importance of poor countries nearly doubled (from 18 per cent of the world total to 33 per cent).[21] Suddenly China's economy became the third largest in the world. Today if you work out world GDPs using exchange rates the G7 rich countries account for two-thirds of the world's GDPs, and there are no poor countries among the five largest world economies; but if you use relative purchasing power the G7 only account for 45 per cent of the world's combined GDPs, and China and India come in as the second and fourth largest economies in the world.[22] It is sometimes said that 'democracy is in the counting'. That is no less true of economics than it is of politics, and all too often poor countries have been left out of the counting.

The Third World debt crisis

The two forces that have been most responsible for forcing economic globalization onto poor countries, in recent decades, have been the Third World debt crisis and world trade negotiations.

The Third World debt crisis has been a particularly irrepressible globalizing force on poor countries. Poor countries can't sign on to a loan from the World Bank or the IMF unless they agree to a package of structural adjustment measures designed to open them up to the global marketplace. These measures include tariff cuts, minimal controls on foreign investment, currency devaluation and low government spending. Today about ninety countries, a full 40 per cent of all the countries in the world, either have been, or still are, subject to such World Bank- and IMF-mandated economic adjustment.[23] This means the IMF and the World Bank have become the de facto economic managers of nearly half the world's economies.

The Third World debt crisis had its origins in the early 1970s. Until then poor countries had only borrowed modest amounts and nearly always from official sources (such as the IMF and the World Bank). Until then rich countries had also been reluctant to extend much money, in any form, to poor countries. But during the 1970s capital controls were relaxed and a new, lightly regulated Eurodollar capital market took off in London increasingly fed by surplus Middle Eastern capital earned from increased oil prices. At the same time raw material export prices earned by poor countries were enjoying steep increases and for the first time since the Second World War poor countries looked like attractive customers to rich-country banks. The stronger raw material prices gave poor countries some economic clout and some even began calling for a 'New International Economic Order'. The result of the new interest by rich-country banks was that poor countries became significantly indebted to them for the first time since the Second World War and Third World debt nearly quadrupled between 1970 and 1980 (to just over US$1,000 billion).[24] The debts looked like a good deal at the time, and they gave poor countries a lot of latitude with the purposes they could borrow money for, but they locked poor countries into the world economy like never before. The loans came at a price. They meant that poor countries could no longer follow the path of economic self-reliance that many had followed since the Second World War. They meant that poor countries had to export (mainly raw materials) to the hilt to be able to meet their new debt repayments. Rich-country banks were happy though. Banks like Citicorp and Bankers Trust made up to 80 per cent of their profits from Third World loans at the time.[25]

By the late 1970s the new poor-country debts were looking shaky. The raw material export prices earned by poor countries began to plummet at the same time as interest rates in rich countries began to be ratcheted up in a radical, new (monetarist) strategy designed to wipe out the inflation of the 1970s. The debt strategy was also undermined by a large volume of capital leaving poor countries as local investors became increasingly nervous about their home economies and sought safer overseas economies to invest in (this is sometimes called 'swallow capital' by the anti-globalization movement). The debt strategy was further undermined by falling currencies which increased the value of the debts. It must also be said that the loans were sometimes used for dubious purposes such as increased military spending and corruption of government officials, which further worsened the debt crisis.

The Third World debt crisis first erupted in 1982 when Argentina suspended repayments on its foreign loan following its defeat in the Falklands War, closely followed by a default by Mexico. Since then the Third World debt crisis has continued unabated with major crises involving Mexico in 1994, East Asia in 1997, Russia in 1998, Brazil in 1999 and Argentina in 2002, to name but a few. There have been a series of strategies to deal with the crisis, including the Baker and Brady plans in the 1980s and the Highly Indebted Poor Countries Initiative in the 1990s, but none ended up significantly reducing Third World debt and, most crucially, none tackled the underlying systemic problems behind the debt crisis. All the plans ignored the fact that while most of the world's production, trade and capital flows remain concentrated in the triad of Western Europe, East Asia and North

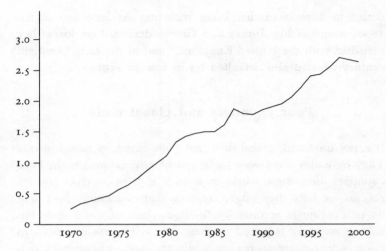

Source: Worldwatch Institute, *Vital Signs 2002–03*, Earthscan, London, 2002, p. 53.

Figure 5.3 Third World and Eastern bloc
foreign debt (US$ trillion; 2000 dollars)

America poor countries simply can't afford, in the long run, to service their foreign debts. Historically, however, rich countries have demonstrated that when they really want to, they are able to enter into significant debt forgiveness. In 1953 rich countries forgave half the foreign debt of the then newly created Federal Republic of Germany to give it a head start as an independent economy.[26]

As things stand today, Third World debt is about two and a half times its level of 1980 (US$2,530 billion).[27] The heaviest debt-servicing burden falls on sub-Saharan African countries to whom private banks will generally no longer lend. The Third World debt crisis of the last three decades is not the first time poor countries have defaulted on loans to rich countries, however. Like many things in global economics, Third World debt default is a problem that keeps recurring. As long ago as the 1870s countries like Turkey and Greece defaulted on loans they then had with the United Kingdom,[28] and in the early twentieth century Mexico also defaulted on its foreign loans.

Poor countries and global trade

It is not only with global debt that poor countries have lost out. They have also done very badly out of international trade. Poor countries often view world trade as a 'rich man's club' and it's easy to see how they might arrive at that conclusion. Not only do rich countries account for the lion's share of world trade but it is increasingly balanced in their favour. The trade deficits of poor countries are increasing while the trade surpluses of rich countries are also increasing. One report has found that for poor countries as a whole (excluding China) average trade deficits in the 1990s were three percentage points higher than they were in the 1970s despite the fact that they were experiencing slower economic growth.[29] And world trade is increasingly concentrated around the three 'triad' mega-regional trade blocs of North America, East Asia and Western Europe.

After the Second World War poor countries argued to rich countries that their development needs should have at least as high a priority as the post-war reconstruction of Europe. They were particularly hoping to get access to World Bank funding. But the rich countries that dominated the World Bank at the time decided the reconstruction of Europe would have first priority and an opportunity was lost to bring poor countries into the 'tent' of world economic prosperity.[30] This rebuff, and others, like the US rejection of the International Trade Organization and its Havana Charter, saw many poor countries become introspective and relatively unconcerned with connecting with the world economy after the Second World War. South American countries in particular focused on building up a high level of national economic self-reliance throughout the 1950s and 1960s reinforced by significant barriers to imports. After rejection by the dominant rich countries of the post-war world, poor countries also set about forming their own political/financial organizations. One of them was the Group of Seventy-seven (G77), named after the number of poor countries that signed the Joint Declaration of the Developing Countries made to the General Assembly of the United Nations in 1963. The G77 declaration made clear the frustration of poor countries with the direction of world trade. Among other things, it said: 'instead of helping the developing countries to promote the development and diversification of their economies, the present tendencies in world trade frustrate their efforts to attain more rapid growth'.[31] Poor countries also established the United Nations Conference on Trade and Development (UNCTAD) with an inaugural meeting in 1964. Poor countries saw UNCTAD eventually becoming their international economic forum, their equivalent of the rich-country Organization for Economic Cooperation and Development (OECD).

The trade power of poor countries increased, briefly, during the 1970s when the prices of many raw material exports from poor countries surged. The price bargaining power of the oil-exporting OPEC countries gave poor countries new confidence, as well as leading many to believe that they could engage the world economy, on their own terms, after all. Poor countries began to believe that a 'New International Economic Order' was possible. In 1976 UNCTAD even tried finally to address the ongoing problem of ever-decreasing raw material export prices by setting up eighteen specific raw material agreements supported by a US$6 billion fund.[32] But the world recession of 1981–82, and the start of the Third World debt crisis, deflated confidence and the poor countries began to slip behind again. The 1980s are sometimes referred to as the 'lost decade' of poor countries.

Ironically it was the brief period of trade strength enjoyed by poor countries during the 1970s that was to be their undoing. Their new 1970s' export strength lulled them out of the trade self-reliance they had followed during the previous two decades. They began to borrow from rich countries on the strength of their export boom, which locked them into a need to keep exporting as much as possible to finance their loan repayments. The result was that poor countries were forced to become more engaged with the world economy than they had ever been since the Second World War. This engagement was pushed along by the World Bank and the IMF, which generally made their loans to poor countries conditional on greater connection with the world trade network. This resulted in a record number of poor countries taking part in the Uruguay Round of trade negotiations between 1986 and 1993. Poor countries were told they would be left behind if they didn't take part in the Uruguay Round and that its 'rules based' system was the best insurance policy they could get in a world trade system often dominated by the major trade powers. Poor countries were also coaxed into the Uruguay Round by promises of compensatory measures to offset the negative effects of trade liberalization on poor countries that imported most of their food (which didn't happen) and by promises of real progress happening, for the first time, on access to rich-country textile and agricultural markets (which didn't amount to much). By the beginning of the twenty-first century many poor countries had become cynical about the benefits of engagement with the world trade system. Poor countries often feel they are stuck in the system through their ongoing need to finance foreign debt, the loan conditions imposed by the IMF and the World Bank and their membership of the WTO. The frustration about the pace, direction and lopsided benefits of globalization came to a head at the WTO trade talks held at Cancún in September 2003, in which a group of poor countries, the G21, led by Brazil, China and India, managed successfully to scuttle the talks and to stand up to rich countries for the first time. This may mark the return of economic assertiveness by poor countries not seen since the 1970s, which may eventually see renewed calls by them for a 'New International Economic Order'.

Trade winners and losers

Poor countries don't necessarily speak with one voice on economic globalization and some countries that were once poor
have undoubtedly done well out of it. Throughout both the
1990s and the 1980s the value of exports from poor countries
expanded more rapidly than those from rich countries. Both of
these decades of faster export growth meant that an increasing
share of world trade went to poor countries. But this masks
the full story. The reality is that the fruits of increasing world
economic engagement enjoyed by poor countries have been
extremely unevenly divided between them, leading many to
claim that poor countries are increasingly separating into 'Third'
and 'Fourth' worlds. So-called 'tiger' economies like Singapore,
South Korea, Taiwan and Hong Kong have been the big poor-
country winners from economic globalization with the result
that they are no longer generally seen as poor countries. They
have entered the ranks of rich countries: they have grown from
poor countries to rich ones in an amazingly short period of
time that would have been undreamed of a few decades ago. But
economies like them are the exception, and most poor countries haven't experienced any trade improvement at all over the
past few decades. East Asia, in fact, accounts for nearly all the
improvement in trade market share achieved by poor countries
throughout the 1990s.[33] What trade performance improvements
have been recorded in other regions of the world were largely
the result of the performance of a few other select economies,
like Mexico, whose trade increases account for nearly all of the
increases of South America. While East Asia saw its share of world
exports more than double throughout the 1990s, other major
regions, like sub-Saharan Africa, saw their market share decline,
while others, like South Asia, saw virtually no improvement in
their market share.[34] Over the past twenty years the forty-nine
poorest countries in the world have seen their share of world
trade fall by about half.[35]

Much of the trade increase recorded by poor countries has been the result of rapid reductions in trade barriers throughout the 1990s – reductions much more rapid, during that decade at least, than those that took place in rich countries. By the end of the 1990s average tariffs in South Asia and sub-Saharan Africa were only half their levels of the early 1980s and in South America and East Asia they were only a third.[36] These deep cuts affected not only the trade health of poor countries but also the financial health of their governments. Most poor countries have fairly crude taxation systems and import tariffs have traditionally been a major source of revenue for poor-country governments; so the tariff cuts meant significantly less government revenue for many poor countries.

Like the overall trade performance of rich countries, the mix of exports coming out of poor countries tells one story, at first glance, then a very different one when the detail is examined. Traditionally primary produce and textiles have made up a large proportion of poor-country exports. But today manufactured goods make up most of the exports from poor countries. At the start of the 1980s manufactured goods accounted for only a quarter of total poor-country exports but today they account for about four-fifths.[37] At first this sounds positive: it should mean that a lot of value-adding is happening in poor countries. In some countries it does mean just that, but in most poor countries it doesn't. Just as overall trade improvement for poor countries is concentrated in East Asia, so too is the improvement in poor-country manufactured exports. East Asia in fact accounts for more than three-quarters of all the manufactured exports that leave poor countries.[38] No more than ten poor (or former poor) countries of East Asia account for about 80 per cent of all poor-country manufactured exports, while the other 160-odd poor countries in the world account for the other 20 per cent. To add insult to injury, very little of the export manufacturing that has found its way into poor countries has involved much value-adding. In fact in the 2002 *Trade and Development Report* released by UNCTAD the organization claimed that even though the share of global manufacturing exports from poor countries more than doubled over the past two decades, their share in world manufacturing value-adding increased by only 50 per cent.[39] This means a large proportion of export manufacturing that has found its way into poor countries has not involved any value-adding and has amounted to little more than cheap assembly factories.

Poor-country raw material exports

Of the roughly 160 poor countries that have missed out on any significant export manufacturing bounty, at least half remain highly dependent on the exports of raw materials, of which poor countries still account for a large global share.[40] In 1996, 23 poor countries derived 80 per cent or more of their export income from just one 'commodity' (raw material), a further 21 derived between 60 and 80 per cent of their export income from one commodity, and another 23 derived between 40 and 60 per cent from one commodity[41] – hardly a picture that shows lots of poor countries enjoying a new-found manufacturing export bounty. Raw materials are an insecure foundation for a poor country's exports because, over time, they have tended to fetch increasingly lower prices around the world. Raw material export dependency has hit Africa the hardest; as a continent they are more dependent on the exports of raw materials than any other. During the 1980s the price of Africa's mainly raw material exports, when compared against the price of its imports (its 'terms of trade'), fell more savagely than for any other region of the globe.[42] In a report released by UNCTAD in 2002 the organization said that most of the world's extreme poverty was concentrated in countries that relied on raw materials for most of their export income; in fact it claimed that 79 per cent of the people in the world living on less than US$1 per day were concentrated in those countries.[43]

So, despite more than two centuries of economic globalization, many poor countries remain reliant on raw materials to earn most of their export income. Yet raw material prices are an extremely slippery slope. They are an increasingly heavy weight carried by poor countries that remain unable to develop industries that can export value-added products into today's globalized marketplace. Continuing reliance on raw material exports has been one of the main forces of economic globalization that have kept poor countries poor. Throughout the past century there has been a long-term downward trend in the prices raw material exports fetch, which has known only occasional interruptions. Today non-fuel raw materials only command, on average, prices about half what they commanded in the mid-1970s and only a third of their levels of 1900.[44]

The main problem behind the long-term slide in raw material price is that the world demand for raw materials is getting seriously out of line with world supply. On the supply side poor-country shortages of foreign earnings, needed to pay for imports and debt servicing, have meant poor countries have a big incentive to keep pouring raw materials onto the world market, almost regardless of price, in the desperate hope that sheer quantity will make up for falling prices (often with disastrous consequences for the environment, whose resources are plundered for ever-diminishing returns). Ever more sophisticated development technology has allowed poor countries to open up new mines, develop new plantations and extract more produce from existing farms, and so on, all of which has increased global raw material supply. But on the demand side, the world is consuming raw materials in more and more efficient ways or is increasingly consuming goods and services that don't use a lot of raw materials. The amount of wheat that is needed to make a given quantity of bread is falling, the amount of iron ore needed to make a given quantity of steel is falling, and the world produces ever increasing volumes of paper without increasing its wood use. Plastics and synthetics are replacing metals and natural fibres while increasingly affluent consumers, in particular, are buying services rather than raw-material-intensive goods as their post-war parents did. None of this makes for good news on the raw material export price front. The brief surge in raw material prices during the 1970s didn't last and by the late 1970s the long-term slide in prices resumed and has continued to this day.

Poor-country trade winners

None of this means, however, that some formerly poor countries in East Asia in particular weren't able to jump off the slippery slope of raw material exports and cut some real teeth in manufactured exports. The problem is they didn't do it by following the free-market prescriptions of the rich-country high priests of economic globalization. They did it by following decidedly protectionist development programmes that involved a lot of government intervention. Two of the most successful manufacturing export economies of East Asia have been South Korea and Taiwan. Throughout most of the post-war years both countries had relatively high tariff walls that left most of their domestic economies unexposed to free trade. Both restricted foreign investment (never exceeding more than 2 per cent of total investment in either country), both provided direct and indirect subsidies to local industries (like the famous *chaebol* industries in South Korea), and both had flexible patent laws that allowed local businesses to copy and adapt foreign technologies. Both also insisted on high local content by foreign investors when they did allow them in.[45] But none of this squares with today's rich-country free-trade, non-interventionist formula. In fact it is entirely at odds with it.

Export-processing zones

An area of manufacturing trade that many poor countries have undoubtedly been successful in attracting is export zone industries. These are typically low-tech, labour-intensive industries set up in special zones within poor countries, where often a large number of government concessions like company tax holidays, the supply of infrastructure and minimal labour regulation are extended to attract the industries. In 1970 export processing zones only existed in ten poor countries but their popularity skyrocketed throughout the 1980s and by 1990 at least sixty-three poor countries had them.[46] Many poor countries began courting export zone industries as a way of weaning themselves off a dependency on foreign exchange earnings from increasingly unreliable raw material exports. But foreign companies set up in these export processing zones for one reason and one reason alone – cheap labour. And there is no shortage of cheap labour on offer in poor countries. In countries like Bangladesh garment workers toil for as little as US$1.50 to US$2.00 per day while a woman working a twelve-hour day in El Salvador will work for about US$5 a day.[47] Although these zones bring jobs to their host countries, they often come at a high price. The workers in the zones frequently have no security of employment; they generally work long hours; governments often have to fork out a lot of money to attract the industries; and the export zone industries invariably give little benefit to locally owned businesses. In Mexico, for instance, local inputs only account for about 2 per cent of the value of goods coming out of their *maquiladora* export zones.[48] Most importantly, however, often the export zone industries don't stay. When another poor country starts offering even cheaper wage rates, they often move on. Some of the former stellar performing economies of East Asia, like South Korea, Malaysia, Taiwan and Singapore, began to experience declines in industrial production in 2001 as many export zone industries left for the cheaper labour pool of countries like China. China now has the largest export zone pool of workers in the world, with an estimated 18 million people working, out of a global export zone workforce of about 27 million workers.[49]

Neither the increasingly unequal distribution of world income, nor the ongoing dependency of many poor countries on raw material exports, nor the domination of the world trade network by rich countries, nor the uncertainties of export processing zones, nor the tendency of rich countries to rig trade rules in their favour has stopped poor countries from engaging in world trade and being part of its politics. But the price for them remains high and the gains are at best unevenly distributed, and at worst they are largely non-existent. A study by UNCTAD estimated that the world's poorest forty-eight countries stood to lose between US$300 and US$600 million per year in decreased exports and increased imports as a result of their participation in the Uruguay Round of international trade talks.[50] Echoing the same sentiment, a World Bank report concluded that greater openness to trade had a negative impact on the incomes of the poorest 40 per cent of the population in poor countries with only the richer 60 per cent deriving any benefit.[51]

Rich-country trade losers

So, what at first glance appears to be a world trade network that is somewhat fair to all players is really a club dominated by rich countries that is unfair to all but them. This is not to say that free trade hasn't had its downsides in rich countries. It is dishonest to pretend that free trade has left rich countries completely unscathed. Many labour-intensive manufacturing companies have left rich countries to set up in poor countries where wage rates can be as little as 10 per cent of the rates in rich countries. Garment factories routinely set up in India or Bangladesh, for instance, where they pay wages as low as US$0.25 to US$0.50 per hour.[52] Unsurprisingly, many low-skilled jobs have been lost in rich countries as a result and many remaining jobs have seen declines in their wage rates. In the United States, for instance, it has been estimated that as many as 6.4 million jobs were lost in companies facing intense import competition between the late 1970s and the late 1990s, and that the wages of unskilled workers in the US fell by 20 per cent in after-inflation terms between the mid-1970s and 1998 as a result.[53]

Aid to the rescue?

Given that poor countries are increasingly being left behind in the world economy, and further given the world's resultant horrendous levels of absolute poverty, it would be hoped that foreign aid would come to the rescue. Despite some isolated successes, however, aid has proven ineffective at righting the wrongs of economic globalization. In both quantity and quality terms foreign aid is wanting and has done little to put an acceptable face on economic globalization.

Before the Second World War foreign aid was relatively unknown around the world. The modern-day tradition of aid was begun by the Marshall Plan aid given by the United States to (non-Communist) European countries recovering from the Second World War. Marshall Plan aid was very significant, representing as much as 5 per cent of the GDPs of the recipient countries.[54] During the 1960s the then newly formed G77 group of poor countries began agitating, largely through the United Nations, for a level of ongoing international aid equal to 1 per cent of the GDPs of donor countries. In 1970 the United Nations ended up adopting a diluted target of 0.7 per cent of donor GDPs. However, in 2000 the fifteen largest donor countries in the world gave less than a third of that target, 0.22 per cent, well down on the 0.33 per cent given in 1992 – itself less than half the 0.7 per cent target.[55] Only four countries gave more than the 0.7 per cent target in 2000: Denmark, the Netherlands, Sweden and Norway.[56] The largest donor, the United States, gave only 0.1 per cent.[57] Despite the stinginess of aid, however, many poor countries are very dependent on it. In 1997 aid equalled 10 per cent, or more, of the GDPs of at least twenty-five poor countries, nearly all of them African.[58] The World Bank and the United Nations believe that if there is to be any chance at all of achieving the goal of halving the number of people living in extreme poverty in the world by 2015, rich-country aid needs to double (from about US$50 billion to at least US$100 billion per year).

Table 5.2 Aid given by top fifteen world donors, 1992 and 2000 (as share of GNP and US$ million)

	1992 aid		2000 aid	
	% of GNP	$ million*	% of GNP	$ million*
Denmark	1.02	1,621	1.06	1,664
Netherlands	0.86	3,207	0.84	3,135
Sweden	1.03	2,865	0.80	1,799
Norway	1.16	1,483	0.80	1,264
Belgium	0.39	1,014	0.36	820
Switzerland	0.46	1,327	0.34	890
France	0.63	9,634	0.32	4,105
United Kingdom	0.31	3,778	0.32	4,501
Japan	0.30	12,990	0.28	13,508
Germany	0.39	8,834	0.27	5,030
Australia	0.35	1,182	0.27	987
Canada	0.46	2,930	0.25	1,744
Spain	0.26	1,769	0.22	1,195
Italy	0.34	4,802	0.13	1,376
United States	0.20	13,640	0.10	9,955
All countries	0.33	73,055	0.22	53,737
UN target	0.7			

* in 2000 US$

Source: Worldwatch Institute, *Vital Signs 2002–2003, The Trends that Are Shaping Our Future*, London, Earthscan, 2002, p. 119.

Yet not only is the quantity of aid wanting; so too is the quality. A lot of aid is used for strategic political purposes. The United States rewards countries like Pakistan, which helped during its so-called 'war on terrorism', with extra aid, while Japan routinely threatens to reduce the aid of small Pacific countries that vote against it in the International Whaling Commission. And if there

aren't political strings attached to aid, there are frequently economic ones. A large proportion of aid is tied to the commercial
benefit of companies in donor countries. Since the 1970s there
have also been a lot of economic structural adjustment strings
attached to aid (like those attached to IMF and World Bank
loans).[59] A lot of aid gets gobbled up by technical advice from
donor country experts.[60] And as little as just 1 or 2 per cent
of bilateral aid can end up being spent on essential health and
education in recipient countries.[61]

The net combined effect of aid, foreign debt interest payments
and raw material export price losses has been calculated by the
United Nations Development Programme. They claim that while
US$50 billion in aid flows from rich countries to poor ones
each year, poor countries lose about US$500 billion each year in
interest payments and raw material price losses.[62] You can't rely on
foreign aid to fix the shortcomings of economic globalization.

Ecological debt

In recent years the anti-globalization movement has campaigned
around a combined social, environmental and economic debt it
argues is owed by rich countries to poor countries, which it calls
an 'ecological debt'. The debt has been built up over centuries by
rich countries plundering the social and environmental resources
of poor countries, the plundering being made possible by economic globalization. It recognizes the debt built up through today's exploitation of cheap labour in poor countries and through
slave labour during the colonial period. It recognizes the massive
use rich countries have made of the minerals, farm produce and
timber in poor countries, made cheaper, and more readily available, by economic globalization. It recognizes the pollution rich
countries have pumped into, or onto, the air, land and water of
poor countries, often as globalization-induced pollution such as
transport-related greenhouse gas emissions. And it squarely recognizes that economic globalization perpetrates, and increases, the

ecological debt through Third World debt, IMF/World Bank/ donor-driven structural adjustment, foreign investment, distorted trade rules, ever-plummeting raw material prices and exploitative WTO agreements like those covering global patents and the global trade in services. The anti-globalization movement says that this ecological debt, owed by rich countries to poor ones, is larger than the economic debt owed by poor countries to rich ones. It is a debt that tries holistically to capture all of the net effects of economic globalization, reminding us along the way that economic globalization has only been possible because rich countries have been able to exploit poor ones.

Too much of economic globalization is justified by reductionist arguments that look at specific costs and benefits. The concept of an ecological debt steps beyond this narrow thinking and comes up with a big-picture scorecard that unambiguously has the rich owing the poor.

Notes

1. Ankie Hoogvelt, *Globalization and the Postcolonial World: The New Political Economy of Development*, Palgrave, London, 2001, p. 90.
2. David Landes, *The Wealth and Poverty of Nations*, Abacus, London, 1998, p. xx.
3. Centre for International Economics, *Globalisation and Poverty: Turning the Corner*, Commonwealth of Australia, Canberra, 2001, p. 9.
4. In 1999 even the World Bank concurred that 3 billion were living on less than $3 a day. World Bank, *World Development Report 1998/99*, Oxford University Press, New York, 1999, p. 117.
5. William F. Fisher and Thomas Ponniah, eds, *Another World is Possible: Popular Alternatives to Globalization at the World Social Forum*, Zed Books, London, 2003, pp. 110, 152.
6. George Monbiot, *The Age of Consent: A Manifesto for a New World Order*, Flamingo, London, 2003, p. 17.
7. Kevin Watkins et al., *Rigged Rules and Double Standards: Trade, Globalisation and the Fight Against Poverty*, Oxfam International, Washington DC, 2002, p. 245.
8. Mike Moore, *A World Without Walls: Freedom, Development, Free Trade and Global Governance*, Cambridge University Press, Cambridge, 2003, p. 36.

9. Ibid., p. 245.

10. Mary Jordan and Kevin Sullivan, 'Trade Brings Riches But Not to Mexico's Poor', published by Deb Foskey via WTO Watch email list (debf@webone.com.au), 5 April 2003 (#147). (For archive copy, see www.nwjc.org.au/avcwl/lists/archives.html.)

11. Gustavo Capdevila, 'Africa: UNCTAD Criticizes New IMF–World Bank Poverty Approach', published by Deb Foskey via WTO Watch email list (debf@webone.com.au), 3 October 2002 (#96). (For archive copy, see www.nwjc.org.au/avcwl/lists/archives.html.)

12. Mark Drajem, 'No IMF Tears for Argentina', *The Age*, 6 January 2003.

13. Michael Dynes, 'Fraud Fears as Nigeria Goes to Polls', *The Australian*, 11 April 2003, p. 12.

14. 'Wealth Wars', *The Economist*, 23 March 1996, p. 35.

15. Watkins et al., *Rigged Rules*, p. 37.

16. Pam Woodall, 'A Game of International Leapfrog', *The Economist*, 1 October 1994, p. 10, Survey.

17. World Bank, *World Development Report 2002*, Oxford University Press, New York, 2002, p. 239.

18. Robert Went, *Globalization: Neoliberal Challenge, Radical Responses*, Pluto Press, London, 2000, p. 45.

19. Hoogvelt, *Globalization and the Postcolonial World*, p. 84.

20. World Bank, *World Development Report 2002*, pp. 238, 239.

21. Woodall, 'International Leapfrog', p. 7,.

22. The Economist, *Pocket World in Figures 2002 Edition*, Profile Books, London, 2001, p. 24.

23. Walden Bello, *Deglobalization: Ideas for a New World Economy*, Zed Books, London, 2002, p.68.

24. Worldwatch Institute, *Vital Signs 2001-2002: The Trends that Are Shaping Our Future*, Earthscan, London, 2001, p. 59.

25. Nicholas Guyatt, *Another American Century? The United States and the World After 2000,* Zed Books, London, 2000, p. 8.

26. Eduardo Gudynas, 'Fifty Years Forgetting London', published by Deb Foskey via WTO Watch email list (debf@webone.com.au), 11 May 2003 (#159), p. 1. (For archive copy, see www.nwjc.org.au/avcwl/lists/archives. html.)

27. Worldwatch Institute, *Vital Signs 2002-2003*, p. 63.

28. A.G. Kenwood and A.L. Lougheed, *Growth of the International Economy 1820–1990: An Introductory Text*, Routledge, London, 1992, p. 125.

29. Martin Khor, *Rethinking Globalization: Critical Ideas and Policy Choices*, Zed Books, London, 2001, p. 33.

30. Kenwood and Lougheed, *Growth of the International Economy*, p. 168.

31. Ibid., p. 222.
32. John Madeley, *Hungry for Trade: How the Poor Pay for Free Trade*, Zed Books, London, 2000, p. 66.
33. Watkins et al., *Rigged Rules*, p. 124.
34. Ibid., p. 69.
35. Monbiot, *The Age of Consent*, p. 203.
36. Watkins et al., *Rigged Rules*, p. 124.
37. Ibid., p. 35.
38. Ibid., p. 71.
39. Jayati Ghosh, 'Why More Exports Have Not Made Developing Countries Richer', published by Deb Foskey via WTO Watch email list (debf@webone.com.au), 23 May 2002 (#60), p. 1. (For archive copy, see www.nwjc.org.au/avcwl/lists/archives.html.)
40. Watkins et al., *Rigged Rules*, p. 39.
41. Worldwatch Institute, *Vital Signs 2001-2002*, p. 122.
42. Watkins et al., *Rigged Rules*, p. 184.
43. Scheherazade Daneshkhu, 'New Approach "Could Halt" Growth in Poverty', *Financial Times*, 19 June 2002.
44. Worldwatch Institute, *Vital Signs 2001-2002*, p. 122.
45. Watkins et al., *Rigged Rules*, p. 232.
46. Madeley, *Hungry for Trade*, p. 269.
47. Watkins et al., *Rigged Rules*, p. 191.
48. Ibid., p. 78.
49. Naomi Klein, *No Logo*, Flamingo, London, 2000, p. 205.
50. Went, *Globalization*, p. 26.
51. Madeley, *Hungry for Trade*, p. 89.
52. Watkins et al., *Rigged Rules*, p. 91.
53. Ibid.
54. Kenwood and Lougheed, *Growth of the International Economy*, p. 242.
55. Worldwatch Institute, *Vital Signs 2002-2003*, p. 119.
56. Ibid.
57. Ibid.
58. World Bank, *World Development Report 1999–2000*, Oxford University Press, New York, 2000, p. 270.
59. David Sogge, *Give and Take: What's the Matter with Foreign Aid?*, Zed Books, London, 2002, p. 126.
60. Ibid., p. 126.
61. Ibid., p. 177.
62. Vandana Shiva, *Protect or Plunder? Understanding Intellectual Property Rights*, Zed Books, London, 2001, p. 23.

CHAPTER 6

RICH-COUNTRY
DOUBLE STANDARDS

Given that rich countries today are generally unabashed supporters of economic globalization, which has been made possible by low barriers to the global movement of trade and capital, you would expect that they had always practised what they preach. In fact they haven't. Historically, rich countries have often avoided allowing the free flow of trade and capital across their own borders when it has suited them. This double standard has been particularly apparent with global trade. During the two centuries since the start of the Industrial Revolution rich countries have generally had a history of protectionism, not free trade, and today they often ask poor countries to make sacrifices in the name of economic globalization that in the past they have not been prepared to make themselves. This makes a mockery of their current-day advocacy of greater global economic engagement.

Rich-country double standards on trade

Throughout the nineteenth century most rich countries built up local industries behind significant tariff barriers (with a brief two decades during the 1860s and 1870s the exception). Many rich countries took the view then, as many poor countries do today, that tariffs were the crucial launching pad for new manufacturing industries that might struggle to survive under free trade. This is known as the 'infant industry' argument of tariff protection. One of the loudest advocates of protectionism during the nineteenth century was the United States, which today parades itself as one of the world's biggest champions of free trade.

In 1791 the first US Secretary of the Treasury, Alexander Hamilton, wrote his famous *Report on Manufactures*, which is still regarded as one of the most elaborate arguments in favour of protectionism ever written.[1] Abraham Lincoln was also an unashamed supporter of protectionism, even when Great Britain was pressuring the United States to reduce its tariff barriers. Lincoln even once said: 'I don't know much about the tariff, but I do know if I buy a coat in America, I have a coat, and America has the money'.[2] The net result of this historic US support for protectionism was the introduction of the US Tariff Act in 1816, then a gradual increase in US tariffs throughout the following five decades, with high tariffs playing a major role in the financing of the American Civil War.[3] After the Civil War, a hero from the conflict, Ulysses Grant, who was US president between 1868 and 1876, even went so far as to say, 'within 200 years, when America has gotten out of protection all that it can offer, it too will adopt free trade'.

In Europe support for protectionism was echoed in countries like Germany that were also keen on nurturing infant manufacturing industries behind high tariff walls. Strongly influenced by the Americans, the German Friedrich List wrote *The National System of Political Economy* in 1841, which was highly critical of free trade and supportive of infant industry tariffs.[4] Even the United Kingdom, which throughout much of the nineteenth century had been a lonely voice for free trade, had Corn Laws during that century that protected local producers of wheat, oats and corn against foreign competition.[5]

Throughout much of the twentieth century many rich countries also followed a policy of tariff protectionism. In the 1920s France, Germany, Italy, Spain, Belgium and the Netherlands were among many European countries that introduced or increased tariffs.[6] The United Kingdom introduced the McKenna tariff act in 1915 to save on transport capacity and to ration foreign exchange during the First World War.[7] This act was reinforced by the Import Duties Act of 1932.[8] In the United States the nineteenth-century legacy of protectionism continued during the twentieth century with the introduction of the Fordney–McCumber tariff in 1922, which raised US tariffs to the highest levels they had ever been,[9] only to be raised yet higher by the famous Smoot–Hawley tariff act of 1930.[10] Whatever you read or hear these days, protected trade, not free trade, has been the norm since the start of the Industrial Revolution, and rich countries are being dishonest in pretending otherwise.

Even well before the Industrial Revolution rich countries vigorously pursued protected trade. The British Navigation Laws of the 1650s restricted the entry of foreign ships into the ports of the United Kingdom, giving the country a near-monopoly in its colonial trade. In the fourteenth century Edward III banned the import of woolen cloth into the United Kingdom to help establish a national weaving industry, a move his successors augmented by banning the export of raw wool and unfinished cloth that might assist infant continental European weaving industries.[11] And in the 1660s and 1670s the finance minister of Louis XIV of France, Jean-Baptiste Colbert, introduced a broad raft of protective tariffs.[12] Rich-country protected trade has a very, very long history.

Today protectionism has a tarnished reputation because many commentators simplistically ascribe the cause of the Great Depression to a major outbreak of protectionism that occurred during the 1930s. This protectionism was kicked along by the US Smoot–Hawley tariff act and the UK Import Duties Act. However, like most things in economics, the real causes of the Great Depression were many and varied and global protectionism had only a minor influence. The real causes of the Great Depression included: punitive First World War reparations extracted from Germany, large currency fluctuations caused by the departure of major economies from the gold standard, the large cost of the First World War, and the 1930s' slide in raw material prices. Other causes included the large inequality in income distribution that existed during the 1930s and a then fashionable obsession by governments of the time with balanced budgets. To this list the renowned US economist J.K. Galbraith adds: bad corporate structures, poor banking structures, and the poor state of economic understanding at the time.[13] To blame the Great Depression on trade protectionism alone, as many free-market commentators do these days, is hugely simplistic and ill-informed.

Rich-country double standards on patents

A similar rich-country attitude of 'do as I say, not do as I do' applies to patents. Today rich countries are very keen to impose strict global patent regimes on poor countries through the Trade Related Aspects of Intellectual Property Rights (TRIPS) agreement. Yet a close examination of their own economic histories reveals that during their formative and post-war reconstruction years rich countries weren't at all keen on universal patent protection.

Between 1765 and 1789 the parliament of the United Kingdom passed strict laws that outlawed the export of either machinery or manufacturing employees.[14] These laws were designed to ensure the UK remained the world's economic superpower. But the United States flouted the patent laws and one Samuel Slater, who went on to become the 'father of American manufacturing', secretly violated them by bringing the knowledge of spinning and weaving to the US from the UK.[15] Thomas Jefferson, the third President of the United States, even explicitly rejected the granting of patents to foreign inventions.[16] Many of today's rich countries, including France, Germany, Canada and Japan, similarly failed to provide patent protection until after 1960.[17] Rich countries wouldn't stand for such poor-country behaviour on global patents today.

Rich-country double standards
on agricultural and textile trade

Rich-country double standards aren't confined to protectionism and patents. Two further areas where their double standards are particularly telling are the trade of agricultural produce and the trade of textiles.

Many rich countries, particularly those of Western Europe, Japan and the United States, have long histories of subsidizing and protecting their farm industries, a legacy that reaches back to well before the Second World War. It's hard to argue that such subsidization and protectionism is anything other than blatantly inconsistent with their support for free trade, but their belief in protecting their farm industries runs deep and they are loath to change the habit. Today rich countries spend US$1 billion a day subsidizing their farm industries, and, despite a commitment made during the Uruguay Round to reduce these subsidies, they have increased over the past decade, not decreased. Today agricultural subsidies account for more than 25 per cent of farm income in the United States, 40 per cent in the European Union and over 60 per cent in Japan.[18] And in the United States farm subsidization is set to increase with the passage of the 2002 Farm Bill, which will pay US$180 billion to US farmers over ten years, resulting in a subsidy increase of US$73 billion over the period.[19] This will take US farm subsidies to more than 40 per cent of total US farm incomes.[20]

Agriculture was kept out of international trade negotiations until the Uruguay Round of trade talks. Introducing agricultural trade into that round proved to be a tortuous affair. There was enormous tension around the issue among poor countries and the 'Cairns Group' of agricultural free-trade nations, on the one hand, and rich agricultural subsidizing nations, like the United States and those of the European Union, on the other. The Uruguay Round's Agreement on Agriculture was straightforwardly a deal stitched up between rich countries, like so many trade deals before it. In this case the deal was mainly struck between the United States and the European Union. Although the deal included several exemptions, it generally required countries to limit the protection they gave their agricultural sector to that which had existed in 1993 and to cut agricultural import barriers and export subsidies by 36 per cent (24 per cent for poor countries).[21] Yet the ink was barely dry on the deal before rich countries began claiming they didn't need to make any changes since they had already fulfilled the terms of the deal; they have since gone on to increase farm subsidization from US$182 billion in 1995 to US$362 billion in 1998.[22]

A similar rich-country double standard applies to the global trade in textiles. Traditionally agricultural and textile exports have been mainstays of poor-country exports, which largely remains the case today. The problem for rich countries is that textiles are large manufacturing export industries for them as well. Rich countries have been sufficiently threatened by poor-country textile exports that they have negotiated, often in secret, international agreements that have limited poor-country textile exports, examples being the Longterm Textile Agreement of 1962 and the subsequent Multi-Fiber Agreement (MFA) of 1974.[23] Like agricultural subsidization, these agreements contradicted the apparent support of rich countries for free trade. Like agricultural subsidization, the MFA was brought into global trade talks for the first time during the Uruguay Round. But also like agricultural subsidization, rich countries made sure the playing field remained well and truly tilted in their favour. Agriculture and textiles only made it into the Uruguay Round at all because rich countries used them as levers to get poor countries to agree to punitive trade measures like the TRIPS and GATS agreements. One European representative even said that they 'considered it appropriate to retain control over [textile] quotas with a view to keeping the possibility of using them as a bargaining chip to obtain better market access in third countries'.[24] Under the Uruguay Round agreement on clothing and textiles, import restrictions into rich countries were to be reduced between 1995 and 2005 with most of the reduction occurring at the end of that ten-year period.[25] Quotas had to be removed from at least 51 per cent of the textile imports into rich countries by January 2002.[26] Yet rich countries could largely determine for themselves which items were first exposed to this liberalization. The result has been that rich countries have been highly selective in the import restrictions they have so far elected to lift, with liberalization often occurring in categories that poor countries don't compete in, such as parachutes and felt hats, or in areas that don't have a lot of added value. By January 2002 only 12 per cent of the liberalization in the US and 18 per cent of the liberalization in the European Union had been applied to higher value textile products.[27]

Not content just to discriminate against poor-country agricultural imports, and to compete with poor-country agricultural exports through heavy subsidization, rich countries are also dumping some of their excess production of farm produce onto poor-country markets. The heavy subsidization of farming in the European Union, in particular, has led to the overproduction of a wide range of agricultural produce that has been dumped onto poor-country markets through selling below the cost of production. Cereals, beef, pork, milk, butter, tomatoes, sunflower oil and sugar are among the products dumped on unsuspecting poor-country markets in this way.[28] Rich-country intransigence over agricultural subsidies like these was one of the main factors that led to the collapse of World Trade Organization talks held at Cancún, Mexico, in September 2003.

One can only be highly sceptical, then, about rich-country demands that poor countries open up their markets to world trade. Historically rich countries have often refused to do this when it suited them and there is no reason why poor countries shouldn't be allowed to do the same today.

Notes

1. A.G. Kenwood and A.L. Lougheed, *Growth of the International Economy 1820–1990: An Introductory Text*, Routledge, London, 1992, p. 68.

2. Kevin Watkins et al., *Rigged Rules and Double Standards: Trade, Globalisation and the Fight against Poverty*, Oxfam International, Washington DC, 2002, p. 59.

3. Kenwood and Lougheed, *Growth of the International Economy*, p. 69.

4. Ibid., pp. 68, 69.

5. Robbie Robertson, *The Three Waves of Globalization: A History of a Developing Consciousness*, Zed Books, London, 2003, p. 113.

6. Ibid., p. 176.

7. Kenwood and Lougheed, *Growth of the International Economy*, p. 176.

8. Ibid., p. 202.

9. Ibid., p. 176.

10. Ibid., p. 192.

11. George Monbiot, *The Age of Consent: A Manifesto for a New World Order*, Flamingo, London, 2003, p. 197.

12. Chris Rohmann, *The Dictionary of Important Ideas and Thinkers*, Arrow, London, 2002, p. 258.

13. John Kenneth Galbraith, *The Great Crash 1929: The Classic Study of that Disaster*, Penguin Books, Ringwood, 1975, pp. 186–202.

14. Vandana Shiva, *Protect or Plunder? Understanding Intellectual Property Rights*, Zed Books, London, 2001, p. 34.

15. Ibid.

16. Watkins et al., *Rigged Rules*, p. 209.

17. Ibid.

18. Ibid., p. 100.

19. Roy Eccleston and Stephen Lunn, 'US to Coddle Farmers at Allies' Expense', *Weekend Australian*, 4–5 May 2002, p. 16.

20. Ibid.

21. John Madeley, *Hungry for Trade: How the Poor Pay for Free Trade*, Zed Books, London, 2000, p. 45.

22. Ibid.

23. Joan E. Spero and Jeffrey A. Hart, *The Politics of International Economic Relations*, 5th edn, Routledge, London, 1997 p. 72.

24. Watkins et al., *Rigged Rules*, p. 108.

25. Ibid.

26. Ibid.

27. Ibid.

28. Madeley, *Hungry for Trade*, p. 70.

PART II

THE POLICY ALTERNATIVES OF THE ANTI-GLOBALIZATION MOVEMENT

CHAPTER 7

THE ANTI-GLOBALIZATION
MOVEMENT

There is a common belief that the anti-globalization movement is only concerned with opposing things. Many people believe it is bereft of any vision of how it would fix the perils of economic globalization. In late 2002 *The Economist* magazine boldly claimed that 'today's militant critics of globalization ... present no worked-out alternative to the present economic order. Instead, they invoke a Utopia free of environmental stress, social justice and branded sportswear, harking back to a preindustrial golden age that did not actually exist. Never is this alternative future given clear shape or offered up for examination.'[1] The second half of this book is devoted to giving the lie to this statement. In the years immediately after the 1999 'Battle for Seattle' protests, in particular, a huge amount of time and energy was invested by the anti-globalization movement in working out coherent alternatives to economic globalization. Although the alternatives still have many rough edges, and major lines of internal disagreement, policies *are* being developed and worked-out alternatives *are* being offered up.

The alternatives are being developed within the various groups that make up the anti-globalization movement, particularly non-governmental organizations (NGOs) and alternative political parties. And they are being developed at gatherings of the anti-globalization movement like the hugely popular World Social Forums and regional social forums which have gathered a lot of momentum in recent years and which have become crucial occasions for discussion and policy formulation. The alternatives do exist and are increasingly developing the confidence to pose a real threat to the present pro-globalization, free-market economic and political orthodoxy.

When the Berlin Wall fell in 1989 many commentators claimed there was no argument but that capitalism had won over communism; it was now a question of what style of capitalism would ultimately triumph. Would it be the minimalist government style of the United States, the more interventionist style of Western Europe, or the more cooperative corporate-government style of East Asia (no one considered poor-country systems worth considering)? Right now it appears as though the minimalist government style of the United States has won. But the darkest hour is often just before the dawn and there are strong signs that the US style of globalization-driven capitalism is imploding. It has never been under more stress. A string of poor countries are lining up against further expansion of the power of the World Trade Organization. There is increasing economic nationalism in countries like Indonesia, Argentina and Brazil. The International Monetary Fund and the World Bank are under unprecedented attack from both the left and the right of politics. After a brief hiatus, after the attacks in New York on 11 September 2001, large anti-globalization protests are once again the norm. Trade talks conducted by the World Trade Organization have now collapsed twice in four years (at Seattle in December 1999 and at Cancún in September 2003). And, most significantly of all for the future of economic globalization, the US economy is itself imploding. It is experiencing a falling currency, ever-increasing trade and current account deficits, a string of corporate collapses and low economic growth. The future looks far from rosy for economic globalization.

The global loss of democracy

Apart from world poverty, the other big loser from economic globalization has been democracy. The democratic loss has occurred on several levels. On a political and economic level there is now a one-size-fits-all recipe for international economic management that is brazenly free market. This global economic template has been pushed by the IMF, the World Bank and the WTO and has also been pushed by virtually every mainstream political party in the world whether their origins were on the left or the right. Most former communist parties of Eastern Europe are now free market, the African National Congress in South Africa is free market, the Democrats and Republicans in the United States are free market, the Congress and Bharatiya Janata parties of India are free market, the Gaullists and Socialists of France are free market, and the Tories and Labour Party of the United Kingdom are free market. People don't have any political options any more. In 1989 US academic Francis Fukuyama even confidently proclaimed that history had ended. Fukuyama argued that we don't have choices any more. In 2002 he said: 'what I was arguing in "The End of History" was that if you want to be a modern society, you don't have a lot of alternatives these days. You are going to be liberal democracy, part of the global economy and market-orientated.'[2] Few would have an argument with the democracy part of his statement (although there are some very questionable liberal democratic voting systems in the world) but the second part, about everyone necessarily being part of the global economy, is truly frightening.

Apart from the loss of choice and democracy at a political level, there has also been a loss of democracy at a local level. Increasingly transnational corporations (TNCs) are ruling the world and are taking away democratic choice from local communities. Ironically the centralization of economic power that TNCs represent is making capitalism functionally similar to Communism. Both represent more and more economic power concentrated into fewer and fewer hands. George Orwell's 'Big Brother' is becoming all too real. The problem is that it wasn't meant to be that way under capitalism. The believers in economic globalization seriously thought it would deliver more choice, not less. In a speech given during a visit to El Salvador in 2002 US President George Bush even said: 'free trade produces liberty and freedom'.

A major backlash against the poverty and loss of choice that economic globalization brings is well and truly under way. People won't take them anymore. Throughout the 1980s and 1990s people were waking up to economic globalization; they needed those decades to work out if it was friend or foe. Increasingly they are realizing that it's foe and they are no longer afraid to say so. This doesn't always make life comfortable, however, for governments that come to power with good intentions but end up pursuing unadventurous globalization policies. In South Africa, for instance, the African National Congress (ANC) came to power with the backing and support of the nation's trade unions and socialist movement, but as the ANC goes further down the free market/pro-globalization path, particularly with privatization, the unions and socialists of the country are breaking with the ANC.

Major backlashes against globalization are not new. The Boston Tea Party, in 1773, was such a backlash, as was Gandhi's mass salt march of 1930. Now a new backlash is happening. Change is under way. And the anti-globalization movement is at the cutting edge of that change.

The anti-globalization movement

The anti-globalization movement is no ordinary movement. In many ways it's not a movement at all. Rather, it's a 'movement of movements'. The anti-globalization movement is not a single organization – it's a collection of many different organizations, individuals and loose coalitions of both individuals and organizations. The individuals are young and old. They are concerned about corporate power, global poverty, sustainable agriculture, global warming, the rights of refugees, the preservation of trees and whales, the rights of people working in sweatshops and any other issue that globalization connects with. The organizations involved in the movement are small and large, formal and informal, hierarchical and nonhierarchical, centralized and decentralized. They represent unions, aid organizations, environment groups, non-mainstream political parties, alternative economic think-tanks, poor-country development movements and many other types of organization. In short, the anti-globalization movement is as diverse as globalization is undiverse. And, given this diversity, it is inevitable that it will have internal disagreement.

There is disagreement about the name of the movement (or even whether it is a movement). Many see the 'anti-globalization movement' tag as a media-driven label that perpetrates the essence of economic globalization, and prefer something like 'the global justice movement', 'the anti-capitalist movement', 'the civil society movement', 'the alternative globalization movement' or 'the movement against global corporatism'.

There is disagreement about tactics. Many like the 'media-grab' power of protests but others prefer less confrontational activism. Some work through political parties; others disagree with working through parties. Some like Internet networking; others prefer neighbourhood networking. Some organizations are very locally based; others are internationally orientated.

There is even disagreement about who the opposition is. Some see it as corporations, others think it is capitalism, others still think it is economic free-marketism. And, as the rest of this book makes clear, there is disagreement about how radical the movement should be, and, as a result, how radical its alternative policies should be.

For some this diversity is maddening, and at times the movement's lack of coherence can definitely be a hindrance. But the diversity is also a strength. It gives the movement flexibility and makes for healthy internal policy debate. It also allows the movement to react quickly to events. Much of the movement responds to events and developments by coordinating via the Internet, often forming temporary coalitions. John Jordan, from the Reclaim the Streets campaign in the United Kingdom, says TNCs 'are like giant tankers, and we are like a school of fish. We can respond quickly, they can't.'[3]

Whether one likes the movement's post-modern, dispersed nature, or not, it is very much a fact of life. Utilized properly, especially with policy development, this diversity can be a strength, not a weakness.

Origins of the anti-globalization movement

The origins of the anti-globalization movement are as complex as the origins of economic globalization itself. One can easily argue that the roots of the present-day movement extend back to at least the 1970s. The 1970s saw the birth of the modern-day peace movement, the birth of the feminist movement, the growth of the Non-aligned Movement, the first United Nations environment summit (in Stockholm in 1975) and the creation of the world's first Green parties (in Australia and New Zealand in 1972).

Crucially, for the future of the anti-globalization movement, the late 1960s and 1970s was the first time since the Second World War that huge movements of people began to question seriously the future of the world's politics, environment, economics and technology. It was the first time in the modern era that people began to ask seriously whether humanity had a future. There were large protests against the Vietnam War and there were massive student protests in Paris. In 1972 the Club of Rome published *The Limits to Growth*, in 1973 Fritz Schumacher published *Small is Beautiful* and in 1968 Paul Ehrlich published *The Population Bomb* – all landmark publications questioning where humanity was heading. All were following a trail blazed by the ground-breaking critique of the effect of poisons, *Silent Spring*, by Rachel Carson, published in 1962.

The 1970s was also a time when the left of politics was still strong. Traditionally the left had always been economically articulate but it was only able to engage with the emerging globalization debate on a level that largely accepted the post-Second World War global economic architecture. The left has traditionally seen the global free movement of goods and people, in particular, as a good thing. Although it had been able to argue a coherent redistributional case since its creation in the late nineteenth century, economic globalization increasingly threw up issues it had no answer for. The Third World debt crisis is sometimes referred to as the first major world economic issue the left had no alternative strategy for. Also, during the 1970s and 1980s a large number of peace, feminist, environment and indigenous peoples' rights organizations began to form that weren't necessarily aligned with the left. These 'secular' organizations challenged the grip the left had traditionally held over progressive issues. Then the fall of the Berlin Wall on 9 November 1989 sealed the socialist movement's fate. Suddenly the old left/right divide no longer seemed relevant. This isn't to say, however, that the left has no part in today's anti-globalization movement. It does. Groups like Global Resistance and the Socialist Workers Party are very active in the movement, but such groups don't dominate alternative political thinking as they once did. Ironically, it could be argued that Karl Marx was the original anti-globalization activist since as early as the mid-nineteenth century he correctly predicted that the new technology of the Industrial Revolution would produce an enormous gulf between rich and poor. But, ultimately, it was Marx's proposed means, rather than his ends (or even his critique), that reached its use-by date.

The 1980s saw the first major stirrings of the present-day anti-globalization movement when the World Bank and the International Monetary Fund became the focus of large-scale protest. Dubious World Bank and IMF projects, such as the Narmada Dam project in India (which the World Bank ended up pulling out of) and the Transmigration project of the Suharto regime in Indonesia, became favourite targets. After the Third World debt crisis broke, the first debt cancellation actions took place.

Some of the momentum of the anti-globalization movement was lost during the first half of the 1990s. Although the decade started well with the Rio Earth Summit in 1992, the movement flagged somewhat, and it failed to speak with a really strong voice against the creation of the World Trade Organization in 1995. It seemed then that most of the world's governments, and many of the world's alternative organizations, had been won over by economic globalization. In the US some (slightly) alternative organizations such as the National Wildlife Federation, the Worldwide Fund for Nature, the Environmental Defense Fund, the Natural Resources Defense Council and the National Audubon Society even backed the signing of the North American Free Trade Agreement (NAFTA) in 1993. When NAFTA came into effect on 1 January 1994, however, the Zapatista National Liberation Army rose up against economic globalization and poverty in the Chiapas region of Mexico. Their uprising provided huge inspiration to the emerging anti-globalization movement. Many North American activists travelled down to Chiapas in the summer after the uprising.

The second half of the 1990s saw pro-globalization forces provide the anti-globalization movement with two important rallying points that were crucial to its development. The first was the Multilateral Agreement on Investment (MAI), which the Organization for Economic Cooperation and Development began work on in 1995. The emerging anti-globalization movement mounted a huge campaign against the MAI, powered by a large amount of Internet networking, that succeeded in burying it in 1998. The next year saw the beginning of a new round of global trade negotiations by the WTO in Seattle in December 1999. Seattle seemed like the perfect venue for the new trade talks. It is the home of iconic global corporations like Microsoft, Amazon.com and Starbucks. It is the second largest shipping container port in the United States. And it has a young, 'new-tech', global culture seemingly perfectly suited to discussions about pushing back the boundaries of world trade. But the expectations became horribly unstuck.

The anti-globalization protests

All hell broke loose at Seattle. Fifty thousand people took to the streets shouting their opposition to the trade talks. It turned ugly. Clouds of tear gas and clashes between banner-waving crowds and police dressed like front-line high-tech soldiers became the dominant images. Many delegates couldn't make it into the talks. Those who did couldn't agree on whether the talks should continue beyond Seattle. The juggernaut of economic globalization faltered, badly, for the first time. A bold new era in the anti-globalization debate had begun.

The WTO doubtless hoped the 'Battle for Seattle' had been a one-hit wonder. But the protests continued. They continued in Washington (against an IMF/World Bank meeting in April 2000), in Chiang Mai (against a meeting of the Asian Development Bank in May 2000), in Melbourne (against a meeting of the World Economic Forum in September 2000), in Prague (against an IMF/World Bank meeting in September 2000), in Quebec City (against the Summit of the Americas in April 2001) and in Gothenburg (against a European Union summit in June 2001), among many other places.[4] The largest protest, by far, was in Genoa, Italy, in July 2001 when a massive 200,000 to 300,000 people hit the streets to protest against a G8 meeting. Two months later, however, the September 11 attacks in New York took place. Although confidently predicted, by some, as the death of the anti-globalization movement, it ended up having only a temporary effect. Big protests began again in 2002, including large ones in Washington (against IMF/World Bank meetings), in New York (against the World Economic Forum), in Sydney (against a WTO mini-ministerial meeting) and in Johannesburg (against the

World Summit on Sustainable Development). Significant demonstrations were also held against the WTO talks held at Cancún
in Mexico in September 2003.

Anti-globalization protests are unstoppable; they have become
the public face of the anti-globalization movement. The problem is
that protests are negative and one-dimensional. They alert people
to the fact that something is horribly wrong with economic
globalization but they don't go any further. As anti-globalization
writer Naomi Klein argues, 'demonstrations themselves aren't a
movement'.[5] Demonstrations will always have a place but they
can't be all that the anti-globalization movement is about.

Policy formulation by the
anti-globalization movement

It didn't take long for the anti-globalization movement to real-
ize the limitations of protest. Several relatively new initiatives
within the movement have attempted to fill the vacuum of
alternatives left by the protests. One has been the creation, and
refinement, of many excellent websites that act as clearing houses
for information on economic globalization. Organizations like
Ralph Nader's Public Citizen in the US, the UK-based New
Economics Foundation, the Malaysia-based Third World Network,
and the Thailand-based Focus on the Global South all publish
volumes of excellent globalization information via their websites,
along with groups like The Transnational Institute, GATSwatch,
Corporations Watch and Multinational Monitor (see websites at
end of the book).

Another initiative has been the staging of a number of
policy forums on globalization alternatives. Groups like the
New Economics Foundation and the International Forum on
Globalization have held such forums. A very ambitious forum
was staged by the Foundation for Ethics and Meaning, in New
York, in May 2000, which attempted to sort out the lack of

unity within the movement once and for all.[6] The most successful forums, however, accept the movement's diversity and haven't
attempted to find a united voice on globalization alternatives.
The largest and most high-profile forums of this type have been
the World Social Forums held in Porto Alegre, Brazil, from 2001
to 2003 and in Mumbai, India, in 2004. They attracted 20,000
people in 2001, then 50,000 people in 2002, and about 100,000
in 2003 and again in 2004. The World Social Forum organizers
specifically prohibit anyone from attempting to speak on behalf
of the forums. They have become a hugely successful convergence
point for the movement. The success of the World Social Forums
has led to the staging of many regional social forums, including a
Middle East Social Forum in Beirut, an African Social Forum in
Bamako, a Pan-Amazonian Social Forum in Belem, an Australian
Social Forum in Sydney, an Indian Social Forum in Hyderabad,
and a European Social Forum in Genoa.

A third policy initiative, on which the remainder of this book
mainly concentrates, is economic globalization policy formulation by non-governmental organizations (NGOs) and alternative political parties within the anti-globalization movement.
The years since the Battle for Seattle, in particular, have seen
an explosion of policy output by these organizations. These
NGOs and political parties include aid organizations, environment groups, debt-relief organizations, development groups, independent research and policy organizations, non-mainstream
'Democratic' parties, as well as Green parties. It must be said
that not all activists within the anti-globalization movement agree
with working with NGOs and non-mainstream political parties.
There have been complaints that anti-globalization forums and
media statements are increasingly dominated by these groups. But
NGOs and non-mainstream political parties have unquestionably
produced some of the best alternative policy work on economic
globalization to date and the spotlight must necessarily turn to
them if one is seriously to consider the future policy direction
of the movement.

NGOs and non-mainstream parties

The place of NGOs and non-mainstream political parties has changed enormously over the past three decades. Generally both are much larger and more effective than ever before. They are also more economically articulate. NGOs have hugely increased in size and number over the past three decades and have developed more credibility as people have become increasingly disillusioned with the ability of governments to solve societal problems. The first NGO was arguably the Anti-Slavery Society, established in 1839.[7] Since then the number of NGOs around the world has experienced massive growth. In 1874 there were 32, in 1914 there were 1,083, in the 1990s there were about 13,000, and today there are about 30,000.[8] Not only have NGOs increased in number; they have also increased in terms of the respect they command. A survey commissioned by the World Economic Forum among 36,000 people in fifteen different countries in 2002 found that the leaders of NGOs commanded more trust and support than United Nations leaders and the government leaders of all major countries.[9]

Non-mainstream political parties aligned with the anti-globalization movement, especially the Greens and left-of-centre Democratic parties, have generally also enjoyed increased popularity over the past three decades. In the European Union, where the Greens are strongest, they have held ministries in most member countries and have also been part of governments in South America and Africa. They have also recently polled well in the United States, Australia and New Zealand and are taking root in more and more countries throughout Asia, the Pacific, Eastern Europe and Africa. Non-mainstream 'Democratic' parties, like the Liberal Democrats in the United Kingdom and the New Democrats in Canada are also polling well (these parties should not be confused, however, with mainstream Democratic parties like the Social and Christian Democrats in Germany and the Democrats in the US, who basically support economic

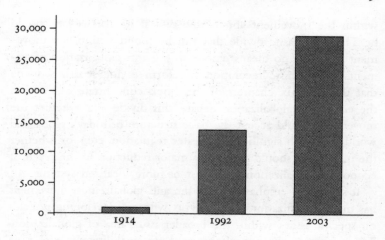

Source: Mike Moore, *A World Without Walls*, Cambridge University Press, Cambridge, 2003, p. 188.

Figure 7.1   Growth of non-governmental organizations in the world

globalization). So, the non-protest 'wing' of the anti-globalization movement has achieved a critical mass and now has the resources, people and sophistication to develop articulate alternatives to economic globalization. It now has the wherewithal to be as economically articulate as the left once was.

The increased popularity and confidence of the anti-globaliza-tion movement has created as many problems as it has solved, however. One major problem that the growth in the number of groups has accentuated is the lack of policy agreement within the movement. This isn't necessarily a bad thing. Many argue that the movement shouldn't rush into finding alternatives, particularly so soon after the Seattle turning point. In any event few oppo-sitional movements in history have ever necessarily had a united, consensual voice. Another major problem has been disagreement within the movement about how radical its alternatives should be. This is a classic divide that can be found within any movement and is by no means unique to the anti-globalization movement. It is a classic 'revolution or reform' divide. It is this divide that the next six chapters of this book concentrate on. Within the economic globalization debate, this divide asks whether the movement should accept the basic structure of today's globalized world (but with significantly greater regulation, etc.), or whether the movement should push for a major reduction in the reach of economic globalization, in favour of more localized systems.

It should be emphasized that the anti-globalization movement has many organizations and activists who are developing policies on specific issues within the broader issue area of globalization. These issues include environmental sustainability, the rights of indigenous people, urban planning, world health, access to shelter, food and water, education, nonviolence, human rights, preservation of local cultures and global migration, to name but a few. Since this book is dedicated to examining economic globalization, these specific issue areas are not discussed here. This in no way diminishes their importance; it simply recognizes that it is not possible to consider properly in one book all the other issues economic globalization touches on.

It should also be emphasized that this book does not attempt to represent the views of every organization in the anti-globalization movement. The following chapters present a representative sample of the views of the organizations in the movement, but since there are thousands of groups it is physically impossible to present all their opinions.

The debate around the moderate/radical divide of economic globalization policies is young. Its youth gives it freshness and vitality and potential for exciting future possibilities. It's a debate that could ultimately decide the future of global economics.

Notes

1. 'Marx after Communism', *The Economist*, 21 December 2002, p. 19.
2. Rodney Dalton, 'Liberal Democracy – That's All, Folks', *The Weekend Australian*, 3 August 2002, p. 24.
3. Naomi Klein, *Fences and Windows: Dispatches from the Front Lines of the Globalization Debate*, Flamingo, London, 2002, p. 22.
4. Walden Bello, *Deglobalization: Ideas for a New World Economy*, Zed Books, London, 2002, pp. 16–17.
5. Klein, *Fences and Windows*, p. 157.
6. Ibid., p. 14.
7. Mike Moore, *A World Without Walls: Freedom, Development, Free Trade and Global Governance*, Cambridge University Press, Cambridge, 2003, p. 188.
8. Ibid.
9. 'POLL: Public Faith in UN, NGOs High; US Ranks Lowest', published by Deb Foskey via WTO Watch email list (debf@webone.com. au), 16 January 2003 (#126), p. 1. (For archive copy, see www.nwjc.org. au/avcwl/lists/archives.html.)

CHAPTER 8

THE FAIR TRADE/
BACK TO BRETTON WOODS SCHOOL

Like the more radical policy school of the anti-globalization movement, the moderate policy school has no formal title. One appropriate title for it, however, is the 'Fair Trade/Back to Bretton Woods' school. This school believes the general structure of today's globalized marketplace is sound but feels its politics are not. It argues that the wrongs of current-day economic globalization could be corrected if the workings of the global marketplace were more regulated and were more rules-based. The Fair Trade/Back to Bretton Woods school believes its policies would take the world economy back to the essence of what the architects of the post-Second World War economic order envisaged at their conference at Bretton Woods in 1944 (which established the International Monetary Fund and the World Bank).

The Fair Trade/Back to Bretton Woods school argues that a level playing field is missing from economic globalization, and that if it were present the global economy could be sustainable. In recent years this school has been particularly vocal about the lack of such a level playing field in world trade and has strongly argued that if world trade was conducted more fairly, millions of people could be lifted out of poverty. Essentially this school believes economic globalization has become corrupted but is redeemable with better world governance through stronger, and fairer, international finance institutions and regulation. The Fair

Trade school mainly stands for political change of economic globalization rather than major structural change (as the more radical school advocates). It takes an attitudinal approach to economic globalization instead of a systemic one.

The bedrock philosophy of this school is close to that of well-known British economist John Maynard Keynes. It is not uncommon, though, for people in the anti-globalization movement to quote Keynes from the early 1930s when he appeared to favour tariffs and protectionism, which are favoured tools of the more radical school in the anti-globalization movement. However, according to his definitive biographer, Robert Skidelsky, Keynes was at times opportunistic, and in general 'Keynes preferred internationalism' and even published a paper in 1941 which explicitly argued that tariffs and subsidies ultimately fail.[1] The IMF and the World Bank are often even referred to as 'Keynes's twins', leaving little doubt where his sympathies ultimately lay, at least in the years immediately preceding his death in 1946. Because of this strong Keynesian flavour the policies of this school connect with the ideology of the post-war left movement. They also resonate with many left-of-centre groups and many poor-country governments.

The organizations in this current don't necessarily see themselves as part of a formal school and therefore have many variations on its basic philosophy. The most conspicuous organizations are several major aid organizations, some environment groups, several unions, some development groups, non-mainstream Democratic parties, as well as some less radical Green parties. They are joined by many groups whose policies address particular facets of economic globalization, such as Third World debt groups and IMF/World Bank reform organizations, but which don't have policies across all the major areas of economic globalization. If any one type of organization stands out in this school it is aid organizations. Many aid organizations do not take a public stand on issues like economic globalization because they fear it could jeopardize their fundraising efforts, but several aid organizations, particularly some from the United Kingdom, have a long history of political engagement that stretches back to the Cold War.[2] It is oversimplifying things, however, to generalize that particular types of organization necessarily belong to this policy school. Some have groups belonging either to the moderate school or to the more radical school but don't have all of their constituent groups necessarily belonging to either. Environmental groups and Green parties are two such types. Like the movement at large, there isn't necessarily any consistency, and in some ways it isn't fair to group together different organizations under the heading of a 'school', but in order to get a big picture idea of the broad policy thrusts of the anti-globalization movement such groupings are useful if not necessary.

Trade

In recent years trade has become a cause célèbre for the moderate/ Fair Trade anti-globalization school. They have no doubt that, if conducted fairly, world trade has the potential to right many of the wrongs of economic globalization, particularly the wrongs of wealth distribution. The organization that has taken the highest profile on 'Fair Trade', of late, has been Oxfam, an aid group that originated in the United Kingdom and that now has offices in most major rich countries. Oxfam readily admits that the way international trade is currently conducted is highly biased against poor countries but argues that 'the increasing integration of developing countries into the global trading system offers the promise of more rapid progress towards poverty reduction',[3] and that, 'managed well, the international trade system can lift millions out of poverty'.[4] It specifically claims that if Africa, East Asia, South Asia and Latin America were each to increase their share of world exports by 1 per cent, 128 million people could be raised out of poverty[5] (about 10 per cent of all the world's population currently living on US$1 a day or less). Oxfam even launched a major Fair Trade campaign in 2002. The Congress of

South African Trade Unions similarly sees trade as a route out of poverty, and advocates the 'lifting of trade barriers against African products by industrialized societies'.[6] Another aid organization, World Vision, also argues that 'for the most part, trade offers very significant net static and dynamic gains over the long term to all countries'.[7] These organizations are by no means alone in their support of Fair Trade. The European Greens, the Liberal Democrat party in the United Kingdom, the New Democrats of Canada, Greenpeace, the Worldwide Fund for Nature and the International Confederation of Free Trade Unions, among others, all join them in advocating rules-based Fair Trade.

Ending rich-country protectionism, allowing special and different treatment for poor countries

The main policy tool the Fair Trade school advocates for sustainable rules-based trade is an end to rich-country protectionism, in the form of subsidies and import restrictions, and the allowance of different trade rules for poor countries ('special and different treatment').

It is a major, and crucial, article of faith for the Fair Trade school that all exports from poor countries should have unhindered access to the import markets of rich countries. Christian Aid argues that 'all exports from least developed countries should be able to enter rich countries duty-free.'[8] Oxfam argues there should be comprehensive duty-free and quota-free access for all products exported by low income countries to rich-country markets by 2005.[9] The German Greens (Bündnis 90/Die Grünen) similarly advocate that one of the two main ways rich countries can help poor countries is by 'opening up their own domestic markets for goods from these countries'.[10] The Liberal Democrats in the UK have a slightly softer line, however, that makes a distinction between agricultural and non-agricultural imports. They argue that non-agricultural imports to rich countries should have all outstanding tariffs removed from them, while rich countries should be prepared to make 'further market access concessions' on poor-country agricultural exports.[11]

Groups advocating Fair Trade through unhindered poor-country export access to rich countries are adamant that trade protectionism is. bad policy, even when it might be advocated to protect rich-country jobs. World Vision says 'workers should not artificially and selfishly protect domestic jobs'.[12] The German Greens bluntly state that they are 'against renationalizing markets'.[13] Such stridency about trade protectionism, however, has brought the school into conflict with the more radical school. Protectionism, as a general policy tool, is a defining difference between the two.

Hand in hand with across-the-board elimination of rich-country import barriers goes the elimination of rich-country agricultural export subsidies (or any type of export subsidy) according to the Fair Trade/Back to Bretton Woods school. Oxfam flatly calls for a comprehensive ban on export subsidies.[14] Like the Liberal Democrats, however, the German Greens are somewhat guarded on the electorally sensitive issue of agricultural trade and argue for a gradual reduction in the 'huge agricultural subsidies' of rich countries.[15]

The Fair Trade school belief in rules-based free trade is not without qualification, however. As part of its belief that the rules need to be tilted more in favour of poor countries it argues that poor countries should have 'special and different treatment' to rich countries that might include longer implementation periods for liberalized trade or less onerous trade rules, and so on. The European Greens argue that poor countries 'require continuing special and different treatment to take account of their relatively weak position in the international trading system'.[16] A widely circulated ten-point global petition, 'WTO: Shrink or Sink', circulated by the Our World is Not for Sale Network in 2001 and 2002, similarly said that 'poor countries should be allowed to protect their economies and therefore be allowed to pursue trade rules that are special and different to those employed by rich countries'.[17]

Protection of national agricultural industries

In a conspicuous break from its general abhorrence of tariffs, however, the Fair Trade school generally advocates poor-country use of tariffs and protectionism to protect their local agricultural industries. The Fair Trade school places a lot of importance, as poor countries often did in the decades immediately after the Second World War, on the ability of poor countries to feed themselves. Despite its high-profile Fair Trade campaign, Oxfam has no problem advocating that 'developing countries have the right to protect their domestic agricultural sectors'.[18] Via Campesina, a global network of peasant and farm organizations, says poor countries should be able to develop 'in favour of domestic self sufficiency in rural development'.[19] The APM World Network advocates what it calls 'Food Sovereignty', which it says should be 'primarily orientated towards the satisfaction of the needs of the local and national markets'.[20] Christian Aid claims that poor countries should be 'free to choose effective import tariffs to ensure they are not flooded with cheap and disruptive food imports'.[21] Similarly Anuradha Mittal, policy director of Food First, argues that 'each country has a right to protect basic food production as it sees fit'.[22]

A further element of special and different treatment for poor countries often advocated by the Fair Trade school marks another departure from its otherwise purist vision of rules-based free trade. This element is the establishment of a global fund that would cushion the financial impact of falling poor-country raw-material export prices. Such a fund would be similar to the funds advocated by the United Nations Conference on Trade and Development (UNCTAD) in the 1970s. They would basically be price support and supply restriction schemes.

The World Development Movement says there should be a fundamental reorientation of the international trading system that would include 'an agreement to support primary prices'.[23] Oxfam advocates the creation of a new institution to oversee global raw material markets coupled with a new system of raw material agreements.[24] Oxfam sees such agreements departing, somewhat, from the proposed 1970s' UNCTAD agreements through a greater emphasis on balancing supply with demand. The Committee for the Annulment of Third World Debt argues that 'mechanisms guaranteeing a better price for the basket of products exported on the world market by developing countries must be introduced'.[25] The Association for the Taxation of Financial Transactions in the Interests of the Citizen (ATTAC) similarly advocates the establishment of a 'Raw Materials Market Stabilization Fund'.[26]

Social and environmental trade clauses

Given the basic belief of the Fair Trade school that properly conducted global trade can be beneficial for all, it is a natural progression for many in the school to advocate the use of special clauses in trade agreements to further their aims. These aims are generally concerned with labour rights and environmental protection. Such trade agreement clauses generally threaten some form of trade retaliation if exporting countries do not uphold bottom-line employment and environmental standards. They recognize the power of world trade agreements and attempt to attach social and environmental agendas to their implementation.

The International Confederation of Free Trade Unions is an advocate of trade agreement clauses, arguing 'the WTO must fully integrate a social, labor, developmental, gender and environmental dimension into the WTO system'.[27] The Worldwide Fund for Nature sees a major tension between trade and international environment agreements and says the only way to resolve that tension is for trade agreements to buttress global environment agreements.[28] Greenpeace also advocates the use of trade agreements to achieve environmental ends. It says that the precautionary principle should be built into decision-making by the World Trade Organization and that the WTO's disputes settlement mechanism should be used to achieve implementation of the Kyoto greenhouse gas emission protocol.[29] It even says: 'if the United States continues to refuse to ratify the Kyoto protocol WTO member states who support Kyoto should also consider bringing that country before a WTO dispute settlement panel'.[30] The United States Greens believe major trade deals need to be updated to include 'more specific environmental, worker, health and safety standards in the text itself'.[31] Echoing the same sentiment, the Green Party of California supports the use of tariffs 'to protect local, state and national health, safety, labor and environmental standards against lower standards in other countries'.[32] These groups feel trade agreements either work for you or against you, so you might as well make them work for you by broadening their ambit.

The future of the IMF, the World Bank and the WTO

Given that the Fair Trade/Back to Bretton Woods school has a belief that the world economic system powered by the World Bank, the International Monetary Fund and the World Trade Organization could work well, if only its politics and rules allowed it, it is not surprising that, generally, the school does not support wholesale scrapping of the World Bank, the IMF and the WTO but instead supports their major reform. If the system, in general, can work given the right parameters, then so too could its public institutions, the school believes. The school doesn't deny that these public world economic institutions have overstepped the mark in the past but it doesn't see that as sufficient reason to get rid of them.

The World Trade Organization

Despite its support of reform, rather than abolition, of the Bretton Woods institutions, the Fair Trade school is not necessarily supportive of how they are run. It is particularly suspicious of the management of the WTO and sees major flaws in its decision-making. The school consistently calls for greater transparency, fairness and accountability in the way decisions are made at the WTO.

Greenpeace says 'transparency, openness and consultation at the WTO urgently need to be improved'.[33] The Liberal Democrats are quite supportive of the WTO, arguing that it is a 'highly effective organization' but that it needs to be more transparent and sensitive to public concerns.[34] The World Development Movement maintains that the WTO needs to be 'radically reformed'.[35] The Our World is Not for Sale's 'WTO: Shrink or Sink' petition said the WTO's dispute settlement system is unacceptable and that future WTO negotiations need to be made 'democratic, transparent and inclusive'.[36] Oxfam says the WTO needs to be democratized and that part of that democratization should be the creation of a fund of about US$250 million to enhance the trade negotiating capacity of poor countries.[37] It also advocates WTO reviews of the impact of trade rules on employment standards.[38] Dot Keet, from the Africa Trade Network, believes the nature and roles of the WTO need to be reformed and that it should be made subordinate to the United Nations.[39] The European Greens say the decision-making of any international financial body needs to be democratic, transparent and inclusive.[40] Canada's New Democrat Party says binding and enforceable rules that protect human rights, labour standards, cultural diversity and the environment need to be in place before any more trade deals are signed.[41] The APM World Network says there needs to be an international appeals court established that is independent of the WTO.[42] Christian Aid probably sums up the feeling of most in the school by arguing that the WTO needs not so much to be reformed as to have its focus narrowed so that its rules no longer impinge on national sovereignty.[43] It also advocates that 'all major decisions must be taken with the active participation of all WTO members, ending the practice of rich countries agreeing deals behind closed doors'.[44]

So, there is respect for the potential of the WTO within the Fair Trade school, but general agreement that the organization needs to do more to include poor countries in its decision-making, needs to be much more transparent to the world's public in general, and needs to have a narrower and more accountable focus. There is generally a sense that the WTO should be refined and contained.

No new issues

The Fair Trade school belief in containment of the WTO is particularly apparent in its consistent claim that no more issues should be introduced into WTO negotiations. It feels that the tentacles of the WTO already spread further than they should and that they should not be allowed to spread even further into new areas of influence like protecting the rights of foreign investors and government purchasing.

The European Greens argue that no new trade negotiations should be commenced, of the sort begun in Doha in 2001, particularly in areas such as foreign direct investment, government procurement, trade transparency and biotechnology.[45] Lori Wallach of Public Citizen argues the current round of trade negotiations should be stopped.[46] The World Development Movement says: 'rich countries must stop the pressure for an expansion of the WTO's powers. Instead of negotiations on new trade rules the WTO, and its agreements, need to be radically reformed.'[47] The Our World Is Not for Sale's 'WTO: Shrink or Sink' petition flatly proclaimed 'there should be no new trade negotiation rounds and no new issues should be embraced by the WTO.'[48]

Services and patent agreements

The Fair Trade school's desire to contain the (reformable) WTO goes beyond a desire that it should not spread its influence into new issues. The school also feels that it has already gone too far

on some issues, particularly services and patents. The school feels
the General Agreement on Trade in Services (GATS) and the
Trade Related Aspects of Intellectual Property Rights (TRIPS)
agreements already go too far and that the boundaries of these
two agreements need to be pulled back.

On the GATS agreement, the World Development Movement
advocates that 'no further GATS negotiations should take place
while there are still grave concerns over the impact of this
agreement on the poor'.[49] 'WTO: Shrink or Sink' bluntly said
the GATS agreement should be scrapped and that areas such as
health, education, energy distribution and other basic human services should not be subject to international free-trade rules.[50]

A similar feeling extends to the TRIPS agreement. Probably
more so than the GATS services agreement, the Fair Trade
school believes the TRIPS intellectual property agreement has
robbed poor countries of access both to affordable medicines and
to plant products long considered communal property in poor
countries. World Vision argues that the TRIPS agreement needs
to be brought into line with the Convention on Biodiversity
and that innovative solutions are needed to ensure poor countries
are left without major financial burdens from rich-country-style
patents.[51] They also say the TRIPS agreement should provide
for poor-country parallel importing of essential drugs.[52] The
German Greens say 'the South's biological diversity must be
withdrawn from the reach of the private companies which are
attempting to patent it.'[53] Greenpeace argues: 'there should be no
patents on life forms.'[54] Christian Aid says to prevent biopiracy
in poor countries' companies wanting to take out new patents
of poor-country plant products must first get the consent of
the original poor-country users.[55] The Free Software Foundation
wants a major stand taken against global software corporations
through software being made freely available 'so as to ensure it
is shared and improved'.[56] Oxfam has particularly detailed policy
proposals on intellectual property rights in poor countries. It
says the duration of patents operating in poor countries should

be reduced, that poor-country public health interests should have priority over patent rights (including being able to access drugs from the cheapest source), that plants essential for food should not be patentable, that poor countries should be able to develop their own unique plant patent systems, and that the TRIPS agreement should be brought into line with the UN Convention on Biological Diversity and the International Treaty on Plant Genetic Resources for Food and Agriculture.[57] Oxfam, however, doesn't necessarily want the TRIPS agreement scrapped and prefers to campaign on 'wedge' issues, such as poor-country access to essential medicines, as a way of forcing broader change to the TRIPS agreement.[58]

The IMF and the World Bank

In keeping with its calls for WTO reform, the Fair Trade school also calls for major changes, as well as some scaling back, to be applied to the IMF and the World Bank. Again, they haven't completely lost faith in these institutions but they feel both need major overhauls and that both have already gone too far.

On the fiftieth anniversary of the IMF and World Bank in 1994 a network of mainly US-based anti-globalization groups, calling itself 50 Years is Enough, was formed to campaign for major reform of the two institutions. Four of their five major policy platform points dealt with overhauling the IMF and the World Bank. They called for:

- Openness and accountability of the Bretton Woods institutions and the systematic integration of affected women and men into the formulation, implementation, monitoring and evaluation of World Bank and IMF projects.
- A major reorientation of World Bank- and IMF-financed economic policy reforms to promote more equitable development based upon the perspectives, analysis and development priorities of women and men affected by these policies.

- An end to environmentally destructive lending and support for more self-reliant, resource-conserving development.
- The scaling back of the financing, operations, role and, hence, power of the World Bank and the IMF and the rechannelling of financial resources thereby made available into a variety of development assistance alternatives.[59]

Another group that has developed detailed, specific policies on reform of the IMF and World Bank is the Bretton Woods Project. Among its recommendations are:

- IMF and World Bank executive board seats should be re-allocated so that creditor and debtor countries have equal representation and all countries should be able to represent themselves (through a rotational system).
- No one country should have a veto on the executive boards of the IMF and the World Bank.
- Agendas and minutes of executive board meetings should be made available to the public, with members' positions indicated by formal votes.
- The heads of both the IMF and the World Bank should be determined on merit, not nationality.
- The United Nations should have greater powers to ensure the IMF and World Bank pay respect to the jurisdiction of other agencies.[60]

Other groups with views on the future of the IMF and World Bank include the International Confederation of Free Trade Unions, which says the IMF and World Bank should stop their policy of refusing loans to governments that want to retain public control and ownership of essential public services.[61] The Liberal Democrats argue that a review of the IMF should be conducted which takes into account 'the appropriate pace at which it is reasonable for a country to adjust to the sudden withdrawal of private finance without damaging its economy and society'.[62] Via Campesina argues that 'international financial institutions must be democratized and made to serve the real needs of the majority of people'.[63] The German Greens break slightly from the rest of the Fair Trade school by calling for an expansion (coupled with consolidation) of international financial institutions. They also call for greater transparency in financial markets in order to decrease the risk of currency speculation.[64] Oxfam links reform of the IMF and the World Bank to global trade reform by advocating that 'IMF–World Bank programs should not impose further loan conditions requiring trade liberalization' and that 'rich countries should reciprocate past liberalization undertaken by developing countries under IMF–World Bank conditions by making equivalent reductions in their own import barriers'.[65] Joshua Karliner from Corpwatch, and Karolo Aparicio from Global Exchange, see a democratic separation of powers issue with the IMF, World Bank and transnational corporations. They think there should be a fundamental separation between the IMF/World Bank and global corporations as there should be between national governments and corporations.[66] François Houtart of the World Forum for Alternatives believes the IMF and World Bank should be turned into mere regulatory bodies.[67]

Like most in the anti-globalization movement, Hector de la Cueva, from Alianza Social Continental, simply calls for a 'rejection of structural adjustment programmes'.[68] The Committee for the Annulment of Third World Debt echoes this call by arguing that structural adjustment programmes 'must ... be cancelled and replaced with policies aimed at satisfying basic human needs'.[69] The Committee for the Cancellation of Third World Debt also says structural adjustment policies should be abandoned.[70]

Debt cancellation

A very conspicuous area in which the Fair Trade school feels the IMF and the World Bank have gone too far is that of Third World debt. There is a universal belief in the school that current Third World debt levels are unsustainable and that some portion (if not all) should be cancelled. This policy is probably the most publicly known policy of the anti-globalization movement and it echoes throughout all their policy documents regardless of whether the policies in question come from the moderate or the more radical anti-globalization movement school.

One of the most high-profile organizations calling for Third World debt relief has been Jubilee 2000. Like many organizations in the anti-globalization movement they do not have policies on all aspects of economic globalization and prefer to concentrate on advocacy in their particular issue area of Third World debt. Jubilee 2000/USA calls for 'definitive cancellation of the crushing international debt in situations where countries burdened with high levels of human need and environmental distress are unable to meet the basic needs of their people'.[71] They also argue that such debt relief should not be conditional on policy reforms. Someone who has campaigned, and written, for many years on Third World debt is British author Susan George. She says the banks and institutions that originally issued the Third World's debt have been 'richly rewarded' and 'are in no danger if the debt is markedly reduced, cancelled or converted to provide for genuine development'.[72]

The European Greens say the IMF, World Bank and regional development banks must convert the Third World debts owed to them into regional development programmes for sustainable development.[73] The 50 Years Is Enough Network says Third World debt should be reduced 'to free up additional capital for sustainable development'[74]. Anuradha Mittal, from Food First, says Third World debt cancellation is the most effective short-term way to inject badly needed capital into poor countries.[75] The International Confederation of Free Trade Unions advocates comprehensive rescheduling of Third World debt, including a poor-country ability to enact 'debt standstills' if their circumstances require.[76] The Congress of South African Trade Unions calls for 'an end to the debt burden on the poorest countries'.[77] The Committee for the Annulment of Third World Debt simply states that 'the Third World's external public debt must be cancelled'.[78] The Social Movements' Manifesto says: 'we demand unconditional cancellation of the debt and reparation payments for historical, social and ecological debts'.[79] The Liberal Democrats advocate a 'bailing in' strategy for Third World debt where interest and capital repayments would be frozen until the relevant lenders are forced to negotiate a reduction in their claims.[80] Interestingly, however, the Liberal Democrats also advocate a form of debt reduction conditionality where cancellation would turn on the relevant debtor country adopting a firm commitment to poverty reduction and the upholding of human rights.[81]

Capital market and TNC regulation

In contrast to its view that global trade should generally be unhindered (but more equitably operated and regulated), the Fair Trade/Back to Bretton Woods school is generally in favour of controls on the flow of capital around the world. Although this is somewhat inconsistent with its approach to trade, it is a line in keeping with the original intent of the Bretton Woods architects of the post-Second World War international economic order. Global capital movements were tightly controlled when the Bretton Woods delegates sat down to their deliberations in 1944, and remained so for three decades. It was very much envisaged by Keynes et al. that a stable world economic order would not allow the free movement of capital.

ATTAC argues, in a very straightforward way, that 'it is ... necessary to introduce capital control measures on an international scale'.[82] The International Confederation of Free Trade Unions says there should be a 'recognition of the rights of governments to control foreign capital flows in the interest of macro-economic and social stability'.[83] The Congress of South African Trade Unions similarly argues for the introduction of 'rules on movement of capital that will not only challenge the speculative character of many portfolio flows, but will shift the balance of power that capital has gained through free movement of capital back to democratic institutions'.[84] The European Greens advocate a looser regime of 'regulation to achieve more control over the ever-increasing power of the financial markets'.[85] The Australian Democrats take a more nation-specific line and argue for a 'far stronger' national Foreign Investment Review Commission.[86] The Committee for the Annulment of Third World Debt also advocates general control over the movement of capital around the world.[87]

Aid groups tend to take a narrower policy line than other groups in the Fair Trade school when it comes to capital control policies, often restricting their support to greater regulatory control of only foreign investment. There are three main forms of global capital: foreign direct investment, sharemarket (portfolio) investment, and loans. Presumably aid groups are comfortable, then, with sharemarket and international loans remaining unregulated at an international level. Christian Aid says poor countries should be allowed to have full regulatory power over foreign investment.[88] World Vision argues that foreign investment should not be uncritically accepted by poor countries but should, instead, be subject to comprehensive economic and social cost–benefit analysis.[89] Consistent with Christian Aid and World Vision, Oxfam says 'governments should retain the right to regulate foreign investors.'[90]

Different types of capital control

In general capital controls can be price-based, quantity-based or a mix of the two.[91] Price-based controls make specific forms of capital movement more expensive with a view to reducing those types of capital flow. Quantity-based controls, as the name suggests, simply limit the volume of foreign capital that is allowed to move across borders. Among quantity-based controls two of the most frequently quoted types of control are those introduced by Chile and Malaysia during the 1990s. The Liberal

Democrats even say that they support 'the so-called Chilean tax which would involve developing countries levying a reserve requirement on capital inflows'.[92] The Chilean measures operated between 1991 and 1998 required, among other things, that if foreign loan funds were invested in Chile, an amount equal to 20 per cent of the funds (increased to 30 per cent in 1992) had to be lodged with the Chilean central bank for one year if the loan ran for a year or more.[93] The rate was reduced to 10 per cent in 1998, before being abolished later the same year. It was ironic that Chile, of all countries, should have used such controls because it was one of the first poor countries to embrace free-market globalization following the *coup d'état* staged by Augusto Pinochet in 1973.

In 1998 Malaysia introduced capital controls that were both quantity- and price-based in response to the 'Asian meltdown' which began the year before. Their controls pegged the local currency, the ringgit, to a fixed rate against the US dollar, banned offshore trading in the ringgit, limited purchase of foreign funds to specific purposes such as payment of salaries and dividends, and introduced a requirement that foreign institutional investors in Malaysia had to keep their funds in the country for at least a year before they could withdraw them.[94] The controls allowed Malaysia to climb out of the Asian meltdown more quickly than other Asian countries that did not have capital controls. Prime Minister Mahathir Mohamad justified the measures by saying: 'there are a lot of things we can do now because we don't have to face their [speculators'] actions to stop us. The free market has failed and failed disastrously because of abuses, not because the system is bad.'[95] Capital controls were also successfully employed by China and India during the Asian meltdown.

The main advantage of capital controls is that they allow national economies to pursue economic strategies that are in their own best interests but that may run against prevailing global economic forces. The capital controls put in place by Malaysia, for instance, allowed it to pursue a strategy of fairly high growth that created jobs and restored confidence after the Asian meltdown. Without those controls, however, they would have had to pursue a low growth strategy that would have prolonged their economic agony (as was the favoured strategy of the IMF and the World Bank at the time).

The Tobin Tax

A form of price-based capital control that is universally embraced by all parts of the anti-globalization movement, regardless of the policy school they are from, is the Tobin Tax on speculative foreign exchange transactions. The Tobin Tax is named after Keynesian economist James Tobin, who was a Nobel prizewinner for economics, a professor at Yale University, and once an economic advisor to US President John F. Kennedy. In 1972 he proposed his famous tax as a means of discouraging short-term speculative global capital movements. He said it would 'throw some sand in the wheels' of global financial markets.[96] Tobin originally proposed a rate of 0.25 per cent on short-term flows (excluding trade and long-term investments, etc.) but today groups in the anti-globalization movement generally advocate a lower rate of about 0.1 per cent, which would raise over US$100 billion per year, or nearly twice as much as is given in foreign aid by rich countries each year.

It is almost impossible to find anyone in the anti-globalization movement who does not support the Tobin Tax. It has even been proposed that an international Tobin Tax day be held each year (13 March). The German Greens say they are 'in favour of taxing speculative capital transactions by, for example, applying the Tobin Tax'.[97] The Australian Democrats argue that one of the best ways of discouraging destabilizing foreign currency speculation would be for the Australian government to campaign internationally for a Tobin Tax.[98] The Committee for the Annulment of Third World Debt says a Tobin Tax 'could be used to combat inequality, and to provide public health and education services, food security and sustainable development'.[99] ATTAC says a Tobin Tax could finance an international poor-country development fund and 'would accord greater authority to national monetary authorities, which could in turn focus their attentions on their domestic economic objectives'.[100] Jeff Faux, from the Economic Policy Institute, says 'volatile financial markets must be tamed' and the simplest way to do that is to introduce a Tobin Tax.[101] The Social Movements' Manifesto says: 'we demand the creation of specific taxes such as the Tobin Tax'.[102] The United States Green Party would set a Tobin Tax at between 0.1 and 0.05 per cent, which, they claim, would raise somewhere between US$75 billion and US$250 billion each year.[103]

Ironically, James Tobin himself felt uneasy about his tax being co-opted by the anti-globalization movement and his resultant implied association with it. He favoured free trade as a means of poor-country development and felt the IMF and World Bank should be strengthened, not weakened. A year before his death in 2002 he even said: 'I have been hijacked. I have nothing in common with this revolution against globalization.'[104]

Another form of price-based capital control has been proposed by ATTAC. They propose that all foreign investment around the world, be it in rich or poor countries, should be taxed at a rate varying between about 10 and 20 per cent. They see such a tax evening out some of the competitive devaluation of social and environmental standards that occurs between countries competing for foreign investment.[105]

Control over transnational corporations

Another article of faith for the Fair Trade school is some type of enhanced control over transnational corporations (TNCs), although there is not necessarily agreement about what form this enhanced control should take. Joshua Karliner of Corpwatch, and Karolo Aparicio of Global Exchange, say there should be 'binding rules' on TNC behaviour through the establishment

Box 8.1   The Fair Trade/Back-to-Bretton
Woods agenda

Rich-country protectionism

Rich-country protectionism, particularly against poor-country imports, should cease. Rich countries should also stop subsidizing agricultural exports.

Special and different treatment

Poor countries should be given 'special and different treatment' to rich countries on trade.

Poor-country protection of their agricultural industries

Poor countries should be able to protect their domestic agricultural industries against imports.

Social and environmental trade clauses

Labour and environmental clauses should be attached to international trade agreements that could be used to pressure exporting countries to lift their employment and environmental standards.

Raw material export price support schemes

There should be mechanisms or agreements to stop the on-going slide in global raw material export prices.

No new issues

No new issues should be introduced into present or future global trade negotiations. Trade liberalization should not be pushed any further.

Containment of the TRIPS agreement

The TRIPS agreement should not allow rich countries to patent poor-country practices or plant species, or stop their access to essential generic pharmaceuticals.

Reform of the WTO

The WTO needs to be made more democratic and accountable, with poor countries more able to engage with it. There should be no more back-room trade agreement decision-making by a select few countries.

Reform of the IMF and the World Bank

Both the IMF and the World Bank should be made more transparent and democratic, with a major reorientation of their lending practices.

Structural adjustment loans

There should be no more structural adjustment loans extended by the IMF or World Bank.

Third World Debt

Third World Debt should be substantially, if not completely, cancelled.

Tobin Tax

All countries should introduce a Tobin Tax on speculative currency transfers.

Foreign investment/capital market regulation

There should be greater regulation of the world's foreign investment, if not of the global capital market in general.

TNC regulation

TNCs should be more regulated and accountable, as well as exposed to stronger international competition laws.

International bankruptcy mechanism

There should be an international bankruptcy mechanism established for countries facing a foreign exchange crisis.

of a Framework Convention on Corporate Accountability.[106] The Committee for the Annulment of Third World Debt is more specific and advocates a limit on the proportion of shares foreigners should be able to hold and a requirement that shares bought by foreigners must be held by them for at least a year after purchase.[107] Christian Aid says that poor countries should be able to take the subsidiaries of TNCs operating in their countries to court, and that a 'legally binding code of conduct for TNCs needs to be established enforcing agreed environmental, human rights and development standards'.[108] World Vision says corporate codes of conduct are not always effective and that they should never remove the need for 'well-enforced social, environmental, tax, anti-corruption and labour laws' in poor countries.[109]

Several groups see the main problem with TNCs as being their tendency to assume monopoly powers and therefore approach their regulation in market competition terms. The World Development Movement advocates a 'new set of enforceable international rules' that would ensure proper regulation of TNCs through prohibition of monopolies and cartels, the prevention of unfair competition and the insistence that TNCs pay fair levels of tax.[110] Oxfam similarly argues for 'a new anti-trust investigation agency' established under the auspices of the WTO.[111] It also says that TNCs should 'support social and economic progress in developing countries' through implementation of the Organization for Economic Cooperation and Development's *Guidelines for Multinational Enterprises*.[112] The Liberal Democrats place a lot of store on TNC regulation through international competition policy. They argue that 'governments should be prepared to break down dominant company players' and that 'a strong competition policy is essential to guard against concentrations of market power'.[113] They go on to advocate the establishment of a global Competition Commission that would guard against global monopolies, mergers, cartels and abuses of dominant market positions.[114]

An international bankruptcy mechanism

A final area of policy that the Fair Trade school often pushes is some form of international bankruptcy mechanism. This mechanism would work similarly to US Chapter 11 laws, which allow companies and individuals to file for bankruptcy while, instead of their being wound up, as they would be in many Anglo-Saxon countries, avenues would be explored that would permit the relevant business to keep trading, principally through reorganization and the injection of new funds. In the case of a global bankruptcy mechanism, if a country was having difficulty meeting foreign debt repayments, avenues such as temporary suspension of part of their debt repayments would be explored that could keep the country financially afloat, even to the extent of allowing it to borrow more funds. It would allow countries to go, at least temporarily, outside the original terms of their foreign loans without their creditworthiness and whole relationship with the world finance market being significantly jeopardized. The idea has been around for some time, and in 2002 developed sufficient credence for the IMF to propose a version of it. However, by 2003 it appeared likely the US would block the proposal because they are keen to protect the rights of private lenders.

In essence, then, this is the policy framework of the Fair Trade/Back to Bretton Woods school of the anti-globalization movement. In its own way it is very idealistic. It believes that the free market has corrupted the original vision of the Bretton Woods negotiations and that if we return to that original vision the world financial system will become more sustainable. The school points to the fact that the Bretton Woods system worked reasonably well for three decades until it was torn asunder in the 1970s. They argue that it had a proven formula with a history of proven results. The more radical Localization school, however, argues that the Bretton Woods system didn't necessarily produce good results, and now that it has been corrupted we should take the opportunity to wipe the slate clean and start anew.

Notes

1. Robert Skidelsky, *John Maynard Keynes: Fighting for Britain 1937–1946*, Macmillan, London, 2000, pp. 202, 204.

2. David Sogge, *Give and Take: What's the Matter with Foreign Aid?*, Zed Books, London, 2002, p. 159.
3. Kevin Watkins et al., *Rigged Rules and Double Standards: Trade, Globalization and the Fight against Poverty*, Oxfam International, Washington DC, 2002, p. 239.
4. Ibid., p. 258.
5. Ibid., p. 3.
6. William F. Fisher and Thomas Ponniah, eds, *Another World is Possible: Popular Alternatives to Globalization at the World Social Forum*, Zed Books, London, 2003, p. 76.
7. Brett Parris, *Trade for Development*, World Vision, East Burwood (Australia), 1999, p. iv, downloaded from www.wvi.org in 2002.
8. Mark Curtis, *Trade for Life*, Christian Aid, London, 2001, p. 10, downloaded from www.christian-aid.org in 2002.
9. Watkins et al., *Rigged Rules*, p. 109.
10. Bündnis 90/Die Grünen, *The Future is Green: Alliance 90/The Greens: Party Program and Policy*, Die Grünen, Berlin, 2002, p. 46.
11. Liberal Democrats, *Global Responses to Global Problems*, Policy Paper No. 35, Liberal Democrats, London, p. 17, downloaded from www.libdems. org.uk in 2002.
12. Parris, *Trade for Development*, pp. 56, 61.
13. Bündnis 90/Die Grünen, *The Future is Green*, p. 47.
14. Watkins et al., *Rigged Rules*, p. 10.
15. Bündnis 90/Die Grünen, *The Future is Green*, p. 46.
16. European Greens, *WTO and Corporate Globalisation*, p. 3, downloaded from www.europeangreens.org in 2002.
17. Our World is Not for Sale Network, 'WTO: Shrink or Sink' petition, point 8, downloaded from www.speakeasy.org in 2002.
18. Watkins et al., *Rigged Rules*, p. 120.
19. Via Campesina, *Tlaxcala Declaration of the Via Campesina*, 1996, downloaded from www.virtualsask.com in 2002.
20. Fisher and Ponniah, *Another World is Possible*, p. 166.
21. Curtis, *Trade for Life*, p. 9.
22. Sarah Anderson, ed., *Views from the South: The Effects of Globalization and the WTO on Third World Countries*, Food First/Institute for Food and Development Policy, Oakland CA, 2000, p. 173.
23. World Development Movement, *If It's Broke, Fix It*, 2001, p. 8, downloaded from www.wdm.org.uk in 2002.
24. Watkins et al., *Rigged Rules*, p. 12.
25. Fisher and Ponniah, *Another World is Possible*, p. 35.
26. Ibid., p. 50.

27. The International Confederation of Free Trade Unions, *Joint Statement on Globalisation and the WTO*, 2001, downloaded from www.icftu.org in 2002.

28. Aimee T. Gonzales, untitled paper, Worldwide Fund for Nature, published by Deb Foskey via WTO Watch email list (debf@webone.com.au), 24 March 2002 (#47). (For archive copy, see www.nwjc.org.au/avcwl/lists/archives.html.)

29. Greenpeace International, *Safe Trade in the 21st Century*, 2001, pp. 8–10, downloaded from www.greenpeace.org in 2002.

30. Ibid., p. 9.

31. United States Greens, *Green Party Platform 2000*, section F, downloaded from www.greenpartyus.org in 2002.

32. Green Party of California, *Policy Directions: Platform Summary*, Sacramento, 2001, p. 39.

33. Greenpeace International, *Safe Trade in the 21st Century*, p. 10.

34. Liberal Democrats, *Global Responses to Global Problems*, pp. 16, 18.

35. World Development Movement, *If It's Broke, Fix It*, p. 1.

36. Our World is Not for Sale Network, 'WTO: Shrink or Sink' petition, point 9.

37. Watkins et al., *Rigged Rules*, pp. 4, 16.

38. Ibid., p. 204.

39. Fisher and Ponniah, *Another World is Possible*, p. 52.

40. European Greens, *WTO and Corporate Globalisation*, p. 3.

41. New Democrat Party, *Fighting for Fair Trade* policy, downloaded from www.ndp.ca in 2002.

42. Fisher and Ponniah, *Another World is Possible*, p. 169.

43. Curtis, *Trade for Life*, p. 10.

44. Ibid., p. 8.

45. European Greens, *WTO and Corporate Globalisation*, p. 3.

46. Fisher and Ponniah, *Another World is Possible*, p. 54.

47. World Development Movement, *If It's Broke, Fix It*, p. 1.

48. Our World is Not for Sale Network, *WTO: Shrink or Sink* petition, point 1.

49. World Development Movement, *If It's Broke, Fix It*, p. 8.

50. Our World is Not for Sale Network, *WTO: Shrink or Sink* petition, point 3.

51. Parris, *Trade for Development*, p. vi.

52. Ibid.

53. Bündnis 90/Die Grünen, *The Future is Green*, p. 134.

54. Greenpeace International, *Safe Trade in the 21st Century*, p. 10.

55. Curtis, *Trade for Life*, p. 10.

56. Fisher and Ponniah, *Another World is Possible*, p. 148.

57. Watkins et al., *Rigged Rules*, pp. 236–7.

58. Fisher and Ponniah, *Another World is Possible*, p. 140.

59. 50 Years is Enough Network, *50 Years is Enough Platform*, downloaded from www.economicjustice.org in 2002.

60. The Bretton Woods Project, 'Civil Society Statement on World Bank/IMF Governance', published by Deb Foskey via WTO Watch email list (debf@webone .com.au), 14 March 2003 (#141). (For archive copy, see www.nwjc.org.au/avcwl/lists/archives.html.)

61. The International Confederation of Free Trade Unions, *Global Unions' Statement: The Role of the IMF and World Bank*, 2001, p. 3, downloaded from www.icftu.org in 2002.

62. Liberal Democrats, *Global Responses to Global Problems*, p. 4.

63. Via Campesina, *Tlaxcala Declaration of the Via Campesina*, p. 2.

64. Bündnis 90/Die Grünen, *The Future is Green*, p. 47.

65. Watkins et al., *Rigged Rules*, p. 11.

66. Fisher and Ponniah, *Another World is Possible*, p. 57.

67. François Houtart and Francois Polet, *The Other Davos: The Globalization of Resistance to the World Economic System*, Zed Books, London, 2001, p. 7.

68. Fisher and Ponniah, *Another World is Possible*, p. 53.

69. Ibid., p. 34.

70. Houtart and Polet, *The Other Davos*, p. 39.

71. Jubilee 2000/USA , *Jubilee 2000/USA platform*, downloaded from www.j2000usa.org in 2002.

72. Susan George, *The Debt Boomerang: How Third World Debt Harms Us All*, Pluto Press, London, 1992, p. 171.

73. European Greens, *WTO and Corporate Globalisation*, p. 4.

74. 50 Years is Enough Network, *50 Years is Enough Platform*.

75. Anderson, *Views from the South*, p. 172.

76. The International Confederation of Free Trade Unions, *Global Unions' Statement: The Role of the IMF and World Bank*, p. 10.

77. Fisher and Ponniah, *Another World is Possible*, p. 69.

78. Ibid., p. 32.

79. Ibid., p. 350.

80. Liberal Democrats, *Global Responses to Global Problems*, p. 15.

81. Ibid., p. 5.

82. Fisher and Ponniah, *Another World is Possible*, p. 44.

83. The International Confederation of Free Trade Unions, *Global Unions' Statement: The Role of the IMF and World Bank*, p. 10.

84. Fisher and Ponniah, *Another World is Possible*, p. 69.

85. European Greens, *Greening the Economy*, p. 3, downloaded from www. europeangreens.org in 2002.

86. Australian Democrats, *Economic Independence* policy, p. 2, downloaded from www.democrats.org.au in 2001.

87. Fisher and Ponniah, *Another World is Possible*, p. 36.

88. Curtis, *Trade for Life*, p. 9.

89. Brett Parris, *Foreign Direct Investment and Corporate Codes of Conduct in National Development Strategies*, World Vision, East Burwood, Australia, 2001, p. 5, downloaded from www.wvi.org in 2002.

90. Watkins et al., *Rigged Rules*, p. 238.

91. Kavaljit Singh, *Taming Global Financial Flows: A Citizen's Guide*, Zed Books, London, 2000, p. 122.

92. Liberal Democrats, *Global Responses to Global Problems*, p. 4.

93. Singh, *Taming Global Financial Flows*, pp. 161–2.

94. Ibid., pp. 140–41.

95. Ibid., pp. 141–2.

96. Ibid., p. 197.

97. Bündnis 90/Die Grünen, *The Future is Green*, p. 47.

98. Australian Democrats, *Economic Independence* policy, p. 2.

99. Fisher and Ponniah, *Another World is Possible*, p. 33.

100. Ibid., p. 45.

101. Ibid., p. 89.

102. Ibid., p. 351.

103. United States Greens, *Green Party Platform 2000*, section F.

104. Obituary, 'Economist Built on the Work of Keynes', *The Australian*, 22 March 2002, p. 14.

105. Fisher and Ponniah, *Another World is Possible*, p. 46.

106. Ibid., p. 60.

107. Ibid., p. 48.

108. Curtis, *Trade for Life*, p. 9.

109. Parris, *Foreign Direct Investment*, p. 1.

110. World Development Movement, *If It's Broke, Fix It*, p. 8.

111. Watkins et al., *Rigged Rules*, p. 258.

112. Ibid., p. 205.

113. Liberal Democrats, *Global Responses to Global Problems*, p. 19.

114. Ibid., p. 19.

CHAPTER 9

THE LOCALIZATION SCHOOL

In policy terms, the radicals within the anti-globalization movement are represented by what is probably best called the 'Localization school'. As the name suggests, the bedrock philosophy of this school is that local economies (be they local, regional or national) should be the centre of economic activity, not the international economy. The effect of Localization policies would be to shrink significantly the size of world economic activity, and therefore the reach of economic globalization, although the Localization school acknowledges there will always be a need for some residual global economic activity.

Localization is a policy philosophy that asserts that economic globalization has taken power away from local economies. It is therefore time to put local economies back at the centre, even if that means using instruments such as tariffs, restrictive capital controls and significant re-regulation of TNCs, the school argues. Localization does not stand for isolationism, and the school generally acknowledges that some aspects of internationalism need to be retained. The Localization school mainly stands for major structural change of economic globalization rather than just political change. It has a much more systemic approach to globalization than the Fair Trade school. The key term in the Localization philosophy is 'self-reliance'. Localization does not aim for local economic self-sufficiency but does aim for local economic self-reliance.

Politically, Localization is an interesting beast. It clearly represents a major break with the internationalist leaning of traditional left philosophy. Some would even argue that its decentralist philosophy has more in common with traditional, anti-centralist, right-wing philosophy than anything else. The Localization school would respond, however, that old left/right analyses of political philosophy are no longer relevant, particularly as the mainstream left and right have united in supporting economic globalization, and a common support for certain structures doesn't imply a common political philosophy.

If Keynes is the ideological 'father' of the Fair Trade school, then Fritz Schumacher, author of the landmark book *Small is Beautiful*, is the ideological father of the Localization school. In *Small is Beautiful* he argues that 'today we suffer from an almost universal idolatry of giantism. It is therefore necessary to insist on the virtues of smallness – where this applies'.[1] It would be wrong, however, to assume that Schumacher thought small structures were always necessarily appropriate. He was very much a relativist and qualified his philosophy by saying small structures were appropriate in a world dominated by large structures. He also argued in *Small is Beautiful* that 'if there were a prevailing idolatry of smallness, irrespective of subject or purpose, one would have to try and exercise influence in the opposite direction'.[2]

Advocates of Localization

The Localization school has a number of significant backers and has grown significantly in popularity in recent years. Although aid organizations and non-mainstream Democratic parties tend to support the Fair Trade school, environmental groups and Green parties, in particular, are split between the Localization and Fair Trade schools. Friends of the Earth breaks with Greenpeace and the Worldwide Fund for Nature in supporting Localization, for instance. Similarly, the Green parties of England and Wales, Ireland

and South Africa break with their European, German and US counterparts in supporting Localization.

Friends of the Earth argues that 'countries and communities should have the option to select those economic mechanisms that they believe best suit their economic, social, cultural and environmental needs at any one time. These decisions should be made with a view to optimizing economic activity and maintaining a degree of self-reliance'.[3]

The Green Party of England and Wales declares: 'Green policies are based on the principle that we need to reduce to a minimum the overall volume of international trade, and to revitalize local communities by promoting self-reliance, economic, social, and political control, and environmental sustainability.'[4] Similarly the Irish Greens (Comhaontas Glas) advocate a 'new protectionism' with 'more support given to self-reliant local and regional economies'.[5] The Green Party of South Africa echoes these calls by arguing that 'increased economic cooperation must be accompanied by much greater economic self-reliance for regions and nations. Self-reliance provides an alternative to the present level of unsustainable and inequitable international relationships.'[6]

Another conspicuous proponent of Localization is the International Forum on Globalization (IFG), a US-based alliance of leading activists, scholars, economists and researchers representing over sixty organizations in twenty-five countries. The IFG says 'all decisions should be made at the lowest level of governing authority'.[7] It also says that Localization policies 'seek to achieve maximum self-reliance nationally and regionally' and that they attempt 'to reverse the trend toward the global by discriminating actively in favour of the local in all policies'.[8]

The person who is probably the most famous long-time advocate of Localization is Colin Hines, a British activist who was once head of Greenpeace's International Economics Unit. He is also a fellow of the IFG and is author or co-author of several books including *Localization: A Global Manifesto* and *The New Protectionism: Protecting the Future against Free Trade*. Hines describes Localization as 'a process which reverses the trend of globalization by discriminating in favour of the local'.[9] He says the term 'local' mainly applies to part of a nation but can also apply to a whole nation or even, on occasion, to a regional grouping of nations.[10]

Another author/activist advocate of Localization is David Korten, author of *When Corporations Rule the World* and *The Post-Corporate World: Life after Capitalism*. He argues 'now we must create living economies based on locally-rooted ownership and deeply held human values of equity, democracy, local and human-scale markets, and personal responsibility.'[11]

Localization aiding democracy

One of the main arguments used in defence of Localization is that it is good for participatory democracy. The Localization school consistently argues that decision-making powers need to be returned to local economies (preferably through adoption of its policies).

The IFG held a 'teach-in' during the Seattle protests of November/December 1999. It said the term 'democracy' was the most consistent theme uniting all the myriad groups that turned up for their teach-in. It said that many adjectives were used to give the term deeper meaning, like 'living democracy', 'participatory democracy', 'new democracy' and 'people's democracy', but democracy was the dominant theme.[12] The IFG argues: 'if democracy is based on the idea that people must participate in the great decisions affecting their lives, then the movement of basic life decisions to distant venues – particularly venues that abhor democratic participation, openness, accountability, and transparency – brings the death of democracy'.[13] It therefore argues that 'bringing governance and economies down to smaller-scale systems – where people are closer to the source of power – offers far greater opportunity and promise for democratic participation than the present model.'[14] Colin Hines says much the same thing by asserting that bringing the production of goods and services as close as possible to their point of consumption will increase economic decision-making power by increasing 'the likelihood of a wide range of peoples' active participation'.[15]

Interestingly, however, neither Hines nor the IFG guarantees that Localization will necessarily always bring greater participatory democracy. The IFG says: 'we are aware that Localization is not a panacea. Localization does not guarantee democracy or equality or human rights; it just makes them far more likely.'[16] Hines concedes almost exactly the same point by arguing that 'local control need not guarantee increased democracy, equality, environmental protection and so on'.[17] So, the Localization school does not assert that less economic globalization and more local control guarantee more democracy; they just claim they increase the chances.

Trade

Although there is some overlap between the Localization and Fair Trade schools, the two areas where they most part company are trade and the future of the International Monetary Fund, the World Trade Organization and the World Bank.

On trade there is little agreement between the two schools. The Fair Trade school believes that given the right rules and moral code global trade can be a force for good that could lift millions out of poverty. The Localization school generally sees global trade as an inherently destructive economic force and believes the only way poor nations will get any richer is through less trade, not more. They see rules-based trade as naive. They believe the world has tried it and it simply doesn't work.

The Irish Greens argue we should be promoting 'a new protectionism for developing local and regional self-reliance'.[18] They believe economic globalization destroys local production and that their new protectionism would 'enable domestic producers to compete while improving social and environmental standards'.[19]

The South African Greens say trade policy should 'increase small-scale, local community import substitution, rather than export promotion'.[20] Caroline Lucas, an English Greens member of the European Parliament, argues that trade policy should be 'part of the reintroduction of protective safeguards for domestic economies'.[21] The Green Party of England and Wales argues that the aim of sustainable trade policy should be 'to introduce import and export controls on a national and/or regional bloc level, with the aim of allowing localities and countries to produce as much of their food, goods and services as they can themselves'.[22] The IFG asserts that 'economic systems should favor local production and markets rather than invariably being designed to serve long distance trade'.[23]

Colin Hines says that goods and services that can't be sourced from within a country should be sourced from neighbouring countries and that long-distance trade should be very much a 'last resort'.[24] He also says tariffs, in the form of import duties, and quotas, in the form of limits on the quantity of goods that can be imported into a country, are the best mechanisms to achieve Localization.[25] Of the two mechanisms, he thinks tariffs are likely to be the most effective. He says quotas are more useful in limiting the importation of goods and services that cannot be locally produced.[26] He says if tariffs are phased in gradually 'they send a clear message to all exporters that they need to reorientate their production towards more local markets'.[27]

The future of the IMF, the World Bank and the WTO

After trade, the area where the Localization and Fair Trade schools least agree is the future of the IMF, the World Bank and the WTO. The Fair Trade school thinks meaningful reform of these three public international finance institutions is possible, while the Localization school will generally only settle for their abolition. Interestingly, however, the Localization school generally calls for replacement of these bodies, rather than abolition with nothing to replace them.

The WTO

There is agreement within the Localization school that the WTO should be abolished, but there isn't agreement, necessarily, about what it should be replaced with. The Green Party of England and Wales would replace the WTO 'with a more accountable, decentralized body which aims to protect and enhance social and environmental conditions, and to develop strong self-reliant regions where individual communities meet more of their own needs'.[28] Colin Hines expresses a similar sentiment. He believes the WTO should be replaced by a 'World Localization Organization' that would administer radically rewritten trade rules that would be enshrined in a new global trade agreement called the 'General Agreement for Sustainable Trade'.[29]

The IFG is less categorical. It gives three replacement options for the WTO:

- the creation of an International Trade Organization, of the sort envisaged at the Havana trade conference in 1947, that embraced global full employment and anti-monopoly goals;
- a return to the type of global trade management that existed before the WTO, where there were non-binding rules and no permanent international trade management body;
- have no global trade management at all but instead have a network of regional trade bodies.[30]

Whatever the WTO is replaced with, however, the IFG argues that future trade agreements, of the sort currently managed by the WTO, must be narrowly defined and should not have the broad-ranging powers they have at present. The IFG says that 'global trade bureaucracies and international finance agencies should not have authority over state or national decision making when it comes to the commons, national heritage resources, the preservation of national choice in domestic services, or fundamental human rights.'[31]

A high-profile activist in the anti-globalization movement who has consistently argued against reform of the WTO (as opposed to its abolition) is Walden Bello, director of the Thailand-based Focus on the Global South organization. He also gives three replacement options for the WTO, all of which are generally more radical than the IFG's:

- a complete decommissioning of the WTO;
- 'neutering' it through its conversion into a purely research-based organization;
- a radical reduction of its powers, turning it into 'just another set of actors co-existing with and being checked by other international organizations, agreements and regional groupings'.[32]

Bello often campaigns on the theme that the WTO, along with the IMF and the World Bank, are driving world economic policy and therefore world social and environmental policy as well. He consistently argues that they shouldn't have this paramount power but should instead be one of a number of global public policy institutions that should keep each other in check. He says that if other international agreements and agencies, such as the United Nations Conference on Trade and Development, multilateral environment agreements, the International Labor Organization, and regional trade authorities such as the Mercosur (Latin America) and ASEAN (Southeast Asia) groupings, had more authority, they could balance out the power of the IMF, the WTO and the World Bank (or their replacements). That would make for 'a more fluid, less structured, more pluralistic world with multiple checks and balances', which would also make for more sustainable poor-country development.[33] Bello cautions against Fair Trade school/WTO-reform policies by arguing that replacing one set of centralized global rules and institutions with another set, albeit a possibly more enlightened set, 'is likely to reproduce the same

Jurassic trap that ensnared organizations as different as IBM, the IMF and the Soviet state'.[34]

The IMF and the World Bank

The Localization school's approach to the future of the IMF and the World Bank is similar to its attitude to the WTO: they need to be replaced, though again there are a number of replacement options proposed.

The Green Party of England and Wales picks up a theme similar to Walden Bello's argument that there needs to be more pluralism in future world economic management. They argue that the present international financial system needs to be replaced by a system 'in which money returns to its proper role as a medium of exchange, not a commodity in its own right'.[35] They say this could result in a reformed IMF and World Bank that are at the centre 'of a global economic system with commercial institutions playing a much diminished role'.[36] The IFG also picks up on Bello's theme. It argues that current global governance is divided between the United Nations (UN) system and the IMF, the World Bank and the WTO. It says that 'the time has come to reshape the system of global economic governance under the auspices of a reformed UN'.[37] It thinks the IMF and the World Bank should be dismantled and replaced with regional bodies, while essential global economic governance functions should be given to a UN 'International Finance Organization'.[38] The IFG claims that such a UN body would 'achieve and maintain balance and stability in international finance relationships, free national and global finance from the distortions of international debt and debt-based money' and 'promote productive domestic investment'.[39]

Walden Bello, for his part, thinks the IMF should be converted into a research agency, with no policy powers, that would monitor capital and exchange rate movements, while the World Bank should stop making loans and should devolve its grant activities to regional institutions.[40]

Colin Hines envisages replacing the IMF with an 'International Central Bank' that would have significant representation from non-governmental organizations.[41] He thinks the World Bank should be replaced by a body with modest development programmes, which would encourage locally based development and also manage commodity price stabilization schemes.[42] The South African Greens call for a 'complete overhaul' of the IMF and the World Bank, making for 'creative alternatives to IMF austerity measures imposed on the world's already most impoverished peoples'.[43]

Capital market and TNC regulation

Like its trade policy, the capital market policies of the Localization school discriminate in favour of the local. The Localization school believes the main source of local investment should be local investors. As with its trade policy, it doesn't rule out some residual amount of non-local investment but it generally believes the current reliance on non-local investment needs to be reduced. On capital market policy, at least, it has much more in common with the Fair Trade school than it does on trade policy. Both schools are somewhat suspicious of global capital, although the Localization school discriminates much more strongly in favour of local investment and generally advocates more radical capital market policies than does the Fair Trade school.

Colin Hines proposes the adoption of an 'Alternative Investment Code' whose basic aim would be 'the regrounding of capital locally to fund the diversification of local, sustainable economies'.[44] He believes domestic investors should be given 'favourable treatment' and that foreign investors should not have the same rights as domestic investors.[45] He also believes that local investment should be encouraged through measures such as ones that guarantee a minimum level of local content in locally produced goods and services, mandated minimum levels of local ownership, preference given to locally produced goods and services, and anti-monopoly laws.[46] Walden Bello advocates similar policies. He believes that 'growth must be financed principally from domestic savings and investment' and that the local market should be the 'principle locomotive of growth'.[47] The IFG argues that 'profits made locally should remain primarily local' and also supports local content rules.[48] In addition it believes capital gains taxes should be increased, especially for short-term investments, and that 'preferential treatment should always be given to local direct investment'.[49]

The Green Party of England and Wales believes capital controls need to be established that ensure the profits made by transnational corporations remain in the country of origin.[50] Caroline Lucas, from the same party, believes a combination of 'controls on capital flows', a Tobin Tax and 'control of tax evasion, including offshore banking centres' should be introduced, allowing money to become localized 'so that the majority of it stays within its place of origin'.[51] The Irish Greens have a fairly radical capital policy that includes the possibility of local areas having their own currencies – what they call 'a parallel system of exchange' – that would make for a more decentralized economy.[52]

Control over transnational corporations

Like the Fair Trade school, the Localization school believes transnational corporations (TNCs) should be more regulated than they are at present. As with their capital market policies, however, the Localization school is generally inclined to go further with TNC regulation than the Fair Trade school.

Friends of the Earth is part of a network of anti-globalization movement organizations that calls for compulsory, and legislated, corporate reporting in a number of key areas, including environmental, labour and human rights issues.[53] The IFG proposes a raft of new TNC regulations, including some that would require TNCs to locate in a local economy to be able to sell there ('site-

Box 9.1   The Localization school agenda

Self-reliance

National and regional economies should be the focus of economic management, not the international economy. Production and investment should be carried out as close to the point of economic activity as possible through a general regime of self-reliance.

Trade

Trade should be as locally based as possible through protectionism using tariffs and quotas.

Investment and capital markets

Investment should be as locally based as possible and capital markets should be regulated in favour of local investment through local content and ownership laws etc.

Abolition of the WTO

The WTO should be abolished and replaced with a more democratic, less powerful, more narrowly defined and transparent body. The new body would be concerned with local production rather than free trade. Alternatively, the WTO could be replaced by regional trade bodies.

Abolition of the IMF and World Bank

The IMF and World Bank should be abolished and replaced with a more democratic, less powerful, more narrowly defined and transparent body. The new body would be concerned with local investment and production as well as balance in international financial relations.

General world economic management

There should generally be more pluralism in world economic management, with international non-financial organizations providing checks and balances against international financial institutions.

> **Greater regulation of TNCs**
>
> TNCs should be more regulated through: restrictions on in-
> ternational profit repatriation, compulsory reporting in non-
> financial areas, site-here-to-sell-here requirements, restrictions
> on patenting and factory closures, tax policies that favour local
> businesses, anti-monopoly laws, greater liability for any social
> and environmental damage they cause, and greater shareholder
> power.

here-to-sell-here' policies), limiting the 'chartering' (incorporation)
of TNCs, and restrictions on the ability of TNCs to close factories and patent life forms.[54] It would also reform tax policies
to favour local businesses, outlaw corporate political donations,
introduce strict anti-monopoly laws, make investors personally
liable for environmental or social harm done by their companies,
and introduce legally enforceable codes of corporate conduct
in areas such as working conditions, the environment, finances
and lobbying activity.[55] The IFG also advocates an end to the
government subsidization of corporations ('corporate welfare'),
as well as the establishment of an 'Organization for Corporate
Accountability' under the auspices of the UN that would provide
information on corporate practices that could form the basis of
legal action and consumer boycotts.[56]

Like the IFG, Colin Hines supports site-here-to-sell-here policies, which he believes would ensure TNCs could no longer use
the threat of moving to another country to win greater concessions.[57] He says that shareholders should have greater opportunities to influence the direction of TNCs and that there should
be strict controls on TNC transfer pricing.[58] Like Friends of the
Earth, he advocates what he calls 'social accounting', where companies would be required to disclose audited information in key
areas like the social and environmental impact of their activities.[59]
Hines, in fact, feels the biggest advantage of Localization policies
is the enhanced control they bring over TNCs.[60]

Caroline Lucas believes that in more protected economies, of the sort advocated by the Localization school, it will be important to have tight local competition policies to eliminate monopolies.[61] The Irish Greens also support 'vigorous use' of anti-monopoly laws against TNCs and believe there should be an international tax treaty to discourage TNCs from avoiding taxes.[62]

This, then, is the agenda of the more radical Localization school – an agenda that refocuses economic activity and priorities around local economies. Some of the Localization school agenda is already being acted upon in some poor parts of the world. In 2002 impoverished street children in Delhi successfully set up their own bank, with over 160 account holders; and in Argentina a network of 'barter clubs', where people meet to exchange goods they have produced themselves, was established in reaction to the country's recent debt crisis. Instead of attempting to rewrite old rules, the Localization school attempts to produce a new set of rules that fly in the face of the international thrust of modern economic globalization.

Notes

1. E.F. Schumacher, *Small is Beautiful: A Study of Economics as if People Mattered*, London, Abacus, 1973, p. 54.
2. Ibid., p. 54.
3. Friends of the Earth, *Towards Sustainable Economics: Challenging Neoliberal Economic Globalisation* (Slovak translation), p. 2, downloaded from www.foei.org in 2002.
4. Green Party of England and Wales, *The Global Economy*, policy no. EC904, downloaded from www.greenparty.org.uk in 2002.
5. Irish Greens (Comhaontas Glas), Economic policy, no. 17.1, downloaded from www.greenparty.ie in 2002.
6. The Green Party of South Africa, *The Global Economy*, p. 1, downloaded from www.greenparty.org.za in 2002.
7. The International Forum on Globalization, *Report Summary – Alternatives to Economic Globalization: A Better World is Possible*, p. 12, downloaded from www.ifg.org in 2002.
8. Ibid., pp. 12, 13.

9. Colin Hines, *Localization: A Global Manifesto*, Earthscan, London, 2000, p. 27.

10. Ibid., p. 27.

11. David Korten, 'Living Economies', *Resurgence* 215, November/December 2002, p. 14.

12. The International Forum on Globalization, *Alternatives to Economic Globalization: A Better World is Possible*, Berrett-Koehler, San Francisco, 2002, p. 54.

13. Ibid., p. 106.

14. Ibid., pp. 117–18.

15. Hines, *Localization*, p. 119.

16. The International Forum on Globalization, *Alternatives to Economic Globalization*, p. 110.

17. Hines, *Localization*, p. 33.

18. Irish Greens (Comhaontas Glas), Economic Policy, no. 17.2.2.

19. Ibid., no. 17.2.3.

20. Green Party of South Africa, *The Global Economy*, p. 1.

21. Caroline Lucas and Colin Hines, *Time to Replace Globalization: A Green Localist Manifesto for the World Trade Organisation Ministerial*, The Greens/ European Free Alliance, London, 2001, p. 16.

22. Green Party of England and Wales, *The Global Economy*, policy no. EC945.

23. The International Forum on Globalization, *Report Summary – Alternatives to Economic Globalization*, p. 12.

24. Hines, *Localization*, p. 64.

25. Ibid.

26. Ibid., p. 65.

27. Ibid., p. 65.

28. Green Party of England and Wales, *The Global Economy*, policy no. EC942.

29. Hines, *Localization*, p. 260.

30. The International Forum on Globalization, *Report Summary – Alternatives to Economic Globalization*, p. 20.

31. The International Forum on Globalization, *Alternatives to Economic Globalization*, p. 102.

32. Walden Bello, *Deglobalization: Ideas for a New World Economy*, Zed Books, London, 2002, pp. 116–17.

33. Walden Bello, *Why Reform of the WTO is the Wrong Agenda*, p. 8, downloaded from www.focusweb.org in 2002.

34. Bello, *Deglobalization*, p. 115.

35. Green Party of England and Wales, *The Global Economy*, policy no. EC960.

36. Ibid.

37. The International Forum on Globalization, *Report Summary – Alternatives to Economic Globalization*, p. 18.

38. Ibid., pp. 19–20.

39. Ibid., p. 20.

40. Bello, *Deglobalization*, p. 108.

41. Hines, *Localization*, p. 144.

42. Ibid.

43. Green Party of South Africa, *The Global Economy*, p. 2.

44. Hines, *Localization*, p. 88.

45. Ibid., p. 90.

46. Ibid.

47. Ibid.

48. The International Forum on Globalization, *Alternatives to Economic Globalization*, pp. 111, 116.

49. Ibid., p. 115.

50. Green Party of England and Wales, *The Global Economy*, policy no. EC981.

51. Lucas and Hines, *Time to Replace Globalization*, p. 16.

52. Irish Greens (Comhaontas Glas), Economic Policy, no. 20.2.2.

53. The International Forum on Globalization, *Alternatives to Economic Globalization*, p. 135.

54. Ibid., p. 143.

55. Ibid., pp. 134, 138, 139, 141, 142.

56. The International Forum on Globalization, *Report Summary – Alternatives to Economic Globalization*, pp. 15, 20.

57. Hines, *Localization*, p. 69.

58. Ibid., pp. 75, 106.

59. Ibid., p. 75.

60. Ibid., p. 217.

61. Lucas and Hines, *Time to Replace Globalization*, p. 16.

62. Irish Greens (Comhaontas Glas), Economic Policy, no. 19.2.2.

CHAPTER 10

GLOBAPHOBES VERSUS GLOBAPHILES

The tension between the Fair Trade and Localization schools is not new. As the policy thinking of the anti-globalization movement has matured, however, the tension has grown more acute and has become quite pronounced in recent years. This can be helpful for the movement if it concentrates minds and creates constructive debate. But the tension can also be destructive. It can make internal disagreement very tribal and oblivious to different points of view. The arguments can become more about loyalties than different philosophies and ways of viewing a problem. The Fair Trade and Localization schools have much more in common than either is generally prepared to admit, although there are significant differences, particularly about trade. For better or worse (probably worse), colloquial labels have been developed for the two schools. Members of the Fair Trade school are known as 'globaphiles' while members of the Localization school are known as 'globaphobes'.

The Oxfam Rigged Rules report debate

In 2002 the tension between globaphobes and globaphiles was brought out into the open with the high-profile launch of Oxfam's Make Trade Fair campaign, which was accompanied by the release of a major comprehensive report it compiled entitled *Rigged Rules and Double Standards – Trade, Globalisation and the Fight against Poverty*. Both in its campaign and in its report Oxfam made no attempt to hide its belief that properly structured, rules-based international trade can lift people in poor countries out of poverty and that disengagement from global trade, as espoused by the Localization school, is bad policy. The *Rigged Rules* report even specifically took on globaphobes by alleging that 'globaphobia is refuted by the evidence of history'.[1] It also claimed that 'a retreat into isolationism would deprive the poor of the opportunities offered by trade' and suggested that globaphobia plays well in rich countries because of insecurity bred by economic globalization.[2]

The release of the *Rigged Rules* report sparked an ideological brawl within the anti-globalization movement. Although the exchange was heated at times, Walden Bello thought it did a great service to the movement by 'pushing the question of our strategy on the trade front to centre stage'.[3] Whether beneficial or not, it generated a lot of heat. Colin Hines said Oxfam's report read like a 'bland script unquestioningly accepting the trade theory of comparative advantage'.[4] Well-known anti-globalization campaigner Vandana Shiva (who is a board member of the International Forum on Globalization) said Oxfam's policies were the same as the 'export first' policies of the World Bank except that they dressed it up in the World Trade Organization language of 'market access'.[5] Food First, a US-based organization that campaigns for food security, said it was disappointed that Oxfam had 'chosen to undermine the demands of social movements and think tanks in the south such as Via Campesina, MST, Third World Network, Focus on the Global South, and Africa Trade Network which have demanded that governments must uphold the rights of all people to food sovereignty and the right to food rather than industry-led export-orientated production'.[6] Walden Bello said Oxfam had the wrong focus and was acting like an agent for the Cairns group of trade liberalizers.[7]

Oxfam wasted no effort in hitting back. Kevin Watkins, principal author of the *Rigged Rules* report, said 'the extreme element of the anti-globalization movement is wrong ... trade can deliver much more (for poor countries) than aid or debt relief'.[8] Watkins denied Oxfam promoted World Bank-style trade liberalization and said the organization did not 'argue for export-led agriculture'.[9] He also said trade market outcomes reflect the policy choices and power relations that lie behind them.[10] He defended his report as one which 'attacks the current course of economic globalization as a motor of greater inequality and poverty'.[11] Above all, Watkins said, he makes 'no apologies for attaching importance to improved market access'.[12]

Short-term versus long-term strategies

At first glance the tension between the Fair Trade and Localization schools appears to be a straightforward ideological one. But several factors influence the two schools, some of which aren't purely ideological. One significant factor is how long term the visions and campaign goals of each school are. Unsurprisingly, the Localization school prides itself on having a truly long-term vision and accuses the Fair Trade school of being obsessed with the short term. During the debate that followed the release of Oxfam's *Rigged Rules* report Walden Bello accused Oxfam of having 'an internal organizational imperative to have a "winnable" short-term campaign'.[13] Oxfam doesn't necessarily deny this charge. At the 2002 World Social Forum, Oxfam seemed quite relaxed about admitting that short-term, achievable goals were important to it. Representatives from the United Kingdom branch of the organization said: 'Oxfam pursues a twin-track strategy, focusing on concrete changes that are achievable in the short term, while also pressing for more fundamental change in the long term. Our experience is that small gains can strengthen rather than undermine the momentum for more fundamental change.'[14] Since many organizations in the Fair Trade school are groups like environmental and aid organizations that generally have large short-term fundraising needs, it is not surprising that these types of groups tend to concentrate on achievable and saleable short-term goals. Nor is it surprising that organizations without these imperatives focus on longer-term and less saleable goals.

A similar tension between groups concerned with short-term, saleable goals and groups concerned with more fundamental, long-term change ran through the global socialist movement from the late nineteenth century onwards. Many socialist movements, particularly those in Western, democratic countries, favoured working through the existing democratic system, which often involved putting up with gradual change. Other groups, like those in Russia, China, Vietnam and Cuba, favoured a complete overthrow of the existing system and the introduction of revolutionary radical change.

Corporate engagement

Another factor that can influence how radical a group within the anti-globalization movement is prepared to be is how willing it is to engage with large corporations and institutions, in what is often known as 'corporate engagement'. This is an extremely vexed issue within the movement. Some organizations argue that you have to engage with powerful corporations and institutions because they are the ones that ultimately make the decisions. Often direct or indirect sponsorship can be an inducement. But many organizations within the anti-globalization movement are opposed to, or are at best suspicious of, corporate engagement, claiming it almost always necessarily involves selling out and diluting one's message. There are no easy answers to the ethical dilemmas thrown up by corporate engagement. In some situations it is worth engaging with public and private institutions if you can achieve real change without losing your integrity, but in other situations you risk becoming part of the problem and 'corporate engagement' can become just another term for expediency.

There is no doubt that organizations in the anti-globalization movement have different attitudes to engaging with organizations directly connected with the economic globalization debate like the IMF and the World Bank. And there is also little doubt that the different attitudes have an effect on policy. Some organizations don't want any direct contact with the IMF and World Bank and prefer to put pressure on them via the public and the media. Other organizations see considerable benefit in directly engaging with them. These organizations include Jubilee 2000 and Oxfam. Jubilee 2000 has regular briefings with both the IMF and the World Bank, while in 2002 Oxfam joined with both organizations in a campaign aimed at getting every child in poor countries into school. In 2003 the director-general of the World Trade Organization, Supachai Panitchpakdi, even proposed that a permanent non-governmental organization advisory committee to the WTO be established – a move that was met with suspicion by many organizations within the anti-globalization movement, particularly those who feared that such a committee would just end up becoming a way of silencing critics of the WTO by assimilating them. Oxfam and Friends of the Earth ended up declining their invitations to join the group (although some groups mentioned in this book accepted, including the Worldwide Fund for Nature, the Third World Network, Christian Aid and the International Confederation of Free Trade Unions). Oxfam wasn't necessarily opposed to consultation with the WTO but said it had envisaged a more 'open-ended' style of consultation rather than the fairly narrow one Supachai Panitchpakdi ended up settling for.[15]

Some of the pitfalls of corporate engagement were highlighted by a campaign Oxfam ran in 2002 aimed at stabilizing the ever-falling price of coffee, on which many poor-country farmers depend. Oxfam targeted coffee giants Kraft (Maxwell House), Proctor & Gamble (Folgers), Nestlé (Nescafé) and Sara Lee (Real Coffee). They demanded the coffee giants help destroy 5 million bags of coffee, to help stabilize its price; and they also

wanted the companies to pay into a poor-country rural diversification fund.[16] Oxfam worked with café giant Starbucks on the
campaign, holding it up as an example of a socially responsible
coffee corporation. Unfortunately, however, it was later revealed,
after criticism of Oxfam's campaign by the Organic Consumers
Association, that Starbucks weren't much different to the other
coffee giants. Starbucks itself ended up admitting it only purchases
about 1 per cent of its coffee through a Fair Trade purchasing
system (no relation to the Fair Trade school) that guarantees
poor-country farmers equitable minimum prices.[17] Oxfam was left
looking silly and its campaign was somewhat discredited because
it didn't sufficiently research the credentials of the corporation it
chose to engage with or the risks of engaging with them.

Rich-country versus poor-country anti-globalization organizations

A third factor that can influence how radical an organization is
inclined to be within the movement is whether it is from a rich
or poor country. There are many radical anti-globalization groups
in rich countries, and many conservative ones in poor countries,
but, if one had to generalize, activists in poor countries tend to
be more radical than activists in rich countries. Poor countries
have generally been hit harder by economic globalization − its
failings are more obvious to them − so it is not surprising that
poor-country groups have a stronger reaction against it. Many
poor-country activists liken economic globalization to colonialism
and often see it as a continuation of colonization. Wangari Maathai,
from the Green Belt Movement of Kenya (and now a member
of the Kenyan parliament), said at the inaugural global conference
of Green parties held in Canberra, Australia, in 2001 (the Global
Greens Conference): 'this animal called globalization is worse
than slavery, it is worse than colonialism'.[18] Likewise, Vandana
Shiva, one of India's leading anti-globalization activists, argues that

'globalization is completing the project of colonization that led to the conquest and ownership of land and territory'.[19]

The generally more radical stance of poor-country activists can affect policy debate within the anti-globalization movement. At the Global Greens Conference, a charter was debated that was intended to be an international policy statement of Green parties. The sections dealing with economic globalization ended up being some of the most hotly debated parts of the charter, particularly a section dealing with reform of the WTO. Conference delegates from poor countries generally wanted to abolish the WTO, while delegates from rich countries generally wanted to reform it. For some time it looked as though no compromise could be reached until the United States Greens successfully proposed a policy that said that Green parties 'support abolition of the WTO unless it is reformed to make sustainability its central goal, supported by transparent and democratic processes and the participation of representatives from affected communities'.[20] The 1999 Jubilee South Summit held in Johannesburg saw similar disagreement between anti-globalization groups from rich and poor countries. A few months before the conference a summit between the seven largest rich countries of the world (the G7) had agreed to reduce substantially the foreign debts of many of the world's poorest countries as long as they undertook further IMF and World Bank structural adjustment reforms (the Heavily Indebted Poor Country Initiative – eventually, however, the initiative only ended up having modest effect). Rich-country groups at the Jubilee South Summit thought the package should be accepted, while poor-country groups thought it should be rejected and the IMF and the World Bank shut down.[21]

Changing fashions within the anti-globalization movement

At the moment the Fair Trade school probably has more support within the anti-globalization movement than the Localization school and it is tempting to think it has always been thus. Like any movement, however, the anti-globalization movement has been subject to lots of mood swings and changes of emphasis and this is particularly apparent in its policy history.

In the 1980s, when modern-day economic globalization was still in its infancy, there was much less concern with globalization and economics in general within the groups that today make up the anti-globalization movement. To the extent that economic globalization was addressed at all, the movement tended to be quite idealistic and fairly radical. In 1984 Jonathon Porritt, then the UK director of Friends of the Earth and a leading member of the (then) Ecology Party, argued in his book *Seeing Green* that 'it's clear that selective protection of the domestic economy will be needed to establish its sustainable basis, and to encourage this country to become far more self-sufficient than it is at present'.[22] In 1986 Johan Galtung, in a book published by the Other Economic Summit, *The Living Economy*, said: 'production for basic needs should be carried out in such a way that the country is at least potentially self-sufficient'.[23]

In the 1990s, however, economic globalization lost its 'shock of the new' and many organizations became more pragmatic in their policy approach to it. The Localization school fell out of favour, to some extent, and increasingly sat more on the edge of the movement. The change in the policies of some Green parties, in particular, make clear the drift towards more pragmatic globalization policies during the 1990s. One Green party for whom the drift has been particularly apparent is the German Greens. In 1983 the (then) West German Greens, Die Grünen, which had only been formed three years before, boldly declared that 'goods should be produced as close as possible to the consumer, in local or regional economic units. This in no way excludes meaningful, albeit reduced, international trade.'[24] Nearly twenty years later, in 2002, however, the German Greens (now Bündnis 90/Die Grünen) had changed their tune after having had members in their national parliament for most of the time since their establishment and having recently cooperated in national coalition government. Today they argue: 'we are against renationalizing markets, just as we are against a European protectionism'.[25] They also say: 'our objective is to keep our national economy competitive without ruining other economies'.[26]

Policies that straddle both schools

The notion of Fair Trade and Localization 'schools' is a device, a means of policy categorization. Although the policies of most organizations in the anti-globalization movement generally tend to fall into either school, some don't. And the policies of some organizations and individuals borrow from both schools. One high-profile activist in the movement who tends to straddle both schools is Martin Khor, director of the Third World Network (based in Malaysia). He advocates a lot of classic Fair Trade school policies, such as rich countries giving greater access to poor-country imports, the establishment of commodity agreements aimed at stabilizing raw-material prices, and protection of poor-country agricultural industries.[27] But he also supports local content rules for foreign investors[28] as well as the poor-country use of tariffs to establish 'infant industries'.[29] In a similar vein, the New Zealand Greens (Green Party of Aotearoa New Zealand) try to take from both schools by saying they support 'a balance between trade and self-reliance'.[30] Like their Antipodean neighbours, the Australian Greens also try to straddle the two schools. They say they support 'the introduction or increase of import taxes and customs duties on goods and services that can be produced in Australia', but they also say they support 'managed international trade'.[31] Given the increasing tension between the Fair Trade and Localization schools it is inevitable, and to some extent understandable, that some organizations should try and borrow from both.

Policies that stand outside the
Localization/Fair Trade divide

Some policies within the anti-globalization movement have no
particular loyalty to either school, and to a large extent stand
outside the Localization/Fair Trade divide. There aren't many of
these policies but those there are seem to approach the problems
of economic globalization from different angles to those of the
two major policy schools. One such set of policies, which deserve
particular attention, come from one-time senior economist with
the World Bank and (radical) Professor of Economics at Louisiana
State University, Herman Daly. He argues that, above all, it is
important to balance trade. He therefore advocates an auctioning system of import licences where the sum of the auctioned
licences would equal that of a nation's sustainable exports.[32] Daly
isn't so much concerned with the volume of international trade as
with the importance of keeping it in balance. He further argues
that balanced trade allows for balanced capital flows. He says: 'if
we have balanced trade there is no need for, or possibility of,
international capital flows.'[33]

Another activist who also argues that balanced trade is crucial
to a future sustainable world economic order is British author
George Monbiot. He argues that the International Clearing
Union idea that Keynes presented to the 1944 Bretton Woods
conference should be reinvigorated.[34] Keynes proposed that all
countries be issued with quotas of an international currency (the
bancor) that would be related to their average trade during the
previous five years. If a country ran up a trade deficit equal to
more than half its quota it would be charged interest, it would be
forced to devalue its currency, and it would also be forced not to
disallow the export of any capital. But the International Clearing
Union would put the same pressure on trade surplus countries by
charging them interest as well, if they exceeded half their quota,
and by forcing them to increase the value of their currencies, and

by also forcing them to allow the export of capital. If they had persistently high surpluses these would be confiscated. Although admitting the idea needs some modern-day refinement, Monbiot argues that the scheme would provide a much-needed mechanism that would put pressure on countries to balance their trade. He suggests a catalyst for establishing the scheme could be a common, unilateral debt default by most, if not all, of the world's current poor-country foreign debt holders.[35]

Another set of policies that sit outside the Localization/Fair Trade schools comes from some progressive members of the modern-day socialist movement. They often disown both the 'state socialist' model of socialism, once pursued by countries like China, Cuba, Vietnam and the USSR, and the 'market socialist' model favoured by many modern-day democratic European communist parties. What they propose instead is a form of 'democratic socialism' where there would be a high degree of participatory democracy in all countries, possibly carried out through a network of self-managing producer, consumer and neighbourhood councils which (presumably) would preside over economies with high levels of state ownership and income redistribution. One advocate of such a socialist system is Alex Callinicos of Global Resistance in Britain, author of *An Anti-Capitalist Manifesto*. He says such a system would allow 'sharing control of productive resources' and would 'reinforce the value of solidarity'.[36]

Much heat has been generated by the rivalry between the Localization and Fair Trade schools. Some of the heat has been useful, but it is now important to step back from the tribal loyalties of the two schools and soberly assess the strengths, weaknesses and common ground, as well as points of divergence between them. The Fair Trade/Localization and globaphile/globaphobe labels are useful, up to a point, but if used obsessively they can mask the common purpose shared by the two schools and can push to the sides the dialogue the two schools need to begin over their areas of genuine disagreement.

Notes

1. Kevin Watkins et al., *Rigged Rules and Double Standards: Trade, Globalization and the Fight against Poverty*, Oxfam International, Washington DC, 2002, p. 23.

2. Ibid., pp. 16, 24.

3. Walden Bello, 'The Oxfam Debate: From Controversy to Common Strategy', published by Deb Foskey via WTO Watch email list (debf@webone.com.au), 7 June 2002 (#63), p. 1. (For archive copy, see www.nwjc.org.au/avcwl/lists/archives.html.)

4. Colin Hines, 'Oxfam's Jekyll and Hyde Approach to Trade Will Worsen the Plight of the Poor', published by Deb Foskey via WTO Watch email list (debf@webone.com.au), 30 April 2002 (#55), p. 2. (For archive copy, see www.nwjc.org.au/avcwl/lists/archives.html.)

5. Vandana Shiva, 'Export at Any Cost: Oxfam's Free Trade Recipe for the Third World', published by Deb Foskey via WTO Watch email list (debf@webone.com.au), 18 May 2002 (#59), p. 2. (For archive copy, see www.nwjc.org.au/avcwl/lists/archives.html.)

6. Nick Parker, 'New Oxfam Campaign Contradicts Developing Country Demands for WTO Reform', published by Deb Foskey via WTO Watch email list (debf@webone.com.au), 17 April 2002 (#51), p. 1. (For archive copy, see www.nwjc.org.au/avcwl/lists/archives.html.)

7. Walden Bello, 'What's Wrong with the Oxfam Trade Campaign', published by Deb Foskey via WTO Watch email list (debf@webone.com.au), 1 May 2002 (#55), pp. 1–2. (For archive copy, see www.nwjc.org.au/avcwl/lists/archives.html.)

8. Patrick Bond, 'Moderates Wilt But Radical South Africans Struggle On', published by Deb Foskey via WTO Watch email list (debf@webone.com.au), 21 April 2002 (#53), p. 1. (For archive copy, see www.nwjc.org.au/avcwl/lists/archives.html.)

9. Kevin Watkins, 'Response to Patrick Bond article', published by Deb Foskey via WTO Watch email list (debf@webone.com.au), 25 April 2002 (#53), p. 1. (For archive copy, see www.nwjc.org.au/avcwl/lists/archives.html.)

10. Ibid., p. 1.

11. Ibid., p. 2.

12. Kevin Watkins, 'Oxfam's Response to Walden Bello's Article on Make Trade Fair', published by Deb Foskey via WTO Watch email list (debf@webone.com.au), 9 May 2002 (#57), p. 2. (For archive copy, see www.nwjc.org.au/avcwl/lists/archives.html.)

13. Bello, 'The Oxfam Debate: From Controversy to Common Strategy', p. 4.

14. William F. Fisher and Thomas Ponniah, eds, *Another World is Possible: Popular Alternatives to Globalization at the World Social Forum*, Zed Books, London, 2003, pp. 140–41.

15. Daniel Pruzin, 'WTO Chief Sets Up Advisory Bodies with Business, NGOs to Boost Dialogue', published by Deb Foskey via WTO Watch email list (debf@webone.com.au), 19 June 2003 (#171), p. 1. (For archive copy, see www.nwjc.org.au/avcwl/lists/archives.html.)

16. Michelle Chihara, 'Drink Coffee? Read This', published by Deb Foskey via WTO Watch email list (debf@webone.com.au), 20 September 2002 (#93), p. 1. (For archive copy, see www.nwjc.org.au/avcwl/lists/archives. html.)

17. Ibid., p. 3.

18. Margaret Blakers, ed., *The Global Greens: Inspiration, Ideas and Insights from the Rio + 10 International Workshop and Global Greens 2001*, Australian Greens, Canberra, 2001, p. 74.

19. Sarah Anderson, ed., *Views from the South: The Effects of Globalization and the WTO on Third World Countries*, Food First Books/Institute for Food and Development Policy, Chicago, 2000, pp. 92, 93.

20. Blakers, ed., *The Global Greens*, p. 196.

21. Walden Bello, Nicola Bullard and Kamal Malhotta, eds, *Global Finance: New Thinking on Regulating Speculative Capital Markets*, Zed Books, London, 2000, p. 74.

22. Jonathon Porritt, *Seeing Green: The Politics of Ecology Explained*, Basil Blackwell, Oxford, 1984, p. 135.

23. Paul Ekins, ed., *The Living Economy: A New Economics in the Making*, Routledge & Kegan Paul, London, 1986, p. 102.

24. Die Grünen, *Purpose in Work – Solidarity in Life: Economic Policy Statement against Unemployment and Social Decline*, Bonn, 1983, p. 7.

25. Bündnis 90/Die Grünen, *The Future is Green: Alliance 90/The Greens: Party Program and Policy*, Berlin, 2002, p. 47.

26. Ibid., p. 46.

27. Martin Khor, *Rethinking Globalization: Critical Issues and Policy Choices*, Zed Books, London, 2001, pp., 30, 45 and 50.

28. Ibid., p. 98.

29. Martin Khor, Report for the United Nations Development Program, p. 3, downloaded from www.twnside.org in 2002.

30. Green Party of Aotearoa New Zealand, 'An Eco-Nation Trades Fairly', from *Thinking Beyond Tomorrow* policy statement, downloaded from www. greens.org.nz in 2002.

31. The Australian Greens, *National Policy 2001*, Canberra, 2001, pp. 69, 71.
32. Herman E. Daly and John B. Cobb, *For the Common Good: Redirecting the Economy towards Community, the Environment and a Sustainable Future*, Green Print, London, 1990, p. 230.
33. Ibid., p. 231.
34. George Monbiot, *The Age of Consent: A Manifesto for a New World Order*, Flamingo, London, 2003, pp. 161–8.
35. Ibid., p. 175.
36. Alex Callinicos, 'Socialism: Political Vision', paper presented at the 'Life after Capitalism' 'conference within the conference' at the World Social Forum, Porto Alegre, 12–28 January 2003, downloaded from www.iso.org in 2003.

CHAPTER 11

DEFICIENCIES OF BOTH SCHOOLS

One can't assume there are no flaws in the arguments of either the Fair Trade or the Localization school. Both have come a long way in recent years, policy-wise, but it doesn't follow that even their core arguments are necessarily always tightly and consistently argued. Although both schools have generally sound arguments, they nevertheless indulge in a fair amount of rhetoric. It follows that the policies of each need discerning examination before being accepted. Neither school necessarily has more consistent arguments than the other.

Deficiencies in Fair Trade school policies

One of the biggest deficiencies in the Fair Trade agenda has to do with its faith in the poverty-relieving potential of trade. The Fair Trade school loudly proclaims that trade has the potential to lift many poor countries out of poverty; however, about three-quarters of the world's trade is accounted for by rich countries and the quarter that isn't takes place among a select few poor countries. This must surely mean that a general, rules-based, freeing up of world trade would mainly benefit a small minority of poor countries and would not have the general global benefit the Fair Trade school claims. The Fair Trade school doesn't, however, tackle the issue of why trade benefits are so concentrated among so few countries; it is therefore hard to have complete faith in its belief that properly managed trade can relieve so much poverty. Even in poor countries that have experienced significantly increased trade over the past decade, like Mexico and China, a huge amount of poverty persists and the claimed potential for trade necessarily to relieve poverty is hard to believe.

There is also a major flaw in the bedrock philosophy of the Fair Trade school. Its dominant credo appeals to values of international fairness based on agreed-upon global rules. It appeals to legalistic notions that say all nations are equal in the eyes of international globalization law. If we had more, and fairer, rules of international economic engagement then all the world's nations could be more equal, so this philosophy argues. But the philosophy can become quite circular. The Fair Trade school says we need more globalization rules because the existing terms of international economic engagement are too often determined by power relationships. Yet it's power relationships that generally decide how rules and laws are written so one can't rely on rules and laws to right the wrongs of power relationships because they often only reflect the power relationships they are based upon. The powerful always write the rules. The Fair Trade school doesn't spend enough time considering this quandary. The Fair Trade school needs to spend a lot more time contemplating the full significance of the power relationships of world trade in the wake of the failed World Trade Organization trade talks held in Cancún in September 2003. If the WTO talks are ever to be revived, the rich countries of the European Union, Japan and the United States have made it clear they will only countenance opening their own agricultural markets up to more imports from poor countries if poor countries open their agricultural markets up to more rich-country imports in return. But this could devastate the agricultural industries of many poor countries and increase poverty, since poverty and agriculture are often closely associated in poor countries.

An equally glaring failing of the Fair Trade agenda is its significant lack of interest in the pollution effects of world trade.
It confidently talks up the poverty-relieving potential of world
trade but almost completely ignores the environmental effects of
moving huge volumes of goods and services around the world.
Given that the average plate of food consumed in Western Europe
travels up to 2,000 miles before it is eaten[1] and that transport
(in general) consumes about 60 per cent of the world's oil,[2] it
is extraordinary how dismissive the Fair Trade school is of the
environmental cost of trade, particularly in this greenhouse-
conscious age. In its 258-page *Rigged Rules* report Oxfam only
devotes one page to consideration of the environmental effects
of trade, and only one paragraph deals with the argument that
more trade, of the sort Oxfam advocates, could lead to more
pollution.[3] Even then all Oxfam says is that rich countries do
most of the world's polluting so this shouldn't be an argument
against more poor-country trade. Oxfam also argues that, in any
event, global warming should be addressed through carbon and
transport taxes. This is not good enough and leaves a major hole
in Oxfam's case.

Another deficiency in the Fair Trade agenda is that it is,
arguably, unrealistic and may, in fact, ironically, be more utopian
than the Localization agenda. The Bretton Woods system, around
which the Fair Trade school revolves, has been in place for more
than fifty years, over which period its rules have become less, not
more, fair. So it is necessary to ask how realistic it is to make
the whole system, somehow magically, fair again after it has been
gradually becoming less fair for more than half a century. An
equitable world trading system requires the altruistic cooperation
of all the world's major trading economies, if not most of the
world's 193 economies in general. With cross-border trade and
investment now at levels higher than ever before, more is at stake
and the chances of altruistic international cooperation are small.
The Localization school agenda has the advantage that much
of it can be implemented unilaterally, but the Fair Trade school

system requires a level of global cooperation that is conspicuous by its absence these days.

The Fair Trade agenda could also, unwittingly, end up giving more power, not less, to transnational corporations. Like the Localization school, the Fair Trade school is generally against more power being accumulated by TNCs. Yet TNCs dominate a lot of world trade: indeed, the largest 500 control nearly 70 per cent.[4] Well-known anti-globalization activist Ralph Nader argues that 'the world doesn't have free trade, it has corporate-managed trade'.[5] So by advocating more, and freer, world trade the Fair Trade school could unwittingly be increasing the power of TNCs and thereby working against its own ends. The Fair Trade school does have separate policies dealing with the regulation of TNCs but they are not necessarily sufficient to ensure TNCs are not made even more powerful through their control of even more global trade. The Fair Trade school would argue they should be able to advocate fairer world trade and less TNC influence, and that the two needn't be mutually exclusive. But at the very least the Fair Trade school needs to place less emphasis on greater world trade and more emphasis on dealing with the greater corporate power that is likely to be associated with it. The school generally needs stronger TNC regulation policies than it has at present.

The call by the Fair Trade school, and many rich-country environmental groups and unions, for clauses to be included in trade agreements that penalize exporting countries that do not have adequate environmental and labour standards is not widely supported by poor-country governments or anti-globalization activists in poor countries. Many see the idea as another example of rich-country protectionism and as another economic globalization tool rich countries might use to penalize poor countries. The accusation that they amount to another form of rich-country protectionism is ironic given how opposed the Fair Trade school is to protectionism. The February 2003 meeting of the Non-Aligned Movement in Malaysia reiterated poor-country objection to trade agreements being used in this way.

A high-profile anti-globalization activist who has long campaigned against environmental and labour trade clauses is Martin
Khor, director of the Malaysia-based Third World Network. He
argues that environmental and labour trade clauses run the risk
of penalizing poor countries and are 'fraught with the dangers of
protectionism'.[6] He also argues that trade-related environmental
measures should not be negotiated through the WTO, and that
whilst many rich-country unions push for labour clauses in trade
agreements, many poor-country unions oppose them.[7] He says
many poor-country governments see their low labour costs as
legitimate comparative advantages rather than evidence of the
exploitation of workers.[8]

Another flaw in the policies of the Fair Trade school relates to
raw material price support schemes. Many organizations in the
school call for varying forms of such schemes for the exports
of poor countries. Given the long-term decline in raw material
export prices, clearly something needs to be done. But the history of international schemes is not good. Such schemes were
attempted on at least four occasions during the twentieth century:
in the 1920s (for products such as wheat, rubber, sugar, copper,
petroleum, lead and zinc); in the 1930s (for products such as tin,
sugar, tea, wheat, rubber, tin and copper); straight after the Second
World War (for products such as sugar, tin, coffee and cocoa);[9]
and latterly in the 1970s (for products such as bauxite, bananas,
copper, tin, coffee and petroleum).

The only arrangement to enjoy any longevity has been the oil
price support scheme of the Organization of Petroleum Exporting
Countries (OPEC), and even that arrangement had long periods
of failure after initial successes in the 1970s and early 1980s. The
problem with all the schemes has been that there are inevitably
producers who want to break ranks and not curtail their exports
in the interests of higher prices. The price support schemes invariably only have a chance of working if global demand for the
relevant raw material outstrips supply, but huge Third World debts
often mean that poor countries can ill afford to restrict their raw

material exports. Sometimes TNCs sabotage the schemes (as happened with the Union de Paises Exportadores de Banana in the 1970s). As an alternative to cutting exports and production the United Nations Conference on Trade and Development tried to establish a US$6 billion raw material price support fund in the 1970s, but rich countries didn't want to help out.[10] Apart from OPEC another long-lasting price support scheme has been the International Coffee Agreement, but that has recently collapsed, partly because poor-country government-controlled exporting boards were abolished as a result of liberalizing pressure from the IMF and the World Bank. None of this means that raw material price support schemes are utterly unworkable, but they have a poor history and most of the problems they have faced in the past are not addressed by the Fair Trade school.

The Fair Trade school's fondness for corporate codes of conduct is also fraught with problems. Although these are increasingly popular in the business world they often don't work. In 2000 the Organization for Economic Cooperation and Development (OECD) released the results of its study of 246 codes of conduct, mainly those of companies and corporate associations. The year before three independent researchers (Kolk, Tulder and Welters) also published the results of their separate assessment of 132 codes of conduct, in the periodical *Transnational Corporations*.[11] The two research projects found that the effectiveness of the codes depended heavily on how specific they were and how they were monitored. Unfortunately most of the examined codes were weak in both areas. Kolk et al. found that 80 per cent of the business group codes and over 50 per cent of the specific company codes they examined were predominantly, or completely, general in nature with no specific targets.[12] The OECD found that 61 per cent omitted relevant information (only one of the 246 examined mentioned tax, for instance), and whilst 71 per cent had monitoring procedures, most of the monitoring was internal and not open to independent, outside scrutiny.[13] So, like raw material price support schemes, the history of corporate codes of conduct is not good; at the very least the Fair Trade school needs to delve more deeply into the specific reasons for its failure to date.

Deficiencies in Localization school policies

The Fair Trade school is by no means alone in having some deficient arguments and policies. The Localization school can be just as guilty of this, at times. A major deficiency of the Localization agenda is that it is forever appealing to universal values of empowerment, democracy, self-control, and so on, but always within a context of local control. Although the Localization school acknowledges that its policies won't necessarily make for greater democracy (they just make it more likely), one often senses that the school doesn't stop to consider, often enough, that an overly rigid highly localized economic world structure could develop a culture of very un-universal values where independent economies could become very parochial. The Localization school prides itself on having an agenda that could be a foundation for a purer type of democracy than we have at present; if all it does is set up lots of highly disconnected economies, it could also set up lots of highly disconnected governments, many of which may be despotic and insensitive about human and environmental rights, and so forth. The Localization school says it supports internationalization but is opposed to economic globalization. These are fine-sounding words but it needs to define them more and develop further safeguards against local economic control becoming a recipe for local tyranny.

Like the Fair Trade school, the Localization school sometimes indulges in very hopeful political thinking. One area where this is particularly apparent is technology transfer. Fritz Schumacher used to remind people that all the ingredients for increased wealth and prosperity can be home grown because, after all, planet earth did not grow more prosperous by importing skills, capital or technology from another planet. Nor does it export to another planet. But, nonetheless, history generally demonstrates that transfers of technology between countries can aid local economic development to a significant degree. For a world made up of many separate, self-reliant economies to work there has got to be a fair degree of technological exchange. Colin Hines even admits that his envisaged localized reorganization of the world economy 'must be underpinned by a commitment by the OECD countries to the two way, free flow of sustainable technologies'.[14] Yet, like much of the rival Fair Trade school agenda, this utopian vision relies on a huge amount of international cooperation and goodwill of a sort the world has never seen before, and therefore this part of the Localization school strategy does not come across as particularly realistic.

British author George Monbiot believes Localization effectively forbids emerging manufacturing industries in poor countries from growing to any significant size because it denies them export markets in rich countries.[15] This, he claims, effectively condemns them to an indefinite reliance on raw material exports.[16] Whilst his criticism wrongly assumes that exports are the only way manufacturing industries can grow, he nevertheless has a point, and the Localization school needs to give more thought to how poor countries can realistically acquire technology and break out of their dependence on raw materials.

One of the most frustrating aspects of the Localization school agenda is that it is extremely generalized, giving few clues as to how it might be specifically applied. The school is often unwilling to commit to detail. Given that the most significant area of disagreement between it and the Fair Trade school is trade, it is unfortunate that the Localization school is not more detailed in what it sees as the feasible limits of its local production agenda. Colin Hines says 'some long distance trade will still occur for those sectors providing goods and services to other regions of the world that can't provide such items from within their own borders'[17] but he doesn't give any examples of goods and services that would be covered by this residual long-distance trade. Hines also says that his critique of today's global capital market 'does not imply that all capital flows should be blocked';[18] but, again, he gives no examples of capital flows that shouldn't be impeded.

One isolated, and laudable, attempt at defining the feasible limits of localized trade has been made by a professor of physics, John Ziman, whose ideas have been adapted by Andrew Simms, an author who has published papers through the British-based New Economics Foundation. Ziman and Simms have developed three groups of concentric circle diagrams, each of which tries to define the production and distribution limits of a localized county, province, region, subcontinent or global market.[19] Simms says the diagrams try to give 'estimates for geo-demographic units that provide sufficient economies of scale for enterprises to succeed, but also give limits beyond which the costs of scale and economic integration can outweigh the benefits'.[20] For the production of goods Ziman and Simms claim that a county (within 20 miles of a consumer or of 100,000 population) can produce its own food crops, cash crops and housing; that a province (within 100 miles of a consumer or of 2 million population) can produce its own building materials, processed food, furniture, hardware and cash crops; that a region (within 500 miles of a consumer or of 50 million population) can produce its own clothes, textiles, small machines and components, electronic devices, steel, oil, gas, coal, civil engineering, books, films and bicycles; that a subcontinent (within 2,000 miles of a consumer or of 1 billion population) can produce its own vehicles, ships, small aircraft and electronic systems; leaving the world to produce only microchips, pharmaceuticals and large aircraft.[21] It is courageous, and practical, commitment to detail like this that can boost the credentials of the Localization school.

The Localization school is equally non-committal, at times, on replacements for the IMF, WTO and World Bank. Both the International Forum on Globalization and Walden Bello give no less than three different options for replacement of these institutions, leaving one confused about which option they really favour.

Colin Hines talks about a 'World Localization Organization' that would administer radically rewritten trade rules enshrined in a new global trade agreement called the 'General Agreement for Sustainable Trade',[22] but few details are given. The Localization school is, however, more detailed in its call for increased regulation of TNCs, with greater accountability, increased liability for social and environmental impacts, and legally enforceable codes of conduct called for. But the school also promotes a 'site-here-to-sell-here' policy for TNCs, which, like its trade policy, must have limits.

Deficiencies common to both schools

No school has a monopoly on flawed thinking. One area where both fall down is the need for any future, sustainable, economic system to have a mechanism that ensures that individual economies necessarily return to balance, in either their trade or capital flows, if they get seriously out of balance. The need for long-term balance is also the main force behind Herman Daly's proposal for auctioned import licences, as well as George Monbiot's call for a reinvigoration of Keynes's International Clearing Union idea.

Countries that run up persistent trade deficits, as many do these days, must pay for them through ongoing imports of foreign capital. Similarly, countries that have persistent net outflows of capital must pay for them with trade surpluses. This is why capital-exporting countries like Japan and Germany run persistent trade surpluses. A rough balance in both the trade and capital flows of particular economies is very important to a sustainable world economy. Yet neither the Fair Trade nor the Localization school sufficiently addresses the important structural imperative of overall economic balance; both need to listen to Herman Daly and George Monbiot. Both indulge in a lot of rhetoric about the desirability of rules-based trade, local economic control, and so on, without addressing the need for external economic balance, regardless of the type of global economic architecture in place.

It is not just balance that a sustainable world economic system needs, however; it also needs structure and more predictability than it has at present. This is another policy area that both schools have given insufficient thought to. To a large extent both schools are obsessed with how much economic globalization there should be, without giving sufficient thought to how it should operate, regardless of its quantity. The world economic order needs more predictability of, say, the sort it had under the gold standard, and it also needs more certainty. Certainty and predictability are key requirements of businesses and investors; they aren't just socially desirable aims. However, both the Localization and Fair Trade models could leave the world with volatile markets (although this is probably less likely under the former). Both schools therefore need to give more attention to how such volatility could be minimized.

Both schools also consistently call for an end to Third World debt. Yet if you get rid of Third World debt without replacing it with a mechanism that would stop it from recurring, then it will just happen all over again. Both schools are often very quantitative in their approach without giving sufficient attention to the quality of their respective visions.

Another major area where both schools are deficient is that of poverty relief for raw-material-dependent poor countries. Poor countries are increasingly separating into 'Third' and 'Fourth' worlds. Increasingly, diverse commentators such as Oxfam, the IMF and the United Nations Conference on Trade and Development all agree that extreme poverty in the world tends to be concentrated in countries that still rely on raw materials for a significant proportion of their export income, and also predominantly among subsistence farmers. But both the Fair Trade and Localization schools are inclined to treat poor countries as one 'job lot' without recognizing the specific challenges that relate to raw-material-dependent countries. It is true that Fair Trade groups like Oxfam address the issue of falling raw material prices, but they don't adequately address the issue of getting poor countries off their seemingly permanent reliance on raw materials. It is also true that the Localization school talks of the need for technology transfer to poor countries, but it doesn't say how this could be realistically achieved. Both schools need to have fewer 'broad brush' policies regarding poor countries and more targeted policies that deal with their specific problems.

The agendas of both the Fair Trade and Localization schools have a major short-term implementation problem inasmuch as both press for 'big picture' global change, yet neither gives many clues about what a country can, and should, do if a party in that country, with a history of opposition to economic globalization, assumes power and wants to make changes but feels hamstrung by the fact that its economy is inexorably linked into the global marketplace. Two recent examples of such have been the African National Congress in South Africa and the Brazilian Workers Party. Both felt caught, economically, when they won power, with the result that both have ended up implementing fairly conservative economic agendas, largely as a result of constraints imposed by economic globalization (although it is probably too early to pass judgement on the new Brazilian government). In South Africa the ANC embraced, and continued, globalization strategies like the removal of barriers to attracting foreign invest-ment, lowering import tariffs and privatizing public assets. The result has been increasing disillusionment with the ANC, with talk of South African unions breaking with the ANC and the possibility of a new major party, to the left of the ANC, being established in the country. In Brazil, the Workers Party president, Luiz Inácio 'Lula' da Silva, wasted no time upon assuming power in 2003 in appointing US-friendly/free-market-friendly people to key economic posts and making a priority of low inflation. Anti-globalization activists are increasingly feeling disillusioned and let down by da Silva (although, again, they should probably suspend judgement for a little longer yet). Yet it's not good enough for the anti-globalization movement to say that both the ANC and the Brazilian Workers Party simply 'sold out'. More country-specific globalization reform steps need to be formulated by the anti-globalization movement so that the world doesn't keep seeing a procession of progressive parties striving for power only to feel economically powerless once they get it.

Yet another area where both schools are somewhat deficient is that of the proper pricing of resources that harm the environment. Both schools acknowledge that if oil, for instance, was priced at a level that reflected all the damage its use does to the environment (at a price level that 'internalized' the cost of its environmental impact) it would be much more expensive and that, in itself, would put a brake on economic globalization. But while both schools give a nod to such 'full cost accounting', neither devotes sufficient energy and detail to it. More quantification of the extent to which the environment subsidizes globalization would help define more clearly what the environmental limits of economic globalization should be.

None of these deficiencies means that either school lacks credibility, but together they mean that whilst a lot of good policy work has been done within the anti-globalization movement since the late 1990s, a lot more still needs to be done.

Notes

1. Walden Bello, *Deglobalization: Ideas for a New World Economy*, Zed Books, London, 2002, p. 113.

2. The International Forum on Globalization, *Alternatives to Economic Globalization: A Better World is Possible*, Berret–Koehler, San Francisco, 2002, p. 165.

3. Kevin Watkins et al., *Rigged Rules and Double Standards: Trade, Globalization and the Fight against Poverty*, Oxfam International, Washington DC, 2002, pp. 60–61.

4. John Madeley, *Hungry for Trade: How the Poor Pay for Free Trade*, Zed Books, London, 2000, p. 91.

5. Ibid.

6. Sarah Anderson, ed., *Views from the South: The Effects of Globalization and the WTO on Third World Countries*, Food First Books/Institute for Food and Development Policy, Chicago, 2000, p. 44.

7. Ibid., pp. 44, 47.

8. Ibid., p. 47.

9. A.G. Kenwood and A.L. Lougheed, *Growth of the International Economy 1820–1990: An Introductory Text*, Routledge, London, 1992, pp. 165, 206, 283.

10. Joan E. Spero and Jeffrey A. Hart, *The Politics of International Economic Relations*, 5th edn, Routledge, London, 1997, p. 228.

11. Brett Parris, *Trade for Development*, World Vision, East Burwood, Australia, 1999, pp. 11–14, downloaded from www.wvi.org in 2002.

12. Ibid., p. 12.

13. Ibid.

14. Colin Hines, *Localization: A Global Manifesto*, Earthscan, London, 2000, p. 33.

15. George Monbiot, *The Age of Consent: A Manifesto for a New World Order*, Flamingo, London, 2003, p. 210.

16. Ibid., p. 216.

17. Hines, *Localization: A Global Manifesto*, p. 64.

18. Ibid., p. 85.

19. Andrew Simms, *Collision Course: Free Trade's Free Ride on the Global Climate*, New Economics Foundation, London, 2000, p. 17.

20. Ibid.

21. Ibid.

22. Hines, *Localization: A Global Manifesto*, p. 260.

CHAPTER 12

THE POLICY FUTURE OF THE
ANTI-GLOBALIZATION MOVEMENT

The anti-globalization movement will never have a united, homogeneous message and should not aim for one. Yet many of the differences between the Fair Trade and Localization schools are rhetorical and some of the differences disappear when the detail is examined. This is not to say the two schools are the same or are different only in terms of emphasis. They are quite different; nevertheless much more could, and should, be done to bring the two closer together.

To bring the two schools closer together, policy-wise, two things need to be done. First, and most importantly, the common ground between them needs to be identified and focused on. The movement potentially has much more in common than it is generally prepared to admit. It needs to question seriously whether much of what it thinks of as fundamental disagreement remains once rhetoric and tribalism are stripped away. Second, in those areas where there is genuine disagreement the movement needs to make sure the agenda of the Localization school reads like a truly long-term version of the Fair Trade school's short-term aims, rather than allowing the two to be entirely inconsistent, and apparently disconnected, with each other. One should be able to look at the Localization school's policies and be satisfied that they read like more radical, long-term versions of the Fair

Trade school's policies. In a few conspicuous areas that isn't the case at the moment.

Common ground between the two schools

Common policies

Despite their differences, the Fair Trade and Localization schools agree on the following broad policy themes:

Third World Debt and IMF/World Bank lending

There needs to be a cancellation of most, if not all, Third World debt and cessation of IMF and World Bank structural adjustment programmes.

Influence of the WTO, World Bank and IMF

The WTO, World Bank and IMF currently drive most international policymaking, including in areas not directly related to economic management. This dominance needs to stop through either reform or replacement of the three international finance institutions.

Regulation of transnational corporations

There needs to be more regulation of TNCs.

No further liberalization

There should be no further global integration of the world's economies and no new issues should be brought into current or future trade negotiations.

Controls on foreign investment/speculation

There needs to be greater regulation, and control, of the world's foreign investment, if not of the world's capital markets in general. There also needs to be more regulation and control of speculative investment including currency speculation. These controls should include a Tobin Tax.

Intellectual property rights

The intellectual property rights of poor countries need to be upheld and should have a higher priority than rich-country intellectual property rights, especially with regard to their access to affordable medicines and their continued ownership of the rights to local plant species and communal practices.

Poor-country protectionism

Poor countries should be able to apply at least limited forms of trade protectionism. In particular they should be able to protect their agricultural industries and possibly also extend at least short-term protection to local, strategic industries that might struggle to survive under completely liberalized world trade.

Philosophies common to both schools

There are also many philosophical overlaps between the two schools. The most significant is that both schools essentially say that society should design the type of economic system it wants, then expect the markets and technology to mould themselves around that design, instead of allowing the markets and technology to drive the design of the world economy as they do at present. Both schools say we must put our ends first, then determine the best means to achieve them, instead of allowing our ends to be driven by the means, as economic globalization currently does.

Both schools also make interesting implicit statements about economic technology. The Fair Trade school asserts that economic technology can be directed and channelled in more sustainable directions. The Localization school, on the other hand, implicitly argues that economic technology can be contained and adapted to smaller scales. Neither school takes technology as a given; both assert that it can be redirected, if not reinvented.

Broader areas of agreement between the two schools

Beyond the narrow, specific areas of agreement within the movement, there are at least two significant, but somewhat controversial, areas where there is a broad measure of agreement between the two schools (although both may hesitate to admit it).

The need for international finance institutions

There is pretty clear agreement between the two schools that something needs to take the place of the IMF, World Bank and WTO, although they disagree about whether they should be reformed or replaced by other versions of these institutions. Although the Localization school advocates abolition of these three institutions, it doesn't advocate leaving nothing in their place. The International Forum on Globalization (IFG) advocates replacing the IMF with an 'International Finance Organization' under the auspices of the United Nations, and Colin Hines advocates replacing the WTO with a 'World Localization Organization', for instance. So there is agreement that some form of international finance organization needs to continue to exist.

Even if the two schools can't agree on what form these finance organizations should take, they can probably agree on Walden Bello's suggestion that whatever type of institution takes their place, it needs to have its influence balanced by other non-financial global authorities that are just as powerful. Both schools need to give more attention to keeping future IMFs, WTOs and World Banks in check instead of being obsessed about whether to reform or replace them.

The need for residual world trade and limited protectionism

The thorniest issue between the two schools is trade. Yet when you look closely at their policies it is obvious that both schools are less than absolute about their respective trade agendas. Organizations subscribing to the Fair Trade school's policies nearly always support protection of poor-country farm industries; they also generally support special and differential treatment of poor-country economies that might allow for some degree of (at least temporary) protectionism. In a similar qualified vein the Localization school does not pretend that the world can rid itself of all international trade and seems relaxed about admitting there will always be some residual world trade.

Thus one could stick one's neck out and say that both schools accept, at least to a degree, that protectionism has its place and that the world will always need some global trade. Confirming this would bring the two schools much closer together on a very vexed issue.

Given that current world trade is highly concentrated around rich countries, one wonders at times whether the broader agendas of the Fair Trade and Localization schools really are as much at odds with each other as it seems. If most trade comes out of, and goes back into, rich countries, then it is hard not to conclude that the Localization agenda of local production would mostly impact on rich-country exports, not poor-country exports as the Fair Trade school often fears. And a lot of the exports that leave poor countries are raw materials, or agricultural produce, that rich countries don't have, or can't produce, so many poor-country exports would necessarily have to fall under the residual world trade that the Localization school concedes will still need to exist under their agenda. There is a lot of potential overlap, then, between the trade agendas of the two schools that simply hasn't been explored and a lot of specific questions that haven't been answered.

Potential areas of greater consistency between the two schools

Despite the common ground, there are unquestionably areas of significant and genuine disagreement between the two schools. This is unproblematic: the two schools should not aim for complete agreement on all issues. Groups like Oxfam make it abundantly clear that they aim for relatively short-term, achievable goals, whereas groups like the International Forum on Globalization present a much longer-term vision. Nearly all alternative causes have groups that push either short- or long-term agendas and this shouldn't be any less the case for the anti-globalization movement. But where there is genuine disagreement the two schools need to make their policies more consistent than they are at present, with more radical policies reading like logical long-term extensions of the more moderate short-term policies rather than seeming to contradict them.

The best way to examine the areas of policy disagreement within the anti-globalization movement is to divide policies into three broad areas: capital market/TNC regulation; management of the IMF, World Bank and WTO; and trade.

Capital market/TNC regulation policies

The policy area that is already reasonably well coordinated between the two schools is capital market and TNC regulation. This could be a template for the other two major policy areas. On capital market and TNC regulation the two schools agree there should be more regulation of both capital markets and TNCs, but the Localization school would go much further on both, which is consistent with its longer-term focus. In this policy area, at least, Localization policies generally read like logical long-term follow-on policies of the short-term Fair Trade policies.

Management of the IMF, World Bank and WTO

The policy area concerning what to do with the IMF, World Bank and WTO falls somewhere in between trade and capital market/TNC regulation in terms of consistency between the two schools. Given that they seem to agree there needs to be some form of ongoing public global finance administration, it is more productive for each school to concentrate on exactly what it wants to see changed in the IMF, World Bank and WTO instead of being obsessed with their replacement or reform. Replacement and reform are means to an end; they are not ends in themselves.

Trade

The area where there is least consistency and agreement between the schools is, of course, trade. It is simply not logical for the Fair Trade school to argue for more trade, particularly for poor countries, while in the long term the Localization school argues there should be less trade. Both schools need a lot more rigour and sophistication in their thinking about trade. Trade is the least developed policy area of the anti-globalization movement. It is unfortunate that it has had a high profile of late. The only way the trade policies of each school will become more consistent and complementary with each other is for both schools to question many of their bedrock assumptions.

The Fair Trade school desperately needs to question its assumptions about the environmental impact of global trade, particularly its part in producing greenhouse and acid rain emissions. Probably the biggest gap in its agenda is that left by its cursory treatment of this issue. Even if the environmental impacts of trade aren't important to the Fair Trade school, it needs to recognize that the world can't forever depend on fossil fuels to power its trade flows. The International Energy Agency, in its *World Energy Outlook 2001*, says that proven global reserves of fossil fuels can meet the world's demand until about 2020 but that beyond that time renewable sources would need to be increasingly relied upon.[1] The Fair Trade school must address what impact this will have on world trade. It has no alternative.

The Localization school also needs to question its assumptions about residual world trade. It is prepared to say that this trade will always need to exist but is rarely prepared to say how significant it should be. It also says there should be transfers of technology to poor countries but does not propose any realistic means through which this could happen. The Localization school is far too general at times, particularly about trade. It's not good enough to declare blithely that there will always be some residual world trade without saying in what areas it might continue: it makes the school's agenda far too open-ended.

The general policy future of the anti-globalization movement

Many reputations and egos have been invested in the Fair Trade and Localization schools. It is to be hoped that pride won't get in the way of meaningful dialogue between the two. Now that a lot of healthy policy formulation has taken place, what is most needed, policy-wise, are forums between the two schools where they concentrate on their differences, and try to work through their inconsistencies, instead of simply talking about the ills of economic globalization to the outside world. Organizationally, the anti-globalization movement will always be together but separate; yet in terms of policies it needs to spend more time and energy on being together without being separate, and ensuring that the agendas of the Fair Trade and Localization schools dovetail. This is not a call for the schools to have the same policies. But they should make sure their policies are complementary.

Engaging with the public

The anti-globalization movement now has enough maturity and confidence to start taking its positive policy message out to the public. Protests don't do this; they only remind the public that something is wrong with economic globalization. If the anti-globalization movement doesn't air its alternatives, it will risk being seen forever as a movement of full-time critics that only speaks to itself. The public often gets very frustrated with alternative groups that knock things without promoting positive alternatives. The anti-globalization movement needs to sell itself more now that it has good, credible alternatives. It needs to get its hands dirty in the often murky battle for the hearts and minds of the general public. What the movement most needs to do now is to get its message out by engaging with the media and political parties. Such engagement is not easy.

To get a positive message out through the media requires a lot of savvy and a fair amount of playing by their rules. This can be extremely frustrating at times. The media don't like complex messages; it is often therefore necessary to reduce complex arguments into short, easy soundbites that the reading, listening or viewing public can comfortably digest. The media also like stories to have 'hooks'. This can sometimes mean using a well-known person to promote a particular story, or attaching an anti-globalization story to a big, colourful event. It can also mean finding snappy 'photo opportunities' to accompany a story. Some in the anti-globalization movement may see media strategies like these as possibly compromising their message, and at times they may involve some measure of compromise, but the downside needs to be weighed against the futility of not getting the message out at all.

The anti-globalization movement shouldn't just depend on the media to get its message out, however. A major problem is that the media are largely owned by a small group of TNCs which have a vested interest in making sure economic globalization continues. So alternative strategies like doorstep campaigning, handing out leaflets at popular venues, neighbourhood meetings and influencing educational texts have to be adopted as well. It is easy to become overly dependent on the media.

Engaging with political parties also involves playing by various rules and realities, many of which can be fairly undesirable. All political parties have to be realistic about how much power they really have and this is often driven by how popular they are with the voting public. Public popularity can mean diluting one's message in order to make it palatable, which, inevitably, often involves a subtle weighing up of the risks of trying to lead public opinion versus the risks of simply responding to it. Often the political parties that potentially have a lot of power play very safe with their messages and can be reluctant to take risks with economic policy in particular. The parties without power will generally take bigger risks with their economic message but they rarely have the clout to implement their agenda. When they do have power, in say a parliamentary balance-of-power situation, they can often only get a small part of their agenda implemented. One dilemma some parties, particularly Green and non-mainstream Democratic parties, have increasingly faced of late is that of cooperating with larger, more conservative parties in forming governments. Such cooperation runs the risk of the smaller, more radical party being seen as propping up the agenda of the conservative and/or unpopular larger party. But the smaller party wouldn't have the opportunity to implement even a minor part of its agenda unless it was in such a potentially fraught political situation. There is no easy answer to this dilemma. In some situations cooperating with larger parties involves too much compromise; in other situations the compromises are worth it. As the anti-globalization movement becomes more popular this sort of dilemma will be faced more and more. Engaging with political parties doesn't necessarily involve joining them; it could involve lobbying them. But parties will only listen to lobbyists if they think there are votes in it for them, which brings one back to the quandary of trying to lead public opinion versus simply responding to it.

Engaging with both the media and with political parties can be dirty, grubby business at times but the anti-globalization movement needs to do more of it, if it is to be effective. It can't afford to create an isolated, detached ideological ghetto for itself.

Engaging with itself

Anti-globalization activists from rich countries, in particular, also need to spend more time talking to poor-country activists and trying to find more common ground with them. Much of the cutting-edge political change that may eventually have a profound impact on the future of economic globalization is taking place in poor countries; the movement can't afford to have rich-country anti-globalization organizations undermining the changes in political thought taking place in poor countries.

All organizations in the anti-globalization movement talk about respect for diversity and difference of opinion. While these should be given their due, they can't be allowed to become a cover for intellectual laziness and an unwillingness to communicate with other parts of the anti-globalization movement. The movement can't rail against the tyranny of economic globalization while setting up its own tyranny based on a right to express one's opinion without listening to the opinion of others on the same side of the debate. There is no shortage of people within the anti-globalization movement who believe it is acceptable for it to present many different policy alternatives – Susan George believes in 'thousands of alternatives', and the Mexican Zapatistas talk of 'one no, many yeses', for instance. Before it presents lots of different options the movement has to ask itself whether it is doing so because it genuinely can't find common ground with other positions or because it just can't be bothered to look due to tribal loyalties and rhetorical habits.

Ironically it may be the forces behind the seemingly irrepressible ongoing integration of the world's economies that may end up doing most to force the anti-globalization movement to conduct a better dialogue between its constituent groups. By 2003 the movement had become very alarmed about the possibility that the Doha Round of trade talks could end up including a new global investment agreement that would include many of the worst elements of the proposed Multilateral Agreement on Investment which it successfully squashed in 1998. In response an anti-globalization movement workshop was held on the issue in March 2003 in Geneva, which, among other things, produced a declaration of opposition to investment treaty negotiations taking place in the Doha Round, signed by more than forty organizations including groups like Oxfam and Friends of the Earth, who generally sit on opposite sides of the Fair Trade/ Localization divide.

Probably the biggest contradiction of the anti-globalization movement, indeed of most alternative movements, is that they generally have a communitarian message but often operate in highly individualized ways and rely on a huge amount of person- alized energy. This individualized way of operating can't be al- lowed to cloud good communication and effective policy formu- lation based on listening as well as advocating. The movement's dedication to diversity needs to be balanced by a commitment to effective communication. It is not good enough to argue that the anti-globalization movement is together-but-separate while ignoring the exciting possibilities that better articulation and con- sistency of policy could bring. Diversity can never be allowed to be an absolute; it has to be balanced with other ideals such as co- operation and communication. The different organizations within the anti-globalization movement jealously guard their autonomy and often (rightly) argue that the movement's decentralized struc- ture is an important counterpoint to the centralized structures of economic globalization. The movement feels it is building a new type of truly participatory democracy. Yet the most critical flaw of centralized structures is that they don't listen to people. The anti-globalization movement needs to make sure that its alterna- tive structures don't suffer from the very same flaw.

Note

1. Worldwatch Institute, *Vital Signs 2002–2003: The Trends That Are Shaping Our Future*, Earthscan, London, 2002, p. 38.

CHAPTER 13

CONCLUSION

The time has long passed when argument, or even large-scale street protest, would be enough, in itself, to turn back, or significantly reform, economic globalization. The impetus for real change will come when economic globalization begins eating away at itself, and the momentum will be pushed along by the protests and alternative policies of the anti-globalization movement.

It is increasingly clear that economic globalization is already eating away at itself.

Economic globalization is eating away at itself in rich countries. It has given rich countries the luxury of ignoring difficult domestic structural change because it has allowed them potentially to live beyond their means by forever borrowing from the rest of the world. Several significant rich countries, including Greece, Iceland, Portugal, Spain, the United States, Australia, New Zealand, the Czech Republic, Hungary and Poland, now borrow massive amounts of money each year from the rest of the world to balance out their weak trade performances, their modest domestic savings rates, and/or their large net leakages of foreign investment and foreign debt income. They are all chalking up persistently high current account deficits. The United States is in a particularly vulnerable situation, with increasing trade deficits, increasing current account deficits, large federal and state government overspending, a falling currency and net foreign liabilities approaching US$3,000 billion. Some commentators are even worried that the US is so vulnerable it will increasingly walk away from world trade negotiations and instead pursue its own unilateral form of world trade that will include protectionism and an emphasis on regional and bilateral trade deals instead of negotiations conducted through the World Trade Organization.

Economic globalization is eating away at itself in poor countries. Nearly half of all the poor countries in the world have been, or are, effectively under the economic management of the International Monetary Fund and the World Bank. After commanding a lot of respect throughout the decades after the Second World War, both institutions have been under unprecedented attack from both the left and the right of politics since the Asian meltdown of 1997. Poor countries spent the 1980s and 1990s coming to terms with economic globalization, and to a large extent gave it the benefit of the doubt during those decades. But now they are cynical. The failed WTO talks held at Cancún in September 2003 showed that poor countries have had enough of rich countries dictating the terms of economic globalization and keeping all the spoils. They showed that, when properly organized and disciplined, poor countries collectively wield enough clout these days to pose a real and serious challenge to rich countries, who ignore it at their peril. Cancún fundamentally changed the power dynamics of economic globalization.

Economic globalization is also eating away at the environment. Global warming is reminding us of the obvious fact that we can't keep moving massive quantities of goods and services around the globe without severely affecting its environment. Also, poor countries hold much of what remains of the world's untouched ecosystems; if we want them preserved we are going to have to find truly sustainable ways of lifting poor countries out of poverty. The Smithsonian Tropical Research Institute has recently estimated, for instance, that up to 40 per cent of the

Amazon's rainforests will be destroyed by 2010 as a result of new, unsustainable Brazilian development strategies.[1]

All this means that the times are increasingly ripe for the anti-globalization movement. It is likely to be success, rather than failure, that will present the greatest future challenges.

The four most profound challenges facing the anti-globalization movement are:

1. The need for the Fair Trade and Localization schools to communicate with each other to produce better articulated and coordinated policies, particularly on trade and the future of the International Monetary Fund, World Bank and World Trade Organization (while respecting the short- and long-term focus of each school). Both also need to address deficiencies in their agendas. In general what is needed is more detail, less rhetoric.

2. The need for rich-country activists to communicate and cooperate with poor-country activists so policies can also be better articulated and coordinated. Otherwise, there is a real possibility they could end up working against each other.

3. The need for positive policy engagement with the general public via the media, political parties and non-media-dependent forms of networking. This involves sober and adroit weighing up of the various rules and realities of both the media and politics in general.

4. The possibility that the anti-globalization message will become assimilated and co-opted by pro-globalization interests, particularly as the message becomes more popular. The only way to make sure this does not happen is for the movement to be more confident about its message, which means facing up to the first three challenges. Recently the concept of 'poverty' has been significantly co-opted by various pro-globalizing forces. George Bush wants to 'attack global poverty'; Tony Blair says he supports 'attacking the causes of global poverty'; and the remaining G8 leaders are apparently dedicated to 'the fight

against global poverty'. Meanwhile, the World Bank is 'fighting grinding poverty'; the World Trade Organization is 'reducing poverty on a worldwide basis'; and the IMF is 'actively combating world poverty'.[2]

The anti-globalization movement has made great strides in recent years in working up coherent, viable alternatives to economic globalization. Most of the work, though, has occurred within organizations; it now needs to occur between them. The movement can no longer allow its commitment to diversity to stand in the way of better internal dialogue. The movement can stay decentralized but it can't stay uncoordinated. With more articulation between the movement's constituent organizations, it can go on to become as potent a force as the newly created labour movement was in the late nineteenth century. Yet without better coordination it could become a footnote to history. The anti-globalization movement is making progress, but it needs to make sure it doesn't develop a litany of blunders and missed opportunities through a lack of intelligent humility, and proper internal and external communication.

One of the most frustrating conclusions one comes to when reviewing the history of world economic integration is that we keep making the same mistakes. There were Third World debt crises in both the nineteenth and twentieth centuries; the slide in raw material export prices is a century-old trend now; world income has been increasingly less equitably distributed for nearly three centuries; and on several occasions during the twentieth century the world went through major convulsions when a major world capital supplier withdrew its money. The mistakes keep recurring and the world keeps dodging the solutions. Unless the anti-globalization movement can get the world to look at long-term, sustainable economic solutions the same mistakes will keep being made over and over again and we will never get it right.

Another equally frustrating conclusion one comes to about economic globalization is that there is often one set of rules for rich countries and another set for poor countries. Rich countries like the United States tell poor countries that their governments shouldn't overspend; yet that is exactly what the US government is doing right now. Rich countries tell poor countries that they should lower their trade and investment barriers; yet in the past rich countries have generally been reluctant to do this themselves, and still refuse to do it with agricultural and textile trade. Rich countries tell poor countries they should give patent protection to foreign companies; yet in years gone by, when it suited them, rich countries have refused to this. The anti-globalization movement should spare no effort in publicizing this hypocrisy.

The twin trade towers in New York were largely the vision of one-time New York governor and US vice-president Nelson Rockefeller, who developed his ideas for their construction in the 1960s (the towers were completed in 1974). Above all else, Rockefeller saw the towers as epitomizing the ability of world trade to bring people together, to make wars redundant because people would be united through a common humanity powered by economic globalization. But the destruction of the towers on 11 September 2001 showed how negative globalization can be. US Secretary of State Colin Powell called the attacks the 'dark side of globalization'. The challenge for the future of globalization is to retain its spirit of internationalism, and its common human bonding, while respecting the separateness and individuality of the world's countries and citizens. In the past, globalization has blindly assumed that no matter what form it took it must inevitably be a force for good. We now know that economic globalization is not necessarily a force for good; it must be managed very carefully and be a force of empowerment, not humiliation. With better internal dialogue the anti-globalization movement can be a pivotal force in making sure restructured, or radically reformed, economic globalization is a force for good.

Notes

1. 'Transitions – Can't See the Forest', *The Weekend Australian*, 5 April 2003, magazine, p. 9.
2. Steve Tibett, 'The West's Rhetoric about Foreign Aid Conceals a Greedy Self Interest', published by Deb Foskey via WTO Watch email list (debf@webone.com.au), 13 July 2003 (#173), p. 1. (For archive copy, see www.nwjc.org.au/avcwl/lists/archives.html.)

USEFUL GLOBALIZATION WEBSITES

General anti-globalization movement organizations

Africa Trade Network www.twnafrica.org
AFTINET www.aftinet.org.au
Aid Watch www.aidwatch.org.au
Bretton Woods Project www.brettonwoodsproject.org
Campaign for Labor Rights www.summersault.com/~agj/clr
Centre for Economic Policy Research www.cepr.net
Center of Concern www.coc.org
Citizens' Network on Essential Services
 www.challengeglobalization.org
Committee for Cancellation of Third World Debt
 www.users.skynet.be/cadtm
Debt Links (links Third World debt groups) www.debtlinks.org
Drop the Debt www.dropthedebt.org
Ecological Debt Campaign
 www.cosmovisiones.com/DeudaEcologica/articulous.html
Economic Policy Institute www.epinet.org
50 Years is Enough www.50years.org
Focus on the Global South www.focusweb.org
Food First www.foodfirst.org
Gats Watch www.gatswatch.org
Global Exchange www.globalexchange.org
Global Policy Network www.gpn.org
Institute for Policy Studies www.ips-dc.org
International Confederation of Free Trade Unions www.icftu.org

International Forum on Globalization　www.ifg.org
International Institute for Sustainable Development　www.iisd.org
International Network on Disarmament and Globalization
　　www.indg.org
International Network for Economic, Social and Cultural Rights　www.
　　escr-net.org
International South Group　www.isgnweb.org
Institute for Agricultural Trade Policy　www.tradeobservatory.org
Investment Watch　www.investmentwatch.org
Jubilee 2000　www.j2000usa.org
Living Democracy Movement　www.transcend.org
Medact　www.medact.org
New Economics Foundation　www.neweconomics.org
Our World is Not for Sale Network　www.speakeasy.org
Peoples' Global Action　www.agp.org
People-Centred Development Forum　www.pcdf.org
Public Citizen　www.citizen.org
Public Citizen's Global Trade Watch/Citizens Trade Campaign
　　www.tradewarch.org
Publish What You Pay　www.publishwhatyoupay.org
Student Alliance to Reform Corporations　www.corpreform.org
The Association for Taxation of Financial Transactions in the Interests of
　　the Citizen (ATTAC)　www.attac.org
Third World Network　www.twnside.org.sg
Tobin Tax Initiative　www.ceedweb.org/noframe.html
United Students Against Sweatshops　www.asm.wisc.edu/usas
Via Campesina　www.viacampesina.org
World Development Movement　www.wdm.org.uk
World Social Forum　www.forumsocialmundial.org.br

Green parties

Australian Greens　www.greens.org.au
Brazilian Greens (Partido Verde de Brasil)　www.partidoverde.org.br
European Greens　www.europeangreens.org
Federation of Young European Greens　www.fyeg.onvaton.org
French Greens (Les Verts)　www.les-verts.org
German Greens (Bündnis 90/Die Grünen)　www.gruene.de
Green Party of Aotearoa New Zealand　www.greens.org.nz

Green Party of Canada   www.green.ca
Green Party of England and Wales   www.greenparty.org.uk
Green Party of South Africa   www.greenparty.org.za
Irish Greens (Comhaontas Glas)   www.greenparty.ie
Italian Greens (Federazione dei Verdi)   www.verdi.it
Mexican Greens (Partido Verde Ecologista de Mexico)
     www.pvem.org.mx
Scottish Green Party   www.scottishgreens.org.uk
Spanish Greens (Confederatión de Los Verdes)   www.verdes.es
United States Greens   www.greenpartyus.org

Non-mainstream Democratic parties

Australian Democrats   www.democrats.org.au
Liberal Democrats (United Kingdom)   www.libdems.org.uk
New Democrats (Canada)   www.ndp.ca

Socialist organizations

Globalize Resistance   www.resist.org.uk
International Socialists   www.internationalsocialist.org
International Socialist Tendency   www.istendency.net
Left Turn   www.leftturn.org
Socialist Workers Party   www.swp.org.uk

Environmental groups

Friends of the Earth   www.foe.org
Greenpeace   www.greenpeace.org
Rocky Mountains Institute   www.rmi.org
Sierra Club   www.sierraclub.org
Worldwide Fund for Nature   www.panda.org

Transnational corporation reform groups

Corporations Watch   www.corpwatch.org
Interfaith Centre for Corporate Responsibility   www.iccr.org
Multinational Monitor   www.multinationalmonitor.org

Program on Corporations, Law and Democracy   www.poclad.org
The Transnational Corporations Observatory   www.transnationale.org
The Transnational Institute   www.tni.org
Transnational Research and Action Centre   www.corpwatch.org

Aid groups

Action Aid   www.actionaid.org
Christian Aid   www.christian-aid.org
Médecins Sans Frontières   www.msf.org
Oxfam   www.oxfam.org
Save the Children   www.scfuk.org
World Vision   www.wvi.org

Anti-globalization commentators

Noam Chomsky   www.worldmedia.com/archive
John Pilger   www.johnpilger.com

Globalization news

www.indymedia.org
Interpress Service   www.ipsnews.net
www.ratical.org
www.redpepper.org.uk
Z Net   www.zmag.org

International public globalization-related organizations

General Agreement on Tariffs and Trade www.worldtradelaw.net
International Labor Organization www.ilo.org
International Monetary Fund www.imf.org
Intergovernmental Panel on Climate Change www.ipcc.ch
United Nations Conference on Trade and Development (UNCTAD)
     www.unctad.org
United Nations Development Program www.undp.org
World Bank www.worldbank.org
World Trade Organization www.wto.org

Suggested Reading

Anderson, Sarah, ed., *Views from the South: The Effects of Globalization and the WTO on Third World Countries*, Oakland CA: Food First/Institute for Food and Policy Development, 2000.

Bello, Walden, *Deglobalization: Ideas for a New World Economy*, London: Zed Books, 2002.

Bello, Walden, Nicola Bullard and Kamal Malhotta, eds, *Global Finance: New Thinking on Regulating Speculative Capital Markets*, London: Zed Books, 2000.

Blakers, Margaret, ed., *The Global Greens: Inspiration, Ideas and Insights from the RIO + 10 International Workshop and Global Greens 2001*, Canberra: Australian Greens, 2001.

Brecher, Jeremy, Tim Costello and Brendan Smith, *Globalization from Below: The Power of Solidarity*, Cambridge MA: South End Press, 2000.

Chossudovsky, Michel, *The Globalization of Poverty: Impacts of IMF and World Bank Reforms*, London: Zed Books, 1999.

Daly, Herman and John B. Cobb, *For the Common Good: Redirecting the Economy Towards Community, the Environment and a Sustainable Future*, London: Green Print, 1990.

Danaher, Kevin and Roger Burbach, eds, *Globalize This! The Battle Against the World Trade Organization and Corporate Rule*, Monroe ME: Common Courage Press, 2000.

Ellwood, Wayne, *The No-Nonsense Guide to Globalization*, Oxford: New Internationalist Publications, 2001.

Fisher, William F. and Thomas Ponniah, eds, *Another World is Possible: Popular Alternatives to Globalization at the World Social Forum*, London: Zed Books, 2003.

Galbraith, Kate, ed., *Globalisation: Making Sense of an Integrating World*, London: The Economist/Profile Books, 2001.

Goldsmith, Edward and Jerry Mander, eds, *The Case against the Global Economy, and for a Turn towards Localization*, London: Earthscan, 2001.

Hines, Colin, *Localization: A Global Manifesto*, London: Earthscan, 2000.

Hoogvelt, Ankie, *Globalization and the Post Colonial World: The New Political Economy of Development*, London: Palgrave, 2001.

Houtart, François and Francois Polet, *The Other Davos: The Globalization of Resistance to the World Economic System*, London: Zed Books, 2001.

International Forum on Globalization, *Alternatives to Economic Globalization: A Better World is Possible*, San Francisco: Berrett–Koehler, 2002.

Jawara, Fatoumata and Aileen Kwa, *Behind the Scenes at the WTO: The Real World of International Trade Negotiations*, London: Zed Books, 2003.

Kenwood, A.G. and A.L. Lougheed, *Growth of the International Economy 1820–1990: An Introductory Text*, London: Routledge, 1992.

Khor, Martin, *Rethinking Globalization: Critical Ideas and Policy Choices*, London: Zed Books, 2001.

Klein, Naomi, *No Logo*, London: Flamingo, 2000.

Klein, Naomi, *Fences and Windows: Dispatches from the Front Line of the Globalization Debate*, London: Flamingo, 2002.

Lucas, Caroline and Colin Hines, *Time to Replace Globalization: A Green Localist Manifesto for the World Trade Organisation Ministerial*, London: The Greens/European Free Alliance, 2001.

Madeley, John, *Hungry for Trade: How the Poor Pay for Free Trade*, London: Zed Books, 2000.

Madeley, John, *Food for All: The Need for a New Agriculture*, London: Zed Books, 2002.

Madeley, John, ed., *A People's World: Alternatives to Economic Globalization*, London: Zed Books, 2003.

Monbiot, George, *The Age of Consent: A Manifesto for a New World Order*, London: Flamingo, 2003.

Moore, Mike, *A World without Walls: Freedom, Development, Free Trade and Global Governance*, Cambridge: Cambridge University Press, 2003.

Neale, Jonathan, *You are G8, We are 6 billion: The Truth Behind the Genoa Protests*, London: Vision Paperbacks, 2002.

Peet, Richard, ed., *Unholy Trinity: The IMF, World Bank and WTO*, London: Zed Books, 2003.

Robertson, Robbie, *The Three Waves of Globalization: A History of a Developing Consciousness*, London: Zed Books, 2003.

Shiva, Vandana, *Protect or Plunder? Understanding Intellectual Property Rights*, London: Zed Books, 2002.

Singh, Kavaljit, *Taming Global Financial Flows: A Citizens' Guide*, London: Zed Books, 2000.

Sogge, David, *Give and Take: What's the Matter with Foreign Aid?*, London: Zed Books, 2002.

Spero, Joan E. and Jeffrey A. Hart, *The Politics of International Economic Relations*, 5th edn, London: Routledge, 1997.

Stiglitz, Joseph E., *Globalization and its Discontents*, London: Penguin, 2002.

Waters, Malcom, *Globalization*, 2nd edn, London: Routledge, 2001.

Watkins, Kevin, et al., *Rigged Rules and Double Standards: Trade, Globalisation and the Fight Against Poverty*, Washington DC: Oxfam International, 2002.

Weatherford, Jack, *The History of Money*, New York: Three Rivers Press, 1997.

Went, Robert, *Globalization: Neoliberal Challenge, Radical Responses*, London: Pluto Press, 2000.

World Watch Institute, *Vital Signs 2003–04: The Trends That Are Shaping Our Future*, London: Earthscan, 2003.

Yergin, Daniel, *The Prize: The Epic Quest for Oil, Money and Power*, New York: Free Press, 1992.

INDEX

Abu Dhabi, 42
acid rain emissions, 64, 200
Africa: aid, 90; bananas, 48; inequality,
72; raw materials, 85; Social Forum,
Bamako, 117; sub-Saharan, 83–4;
Trade Network, 130, 167; TNCs,
42
agriculture, 211; protection, 102; rich
country export subsidies, 46, 55,
100–101, 126; Somalia collapse, 54;
subsistence, 72; trade conflicts, 181
aid: foreign, 140; GDP percentages, 90;
GNP percentages, 91; groups, 138;
organizations, 117, 123; political
strings, 91–2
air traffic: carbon dioxide emissions,
63–4; statistics, 60
Alianza Social Continental, 135
Amazon.com, 114
Amazon, rainforest destruction, 209
American Express, 40
American International Group, 40
Amsterdam, global capital centre, 19
anti-globalization movement: diversity,
111, 113, 194; coordination need,
210
Anti-Slavery Society, 118
Aparicio, Karolo, 135, 141
APM World Network, 127, 130
Argentina, 8, 32, 51, 74; 'barter' clubs,
163; debt crisis 2002, 3, 33; debt

default, 32; economic nationalism,
108; foreign debt default, 28;
poverty, 72; repayments suspension,
78
Asia: 1997 'meltdown', 3, 32, 55–6,
139–40, 208
Asian Development Bank, 115
Association for the Taxation of
Financial Transactions in the
Interests of the Citizen (ATTAC),
128, 137, 141
Association of South East Asian
Nations (ASEAN), 51, 157
Aswan Dam, 3
AT&T, 39
Australia, 8, 29, 47, 171: Centre for
International Economics, 71; debt,
207; Democrat Party, 138, 140;
foreign investment in, 20; Greens,
112, 118, 174; Social Forum,
Sydney, 117
Austro-Hungarian Empire, 21
Azerbaijan, 41

Baker Plan, 78
balanced budgets, obsession, 99
bananas, preferential importation, 48
Bangladesh: farmer bankruptcies, 55;
textile wages, 88–9
Bankers Trust, profits, 78
banking, Crusaders, 18; offshore, 160

bankruptcy, international mechanism proposal, 144–5
Basmati rice, patent, 49
Belgium: foreign investment, 19; protectionism, 97
Bello, Walden, 157–8, 160, 167–8, 188, 197
Berlin Wall, fall, 108, 113
biopiracy, 132
Birmingham, UK, G8 protest, 45
Blair, Tony, 5, 209
Boeing, 114
bond markets, controls relaxation, 26
Bosnia, war, 55
Boston Tea Party, 110
BP, 41
Brady Plan, 78
Brazil, 46, 51, 74, 82; currency crisis 1999, 32; debt crisis, 78; development strategies, 209; economic nationalism, 108; oil, 47; orange juice, 62; Workers Party, 191
Bretton Woods Conference, 23–5, 122
Bretton Woods Project, campaign group, 134
Bush, George W., 110, 209

Cairns Group, 100, 167
Callinicos, Alex, 176
Canada, 8, 59, 99; Foreign Investment Review Agency, 42; hormone-treated beef, 48; New Democrat Party, 118, 125, 130
Cancún, WTO talks, 40, 46, 82, 102, 108, 116, 181, 208
capital controls, 22, 33; types, 137–9; capital markets/flows, 18–21, 188; non-currency controls dismantling, 26–7; regulation, 199
carbon dioxide, world concentrations, 62–4
Carson, Rachel, 112
Chiang Mai protest, 115
Chicago School, 58–9
Chile: capital controls, 138–9; coup, 41
China, 32, 46, 74, 76, 80, 82, 176; capital controls, 33, 139; export

zone, 88; income inequality, 72; poverty, 181; revolution, 169
Christian Aid, 127, 130, 132, 138, 144, 170
Citigroup, 58; Citicorps profits, 78
Clinton, Bill, 58
Club of Rome 1973 report, 112
cocoa, 37
coffee: International Agreement, 185; stabilization price, 170; trade, 37
Colbert, Jean-Baptiste, 98
Columbus, Christopher, 6–7
Committee for the Annulment of Third World Debt, 128, 135–6, 138, 140, 143
communications: global capacity, 15; technology, 35, 38, 60; telegraph, 8
comparative advantage, theory, 167
Congress of South African Trade Unions (COSATU), 125, 136–7
containerization, 60
Convention on Biodiversity, 132
corporate engagement, ethical dilemma, 169–70
Corporations Watch, 116
Corpwatch, 135, 141
Credit First Suisse Boston, 40
Cuba, 176; revolution, 169
Cueva, Hector de la, 135
currencies, 18, 20; controls, 25; dollar-pegged, 139; floating rates, 52; global exchange statistics, 28; local area, 160; overvalued, 32; poor country devaluation, 77; speculation, 135, 140
Czech Republic, debt, 29, 207

Daly, Herman, 54, 175, 189
debtor nations, list, 29, 207
Delhi, street children bank, 163
democracy, 186; global loss, 109; participatory, 153–4, 205
Denmark: aid statistics, 90; World Bank loan, 52
Doha, WTO Round, 13, 38, 40, 44–6, 131, 205

dollar, US, 32, 76; floated, 38; overvalued, 26

Du Pont, 40

dumping, 102

East Asia: capitalist style, 108; manufactured exports, 87; tariff cuts, 84; trade share, 83; 'tiger' economies, 13, 83

Eastern Europe, 32

'ecological debt', 92–3

Ecology Party, 173

economic nationalism, 108

Economic Policy Institute, 141

Economist, The, 107

education: GATS impact, 132; privatization, 50

El Salvador, wage levels, 88

England and Wales, Green Party, 151, 155–6, 158, 160

environment, standards, 183–4; campaigning groups, 151

Environmental Defense Fund, USA, 114

Erlich, Paul, 112

eurodollars, 77

Europe: foreign investments, 20; Greens, 118, 131, 138, 152; oil consumption, 11; trade deficit, 22

European Economic Community, 51

European Social Forum, Genoa, 117

European Union (EU), 59, 118, 181; agricultural protection, 101; GM moratorium, 48 exchange rates: European crisis 1992, 32; floating, 26–7

expansionary economic policies, 22

export processing zones (EPZs), 87–9

exports: booms, 72; concentration, 74; manufacturing, 84; raw materials dependence, 85, 187; subsidies, 101, 126

Fair Trade/Back to Bretton Woods school, 122, 124–7, 129, 131, 133, 135, 137–8, 141, 144–5, 154–5, 157, 166, 168, 180, 183, 186, 194, 198, 201, 209

Falklands War, 28, 78

Fauz, Jeff, 141

feminism, 4

50 Years is Enough, campaign group, 133, 136

First World War, 9–10, 20–21, 23

Fischer, Stan, 58

Focus on the Global South, Thailand, 116, 157, 167

Food First organization, 127, 136, 167

'Food Sovereignty', 127

Ford, Henry, 15

Fordney-McCumber tariff, USA, 98

Foreign Investment Review Commission, Australia, 138

foreign investment: content rules, 174; FDI concentration, 74; regulation, 195; rights, 39

'forward exchange systems', 7

fossil fuels, global consumption, 62–3

Foundation for Ethics and Meaning, New York, 116

Framework Convention on Corporate Accountability, 143

France, 21, 39, 99; foreign investment, 19; political parties, 109; protectionism, 97; World Bank loan, 52

Franco, Francisco, 41

Free Software Foundation, 132

Free Trade Agreement of the Americas, proposed, 51

free-market ideologies, 38

freight, global, 60, 62, 64

Friedman, Milton, 38, 59

Friends of the Earth, 151, 160, 162, 170, 173, 205

Fukuyama, Francis, 109

'full cost accounting', 192

Galbraith, J.K., 99

Galtung, Johan, 173

Gama, Vasco da, 6–7

Gandhi, Mahatma, mass salt march, 110

Gap, clothing company, 15

General Agreement on Tariffs and Trade (GATT), 12, 14; charter, 43; Rounds, 13, 15, 36, 44–5, 48,

50, 82, 89, 100–101, 167; rules
flexibility, 47
General Agreement on Trade in
Services (GATS), 40, 50, 101, 132
GATSwatch, organization, 116
genetically modified food, EU
moratorium, 48
Genoa: European Social Forum, 117;
G8 protest, 115
George, Susan, 136, 204
Georgia, 41
Germany, 21, 99; Federal Republic
debt forgiveness, 79; foreign
investment, 19; Green party, 125–6,
132, 135, 140, 152, 173; political
parties, 118; protectionism, 97;
trade surpluses, 189
Global Competition Commission,
proposal, 144
Global Exchange, 135, 141
'global factory', 15
global institutions, checks and
balances, 197
Global Resistance, 113
globalization: institutions, 35; second
wave, 7, 68; technological change,
60; waves, 6
Gold Standard, 21; 1960s' return, 25;
dollar delinking, 26; emergence, 20;
return to, 22; suspension, 21
Goldman Sachs, 58
Gothenburg: EU summit protest, 45,
115
grain trade, 37; buffer stocks sell-off,
55
Grant, Ulysses, 97
Great Depression, 9–10, 22, 43, 98–9
Greece, debt, 29, 207; loan default, 80
Green Belt Movement, Kenya, 171
Green parties, 112, 117–18, 124–5,
151, 173, 203; California, 129;
Canberra global conference,
171–2; European, 126, 130, 136; less
radical, 123
'Green' revolution, 3
greenhouse gas emissions, 92, 200
Greenpeace, 125, 128, 130, 151;
International Economic Unit, 152

Group of Seventy-seven (G77), 81, 90
Group of Twenty-one (G21), 82;
membership, 46

Hamilton, Alexander, 97
Harvard University, 69
Havana, 1947 conference, 156; Charter,
43, 80
Hayek, Friedrich von, 38, 59
health: GATS impact, 132;
privatization, 50; public, 133
Heavily Indebted Poor Country
Initiative, 56, 78, 172
Heritage Foundation, USA, 56
Hines, Colin, 152–6, 159, 162, 167,
187, 189, 197
HIV/AIDS, drugs, 49
Honeywell, 41
Hong Kong, 13, 83
hot money: real estate, 55; speculation,
28–9
Houtart, François, 135
Hungary, 29; debt, 207

IBM, 39, 158
Iceland, debt, 29, 207
IMF (International Monetary Fund),
12, 24–5, 33, 35–6, 38, 43, 51, 54–6,
58, 64, 76, 82, 108–9, 113, 122–3,
129, 136, 140–41, 145, 154–5,
157, 185, 188, 190, 195, 208–10;
abolition proposal, 161; decision-
making structures, 59; engagement
debates, 170; management
proposals, 199–200; privatization
insistence, 53; reform ideas,
133–4, 143; replacement proposals,
158–9, 197; structural adjustment
programmes, 53, 77, 92, 172; UK
loan 1956, 52; unpopularity, 57
Import Duties Act, UK, 98
import licences, auctioning system,
175, 189
income statistics, national, 70
India, 15, 46, 74, 76, 82; capital
controls, 33, 139; generic drugs,
49; Internet access, 72; plague
outbreaks, 54; political parties, 109;

Social Forum, 117; textile wages, 89; TNCs policy, 42

indigenous peoples rights organizations, 4, 113

Indonesia, 32, 55, 74; economic nationalism, 108; Suharto regime, 114

industrial production, geographical concentration, 73

Industrial Revolution, 6–7, 19, 68

inequality: global, 68–74, 88; national, 89, 99

inflation, 10, 26, 53, 78, 191

intellectual property rights, 132, 196

interest rates, US, 21, 78

International Clearing Union, Keynes proposal, 23, 175, 189

International Coffee Agreement, 185

International Confederation of Free trade Unions, 125, 128, 134, 136–7, 170

International Energy Agency, 62, 200

International Forum on Globalization (IFG), 116, 152–6, 158, 160, 162, 167, 188, 197, 199

International Labor Organization (ILO), 41, 157

International Trade Organization: US rejection, 43, 80

International Treaty on Plant Genetic Resources for Food and Agriculture, 133

International Whaling Commission, 91

Internet: access, 72; networking, 111, 114

Iran, fall of Shah, 11

Ireland: Green Party (Comhaontas Glas), 151–2, 154, 160, 163

Israel, 10

Italy, protectionism, 97

Japan, 8, 15, 26, 36, 59, 99, 181; agriculture protection, 100; aid strings, 91; global capital supplier, 29; trade surpluses, 189

Jefferson, Thomas, 99

Johannesburg, Sustainable Development protests, 115

Joint Declaration of the Developing Countries, 1963, 81

Jordan, John, 112

Jubilee 2000, 136, 170

Jubilee South Summit, Johannesburg, 172

Kanbur, Ravi, 54

Karliner, Joshua, 135, 141

Keet, Dot, 130

Kennedy Round, GATT, 13, 15, 44

Kennedy, John F., 140

Keynes,, John Maynard, 23, 59, 123, 137, 151, 175

Khor, Martin, 174, 184

Klein, Naomi, 116

Korean War, 10

Korten, David, 153

Kraft, 170

Kyoto, emissions protocol, 129

labour: minimal protection, 88; slave, 7, 92; standards, 183–4

Landis, David, 69

Latin America, TNCs, 42

lend–lease arrangements, 23

Liberal Democrat party, UK, 134, 138, 144

Libya, 11

List, Friedrich, 97

loan conditionality, 52–3

local investment: competition policies, 163; favourable treatment, 159–60

Localization School, 145, 150–54, 159, 161, 166, 168, 173–4, 182–3, 186, 191, 194, 201, 209; blueprint, 188

London, global capital centre, 19

Louisiana State University, 175

Lucas, Caroline, 155, 160, 163

Luxembourg, World Bank loan, 52

Lydia, city-state, 18

Maathai, Wangari, 171

Malawi, drought, 55

Malaysia, 55, 73, 74, 88; capital controls, 33, 138–9; Non-Aligned meeting, 183; Third World Network, 116

maquiladora, 88
Marshall Plan, 25, 52, 90
Marx, Karl, 113
Médecins sans Frontières, 49
media, movement strategies, 202
medicines: affordable, 132; generic, 46, 49; global non-access, 71
Melbourne: World Economic Forum protest, 45, 115
Merck, 40
Mercosur, 51, 157
Mexican Yellow Enola Bean, patent, 49
Mexico, 74, 78; currency crisis 1994, 32; foreign debt default, 28, 80; income inequality, 72; poverty, 181; trade, 83; Yellow Enola Bean patent, 49; Zapatistas, 204
Microsoft, 114
Middle East Social Forum, Beirut, 117
military spending, Third World, 78
Mittal, Anuradha, 127, 136
Mohamad, Mahathir, 139
Monbiot, George, 175–6, 187, 189
monetarism, 78
monopoly, anti- laws, 162; prohibition proposals, 144
Morgan, J.P., 58
Mozambique, 69
MST, organization, 167
Multi-Fiber Agreement, 1974, 101
Multilateral Agreement on Investment (MAI), 39–40, 114, 205
Multinational Monitor, 116
Mutual Aid Agreement, UK–US, 23

Nader, Ralph, 116, 183
Narmada Dam project, 113
National Audubon Society, USA, 114
national sovereignty, 130
National Wildlife Federation, USA, 114
Natural Resources Defense Council, USA, 114
Navigation Laws, UK, 98
Nestlé, 170
Netherlands: aid statistics, 90; foreign investment, 19; protectionism, 97;

World Bank loan, 52
New Economics Foundation, UK, 116, 188
'New International Economic Order', 77, 81–2
'new protectionism', 152, 154
New York: twin towers, 211; World Economic Forum protest, 115
New Zealand, 8, 29; debt, 207; foreign investment in, 20; Green Party, 112, 118, 174
nitrogen oxides, 64
Nixon, Richard, M., 26, 30
Non-Aligned Movement, Malaysia meeting 2003, 183
non-governmental organizations (NGOs), 107, 117; global numbers, 118–19
non-violence, 4
North American Free Trade Agreement (NAFTA), 51, 72, 114
Norway, aid statistics, 90

oil, 9, 182, 184; BP pipeline, 41; companies, 42; OPEC, 10–11, 184–5; price movements, 10–11, 26, 62, 77
Organic Consumers Association, 171
Organization for Corporate Accountability, proposed, 162
Organization for Economic Cooperation and Development (OECD), 39, 62, 72, 81, 114, 144, 185, 187; Guidelines for Multinational Enterprises, 41
Orwell, George, 110
Our World is Not for Sale Network, 126, 130–31
Oxfam, 49, 124–8, 130, 132–3, 135, 138, 144, 167–8, 170–71, 182, 190, 199, 205; Make Trade Fair campaign, 166

Pakistan, US aid, 91
Pan-Amazonian Social Forum, Belem, 117
Panitchpakdi, Supachai, 170
Paraguay, 51

participatory democracy, 153–4, 205
    patents: genetic material, 48–9;
    laws, 48, 99; life forms, 132–3, 162;
    TNC domination, 37
Peru, debt repayment limits, 54
petro–dollar, 28
Pfizer, 40
pharmaceutical industry, 40, 49
Philippines, the, 74
Pinochet, Augusto, 139
plant products, communal property,
    132
pluralism, world economic
    management, 157–8
Poland, debt, 29, 207
political parties, 109, 111, 117;
    engagement with, 203
pollution, 92
poor countries: activist radicalism,
    171–2; bank lending to, 52;
    borrowing, 28; cheap factories,
    85; ecosystems, 208; exports, 83,
    125; foreign investment, 31–2;
    medicines access, 46; protectionism,
    196, 198; raw material dependent,
    190; tariff reduction, 77; tariff use,
    127; trade deficits, 80
Porritt, Jonathon, 173
portfolio investments, speculative, 137
Portugal, 29, 207
poverty, 4, 74, 181, 210; absolute, 72;
    backlash against, 110; concept
    co–option, 209; extreme, 85, 90;
    reduction aims, 124; reduction
    rhetoric, 56; relative, 71; relief, 190
Powell, Colin, 211
Prague, IMF protest, 115
Pratt, Edmund, 40
Preston, Lewis, 58
privatization, 50, 191; IMF insistence,
    53; public services, 134
Procter & Gamble, 170
protectionism, 123, 126, 184;
    development programmes, 87; poor
    country, 196, 198; rich countries,
    96–8, 125
protests, 'media–grab', 111
Public Citizen, USA, 116, 131

Qaddafi, Muammar, 11
Qatar, 42
Quebec, Summit of the Americas
    protest, 45, 115

railways, 8, 20
raw materials, 8, 37; export
    dependency, 85, 187; oversupply,
    86; price pressures, 9, 22, 28, 77–8,
    81, 92, 99, 190; stabilization funds/
    price support schemes, 127–8,
    184–5
Reagan, Ronald, 38, 40, 59
Reclaim the Streets, UK, 112
Reconstruction Finance Corporation,
    USA, 24
regional trade deals, 50
relative purchasing power, 70, 76
Rhodes, Cecil, 7
rich countries,, import barriers/
    protectionism, 96, 125–6
Rio Earth Summit, 114
Robertson, Robbie, 6–7, 68
Rockefeller, Nelson, 211
Rubin, Robert, 58
Russia: debt crisis 1998, 32, 78;
    revolution, 169
Rwanda, civil war, 54

Sara Lee, 170
Saudi Arabia, 42, 74
Schumacher, Fritz, 112, 151, 186
Seattle: WTO meeting 1999, 13, 108,
    114; protest, 3, 45, 107, 115, 117,
    119, 153
Second World War, 10, 22–3
self–sufficiency, rural devlopment,
    127
'self–reliance', 150–52, 161
September 11, 2001 attacks, 115, 211
Shiva, Vandana, 167, 171
Silk Road, 6
Silva, Luiz Inácio 'Lula' da, 191
silver standards, 21
Simms, Andrew, 188
Singapore, 13, 73–4, 83, 88
Skidelsky, Robert, 123
Slater, Samuel, 99

Smithsonian Tropical Research Institute, 208
Smoot–Hawley tariff act, USA, 98
'social accounting', 162
Social Movements, Manifesto, 137, 141
Socialist Workers Party, 113
Somalia, agricultural collapse, 54
South Africa, 8, 74; African National Congress (ANC), 109–10, 191; Congress of Trade Unions (COSATU), 125, 136–7; Green Party, 152, 159; Treatment Action Campaign, 49
South America: debt crisis, 53; tariff cuts, 84
South Asia: tariff levels, 84; trade share, 83
South Korea, 13, 15, 55, 73–4, 83, 88; high tariffs, 87; TNC controls, 42
Spain: Civil War, 41; debt, 29, 207; protectionism, 97
spot prices, agreed, 7
Starbucks, 114, 171
Stiglitz, Joseph, 54
stockmarket collapse, 1929, 9, 22
Suez Canal; crisis 1956, 25; opening, 8, 20
Sutherland, Peter, 58
'swallow capital', 78
Sweden, aid statistics, 90
Switzerland, 69; foreign investment, 19
Sydney, WTO protest, 115

Taiwan, 13, 55, 73, 83, 88; high tariffs, 87; TNC controls, 42
tariffs, 84, 123, 174; 'infant industry, 97; positive use, 155; reductions, 14–15; rich world, 96, 125
tax: evasion control, 160; policies, 162
tea, 37
technology, 3–4; transfer, 186–7, 191
Texaco, 41
textiles, 84, 100, 211; subsidies, 101; wages, 88–9
Thailand, 32, 55, 74, 157
Thatcher, Margaret, 26, 38, 59
'the left', 113
Third Word debt, 29, 31, 113, 135, 184,

190, 195; cancellation campaigns, 136–7; crises, 29, 32, 53, 76–7, 81, 114; campaigning groups, 117, 123; defaults, 21, 28; relief, 168; servicing costs/profits, 78–9; temporary repayment suspension, 145
Third World, global export share, 124
Third World Network, Malaysia, 116, 167, 170, 184
'tiger' economies, 13, 83
Tobin, James, tax proposal, 140–41, 143, 160, 196
Tokyo Round, GATT, 44
trade, world: balanced, 175; commercial services, 14; composition, 14, 16; environmental impact, 182, 200; European share, 9; geographical concentration, 80; long-distance, 155, 187; minerals, 9; negotiations, 76; periphery/core template, 37; statistics, 8, 10, 14; WTO rules, 48
Transmigration project, Indonesia, 113
transnational corporations (TNCs), 4, 15–16, 35, 41, 57, 64, 109, 112, 135, 141, 183, 185; codes of conduct, 185; European, 50; list, 61; media ownership, 202; political influence, 39; regulation proposals, 143–4, 160, 162, 183, 189, 195; repatriated profits, 42; statistics, 36–7, Transnational Institute, 116
'transparency', 130; financial markets, 135
transport, 182; air, 63–4; freight, 60, 62, 64; global capacity, 15; global statistics, 60; steam-based, 7; technology, 35, 38
TRIMS, (Trade Related Investment Measures), 50
TRIPS, (Trade Related Aspects of Intellectual Property Rights) 40, 46, 48–50, 99, 101, 132–3; containment, 142
Truman, Harry, 12, 43
Turkey, 29, 41; loan default, 80

Union de Paises Exportadores de
    Banana, 185
Union of Soviet Socialist Republics
    (USSR), 158, 176
United Kingdom (UK): agriculture
    protection, 102; aid organizations,
    124; Bretton Woods negotiations,
    23–4; capital controls relaxation,
    58; Corn Laws, 97; financial
    dominance, 21; foreign investment,
    19–20; IMF loan 1956, 25, 52;
    Liberal Democrats, 118, 125–6,
    130; McKenna Tariff, 98; political
    parties, 109
United Nations (UN), 90, 118, 130,
    134; Centre on Transnational
    Corporations, 41; Conference
    on Trade and Development
    (UNCTAD), 13, 36, 41, 85,
    127–8, 157, 190; Convention
    on Biological Diversity, 133;
    Development Programme
    (UNDP), 69, 92; environment
    summit, 1975, 112; General
    Assembly, 81; Millennium Summit,
    73; system, 158
United States of America (USA),
    8, 15, 51, 145, 181; agriculture
    protection, 100–102; aid, 90–91;
    Bretton Woods dominance,
    23–4; capital controls relaxation,
    58; capitalist style, 108; Chapter
    11 laws, 144; Council for
    International Business, 39; debt,
    29, 207–8; Democratic Party, 118;
    dollar, 28, 38, 139; Endangered
    Species Act, 47; foreign investment,
    25; global lending statistics, 21;
    government overspending, 211;
    Greens, 129, 152, 172; hormone-
    treated beef, 48; household savings
    rate, 29; inequality, 72; job losses,
    89; Marine Mammal Protection
    Act, 47; Meltzer Commission, 56;
    oil self-sufficiency, historical, 11;
    patent law flouting, 99; political
    parties, 109, 118; protectionism,
    97–8, 100–101; R&D spending,

37; railways, 20; savings and loan
    scandal, 32; Tariff Act 1816, 97;
    TNC headquarters, 36; trade
    deficits, 26; Treasury, 57; world
    trade share, 9–10
Uruguay, 8, 51
Uruguay Round, GATT, 15, 38, 40,
    44, 48, 50, 82, 101; Cairns Group,
    100, 167; poor countries' losses,
    89
value-adding exports, 84, 86
Venezuela, 74; oil, 47
Via Campesina, 127, 134, 167
Vietnam, 176; revolution, 169; War, 26,
    38, 41, 112

Wallach, Lori, 131
Washington, IMF protests, 45, 115
'Washington Consensus', 57–9
water: global non-access, 71;
    privatization, 50
Watkins, Kevin, 168
websites, 116
Western Europe: agriculture
    protection, 100; capitalist style, 108;
    TNC headquarters, 36
White, Harry Dexter, 59
World Bank, 12, 24, 33, 36, 38, 43,
    51, 55–6, 58, 64, 71, 74, 77, 80,
    82, 89–90, 108–9, 113, 122–3, 129,
    136, 140, 154–5, 157, 175, 185, 188,
    195, 208–10; abolition proposal,
    161; decision-making structures,
    59; engagement debate, 170;
    European loans, 52; 'export first'
    policies, 167; loan conditionality,
    53, 92; management proposals,
    199–200; reform ideas, 133–4, 143;
    replacement proposals, 158–9, 197;
    SAPs, 172; unpopularity, 57; World
    Development Task Force, 54
World Development Movement, 127,
    130–32, 144
World Economic Forum, 118
World Forum for Alternatives, 135
World Health Organization, 41
World Social Forums, 108, 117, 168
World Trade Organization (WTO),

15, 36, 38, 43, 51, 57–8, 64, 82, 108–9, 115, 128–9, 144, 154–5, 157–8, 167, 170, 172, 184, 188, 208–10; abolition proposals, 156, 161; Cancún talks collapse, 40, 46, 82, 102, 108, 116, 181, 208; containment objective, 131; creation, 114; decision-making, 130; Doha Round, 13; Geneva HQ, 47; management proposals, 199–200; national investment policy, 45; reform ideas, 142; replacement proposals, 197; rules enforcement, 48; Seattle negotiations, 13, 44, 108, 114

World Vision, 125–6, 132, 138, 144
Worldwide Fund for Nature, USA, 114, 125, 151, 128, 170

Yale University, 140
Yom Kippur War, 10

Zapatista National Liberation, Chiapas, 114, 204
Ziman, John, 188
Zoellick, Robert, 51

A BRAVE NEW SERIES

GLOBAL ISSUES
IN A CHANGING WORLD

This new series of short, accessible think-pieces deals with leading global issues of relevance to humanity today. Intended for the
enquiring reader and social activists in the North and the South,
as well as students, the books explain what is at stake and question conventional ideas and policies. Drawn from many different
parts of the world, the series' authors pay particular attention
to the needs and interests of ordinary people, whether living in
the rich industrial or the developing countries. They all share a
common objective – to help stimulate new thinking and social
action in the opening years of the new century.

Global Issues in a Changing World is a joint initiative by Zed
Books in collaboration with a number of partner publishers and
non-governmental organizations around the world. By working
together, we intend to maximize the relevance and availability of
the books published in the series.

PARTICIPATING NGOs

Both ENDS, Amsterdam
Catholic Institute for International Relations, London
Corner House, Sturminster Newton
Council on International and Public Affairs, New York
Dag Hammarskjöld Foundation, Uppsala
Development GAP, Washington DC
Focus on the Global South, Bangkok
IBON, Manila
Inter Pares, Ottawa
Public Interest Research Centre, Delhi
Third World Network, Penang
Third World Network–Africa, Accra
World Development Movement, London

ABOUT THIS SERIES

'Communities in the South are facing great difficulties in coping with global trends. I hope this brave new series will throw much needed light on the issues ahead and help us choose the right options.'

MARTIN KHOR, *Director,*
Third World Network, Penang

'There is no more important campaign than our struggle to bring the global economy under democratic control. But the issues are fearsomely complex. This Global Issues series is a valuable resource for the committed campaigner and the educated citizen.'

BARRY COATES, *Director,*
World Development Movement (WDM)

'Zed Books has long provided an inspiring list about the issues that touch and change people's lives. The Global Issues series is another dimension of Zed's fine record, allowing access to a range of subjects and authors that, to my knowledge, very few publishers have tried. I strongly recommend these new, powerful titles and this exciting series.'

JOHN PILGER, *author*

'We are all part of a generation that actually has the means to eliminate extreme poverty world-wide. Our task is to harness the forces of globalization for the benefit of working people, their families and their communities – that is our collective duty. The Global Issues series makes a powerful contribution to the global campaign for justice, sustainable and equitable development, and peaceful progress.'

GLENYS KINNOCK, *MEP*

THE GLOBAL ISSUES SERIES

Already available

Walden Bello, *Deglobalization: Ideas for a New World Economy*

Robert Ali Brac de la Perrière and Franck Seuret, *Brave New Seeds: The Threat of GM Crops to Farmers*

Greg Buckman, *Globalization: Tame it or Scrap It? Mapping the Alternatives of the Anti-Globalization Movement*

Ha-Joon Chang and Ilene Grabel, *Reclaiming Development: An Alternative Economic Policy Handbook*

Oswaldo de Rivero, *The Myth of Development: The Non-viable Economies of the 21st Century*

Graham Dunkley, *Free Trade: Myth, Reality and Alternatives*

Joyeeta Gupta, *Our Simmering Planet: What to Do about Global Warming?*

Nicholas Guyatt, *Another American Century? The United States and the World since 9/11*

Martin Khor, *Rethinking Globalization: Critical Issues and Policy Choices*

John Madeley, *Food for All: The Need for a New Agriculture*

John Madeley, *Hungry for Trade: How the Poor Pay for Free Trade*

A.G. Noorani, *Islam and Jihad: Prejudice versus Reality*

Riccardo Petrella, *The Water Manifesto: Arguments for a World Water Contract*

Peter Robbins, *Stolen Fruit: The Tropical Commodities Disaster*

Vandana Shiva, *Protect or Plunder? Understanding Intellectual Property Rights*

Harry Shutt, *A New Democracy: Alternatives to a Bankrupt World Order*

David Sogge, *Give and Take: What's the Matter with Foreign Aid?*

Paul Todd and Jonathan Bloch, *Global Intelligence: The World's Secret Services Today*

In preparation

Peggy Antrobus, *The International Women's Movement: Issues and Strategies*

Julian Burger, *First Peoples: What Future?*

Koen de Feyter, *A Thousand and One Rights: How Globalization Challenges Human Rights*

Susan Hawley and Morris Szeftel, *Corruption: Privatization, Transnational Corporations and the Export of Bribery*

Roger Moody, *Digging the Dirt: The Modern World of Global Mining*

Edgar Pieterse, *City Futures: Confronting the Crisis of Urban Development*

Toby Shelley, *Oil and Gas: What Future? What Consequences?*

Kavaljit Singh, *The Myth of Globalization: Ten Questions Everyone Asks*

Vivien Stern, *Crime and Punishment: Globalization and the New Agenda*

Nedd Willard, *The Drugs War: Is This the Solution?*

For full details of this list and Zed's other subject and general catalogues, please write to: The Marketing Department, Zed Books, 7 Cynthia Street, London N1 9JF, UK or email Sales@zedbooks.demon.co.uk

Visit our website at: www.zedbooks.co.uk

Participating Organizations

Both ENDS A service and advocacy organization which collaborates with environment and indigenous organizations, both in the South and in the North, with the aim of helping to create and sustain a vigilant and effective environmental movement.

Nieuwe Keizersgracht 45, 1018 VC Amsterdam, The Netherlands
Phone: +31 20 623 0823   Fax: +31 20 620 8049
Email: info@bothends.org   Website: www.bothends.org

Catholic Institute for International Relations (CIIR) CIIR aims to contribute to the eradication of poverty through a programme that combines advocacy at national and international level with community-based development.

Unit 3, Canonbury Yard, 190a New North Road, London N1 7BJ, UK
Phone +44 (0)20 7354 0883   Fax +44 (0)20 7359 0017
Email: ciir@ciir.org   Website: www.ciir.org

Corner House The Corner House is a UK-based research and solidarity group working on social and environmental justice issues in North and South.

PO Box 3137, Station Road, Sturminster Newton, Dorset DT10 1YJ, UK
Tel.: +44 (0)1258 473795   Fax: +44 (0)1258 473748
Email: cornerhouse@gn.apc.org   Website: www.cornerhouse.icaap.org

Council on International and Public Affairs (CIPA) CIPA is a human rights research, education and advocacy group, with a particular focus on economic and social rights in the USA and elsewhere around the world. Emphasis in recent years has been given to resistance to corporate domination.

777 United Nations Plaza, Suite 3C, New York, NY 10017, USA
Tel. +1 212 972 9877   Fax +1 212 972 9878
Email: cipany@igc.org   Website: www.cipa-apex.org

Dag Hammarskjöld Foundation The Dag Hammarskjöld Foundation, established 1962, organises seminars and workshops on social, economic and cultural issues facing developing countries with a particular focus on alternative and innovative solutions. Results are published in its journal *Develpment Dialogue*.

Övre Slottsgatan 2, 753 10 Uppsala, Sweden.
Tel.: +46 18 102772   Fax: +46 18 122072
Email: secretariat@dhf.uu.se   Website: www.dhf.uu.se

Development GAP The Development Group for Alternative Policies is a Non-Profit Development Resource Organization working with popular organizations in the South and their Northern partners in support of a development that is truly sustainable and that advances social justice.

927 15th Street NW, 4th Floor, Washington, DC, 20005, USA
Tel.: +1 202 898 1566   Fax: +1 202 898 1612
E-mail: dgap@igc.org   Website: www.developmentgap.org

Focus on the Global South Focus is dedicated to regional and global policy analysis and advocacy work. It works to strengthen the capacity of organizations of the poor and marginalized people of the South and to better analyse and understand the impacts of the globalization process on their daily lives.

C/o CUSRI, Chulalongkorn University, Bangkok 10330, Thailand
Tel.: +66 2 218 7363 Fax: +66 2 255 9976
Email: Admin@focusweb.org   Website: www.focusweb.org

IBON IBON Foundation is a research, education and information institution that provides publications and services on socio-economic issues as support to advocacy in the Philippines and abroad. Through its research and databank, formal and non-formal education programmes, media work and international networking, IBON aims to build the capacity of both Philippine and international organizations.

Room 303 SCC Bldg, 4427 Int. Old Sta. Mesa, Manila 1008, Philippines
Phone +632 7132729   Fax +632 7160108
Email: editors@ibon.org   Website: www.ibon.org

Inter Pares Inter Pares, a Canadian social justice organization, has been active since 1975 in building relationships with Third World development groups and providing support for community-based development programmes. Inter Pares is also involved in education and advocacy in Canada, promoting understanding about the causes, effects and solutions to poverty.

221 Laurier Avenue East, Ottawa, Ontario, KIN 6PI Canada
Phone +1 613 563 4801   Fax +1 613 594 4704
Email: info@interpares.ca   Website: www.interpares.ca

Public Interest Research Centre PIRC is a research and campaigning group based in Delhi which seeks to serve the information needs of activists and organizations working on macro-economic issues concerning finance, trade and development.

142 Maitri Apartments, Plot No. 28, Patparganj, Delhi 110092, India
Phone: +91 11 2221081/2432054   Fax: +91 11 2224233
Email: kaval@nde.vsnl.net.in

Third World Network   TWN is an international network of groups and individuals involved in efforts to bring about a greater articulation of the needs and rights of peoples in the Third World; a fair distribution of the world's resources; and forms of development which are ecologically sustainable and fulfil human needs. Its international secretariat is based in Penang, Malaysia.

121-S Jalan Utama, 10450 Penang, Malaysia
Tel.: +60 4 226 6159   Fax: +60 4 226 4505
Email: twnet@po.jaring.my   Website: www.twnside.org.sg

Third World Network–Africa   TWN–Africa is engaged in research and advocacy on economic, environmental and gender issues. In relation to its current particular interest in globalization and Africa, its work focuses on trade and investment, the extractive sectors and gender and economic reform.

2 Ollenu Street, East Legon, PO Box AN19452, Accra-North, Ghana.
Tel.: +233 21 511189/503669/500419   Fax: +233 21 511188
Email: twnafrica@ghana.com

World Development Movement (WDM)   The World Development Movement campaigns to tackle the causes of poverty and injustice. It is a democratic membership movement that works with partners in the South to cancel unpayable debt and break the ties of IMF conditionality, for fairer trade and investment rules, and for strong international rules on multinationals.

25 Beehive Place, London SW9 7QR, UK
Tel.: +44 (0)20 7737 6215   Fax: +44 (0)20 7274 8232
Email: wdm@wdm.org.uk   Website: www.wdm.org.uk

This Book is also Available
in the Following Countries

CARIBBEAN

Ian Randle Publishers
11 Cunningham Avenue
Box 686, Kingston 6,
Jamaica, W.I.
Tel: 876 978 0745/0739
Fax: 876 978 1158
email: ianr@colis.com

EGYPT

MERIC
(Middle East Readers'
Information Center)
2 Bahgat Ali Street,
Tower D/Apt. 24
Zamalek
Cairo
Tel: 20 2 735 3818/3824
Fax: 20 2 736 9355

FIJI

University Book Centre,
University of South
Pacific,
Suva
Tel: 679 313 900
Fax: 679 303 265

GHANA

EPP Book Services,
PO Box TF 490,
Trade Fair,
Accra
Tel: 233 21 778347
Fax: 233 21 779099

MAURITIUS

Editions Le Printemps
4 Club Road
Vacoas

MOZAMBIQUE

Sul Sensações
PO Box 2242,
Maputo
Tel: 258 1 421974
Fax: 258 1 423414

NAMIBIA

Book Den
PO Box 3469
Shop 4
Frans Indongo Gardens
Windhoek
Tel: 264 61 239976
Fax: 264 61 234248

NEPAL

Everest Media Services,
GPO Box 5443
Dillibazar
Putalisadak Chowk
Kathmandu
Tel: 977 1 416026
Fax: 977 1 250176

NIGERIA

Mosuro Publishers
52 Magazine Road
Jericho
Ibadan
Tel: 234 2 241 3375
Fax: 234 2 241 3374

PAKISTAN

Vanguard Books
45 The Mall
Lahore
Tel: 92 42 735 5079
Fax: 92 42 735 5197

PAPUA NEW GUINEA

Unisearch PNG Pty Ltd
Box 320, University
National Capital District
Tel: 675 326 0130
Fax: 675 326 0127

RWANDA

Librairie Ikirezi
PO Box 443
Kigali
Tel/Fax: 250 71314

SUDAN

The Nile Bookshop
New Extension Street 41
PO Box 8036
Khartoum
Tel: 249 11 463 749

TANZANIA

TEMA Publishing Co. Ltd
PO Box 63115
Dar Es Salaam
Tel: 255 22 2113608
Fax: 255 22 2110472

UGANDA

Aristoc Booklex Ltd
PO Box 5130,
Kampala Road
Diamond Trust Building
Kampala
Tel/Fax: 256 41 254867

ZAMBIA

UNZA Press
PO Box 32379
Lusaka
Tel: 260 1 290409
Fax: 260 1 253952

ZIMBABWE

Weaver Press
PO Box A1922
Avondale
Harare
Tel: 263 4 308330
Fax: 263 4 339645